The Anarchy of the
IMAGINATION

PAJ Books

Bonnie Marranca and Gautam Dasgupta,
Series Editors

The Anarchy of the

IMAGINATION

Interviews, Essays, Notes

RAINER WERNER FASSBINDER

Edited by Michael Töteberg and Leo A. Lensing

Translated from the German by Krishna Winston

THE JOHNS HOPKINS UNIVERSITY PRESS

Baltimore and London

Originally published as *Filme befreien den Kopf: Essays und Arbeitsnotizen.*
© Fischer Taschenbuch Verlag, GmbH, Frankfurt am Main, 1984, Mit Genehmigung
des Verlags der Autoren, Frankfurt am Main, and *Die Anarchie der Phantasie: Gespräche und Interviews,* Fischer Taschenbuch Verlag, GmbH, Frankfurt am Main, 1986.

The Johns Hopkins University Press
701 West 40th Street
Baltimore, Maryland 21211-2190
The Johns Hopkins Press Ltd., London

∞ The paper used in this book meets the minimum requirements of the American
National Standard for Information Sciences—Permanence of Paper for Printed Library
Materials, ANSI Z39.48−1984.

Library of Congress Cataloging-in-Publication Data
Fassbinder, Rainer Werner, 1946−
    [Anarchie der Phantasis. English]
    The anarchy of the imagination : interviews, essays, notes / Rainer Werner
Fassbinder ; edited by Michael Töteberg and Leo A. Lensing ; translated from the
German by Krishna Winston.
        p.   cm. — (PAJ books)
    Translation of: Die Anarchie der Phantasis and Filme befreien den Kopf.
    Includes bibliographical references (p.   ) and index.
    ISBN 0-8018-4368-5. — ISBN 0-8018-4369-3 (pbk.)
    1. Fassbinder, Rainer Werner, 1946−   —Interviews. 2. Fassbinder, Rainer
Werner, 1946−   —Germany—Interviews. 3. Motion Pictures. I. Töteberg,
Michael, 1951− . II. Lensing, Leo A. III. Fassbinder, Rainer Werner, 1946−.
Filme befreien den Kopf. IV. Title. V. Series.
PN1998.3.F37A3   1992
791.43′0233′092—dc20   91-41979

Contents

PART IV. Literary Past / Cinematic Present

PART V. Monologues and Confessions

List of Illustrations

Preface

Few directors insinuate their own lives into their films with as much passionate intensity as Rainer Werner Fassbinder. Whether portraying an exploited homosexual in *Fox and His Friends* or a black marketeer who sells Hanna Schygulla a cocktail dress in *The Marriage of Maria Braun,* Fassbinder offers us a cinematic persona that reflects his own personality in fascinating ways. It would be a mistake, however, to assume that Fassbinder's films provide direct access to his biography. Rather, they are autobiographical in the true sense: they attempt to confer shape and meaning on a chaotic, sometimes scandalous life subject to the distortions of what Fassbinder perceived as a catastrophic social and political environment.

Biographies of the director, many of which were rushed into print as soon as possible after Fassbinder's death in June 1982, focused primarily on his injurious and injured existence. Sensational details were blown up, and Fassbinder's cinematic oeuvre, astonishing for its unity and its capacity to illuminate the life, seldom received serious consideration.

But any thoughtful attempt to interpret the filmmaker and his works should include study of his interviews, essays, and working notes, most of which are presented here in English for the first time. They constitute an indispensable record of the self-understanding and self-stylization of this major artist, one of the most remarkable cultural figures to emerge from postwar Germany.

Valuable though they are for the information they contain, the interviews and conversations should not be read naively. For Fassbinder, the interview provided an opportunity not only for communication, but also for aesthetic experimentation. More than once he integrated interviews into the fictional texture of his films. In *A Year of Thirteen Moons,* for example, the camera watches the prostitute Red Zora as she in turn watches Fassbinder giving a television interview. In Fassbinder's segment of the collective film *Germany in Autumn*, we see the director engaged in a virtual interrogation of his own mother on the subject of political repression. In both instances, the visual context and the tension between the actors and their roles lend unexpected dimensions to the interview and complicate interpretation. The actress who plays Red Zora turns out to be Ingrid Caven, Fassbinder's former wife and the woman with whom he claims to have his most important "elective affinity"; and his mother is of course also his actress, with major or minor roles in most of his films.

If we remain mindful of Fassbinder's predilection for manipulating perspectives and provoking his interviewer or possible reader, the interviews and essays in this volume can cast a great deal of light on Fassbinder's intellectual scope and aesthetic opinions. He shows himself capable of shrewd historical judgment, for example, when he offers a balanced assessment of anti-Semitic tendencies in the nineteenth-century bestseller *Debit and Credit* by Gustav Freytag. Now and then Fassbinder also delivers an irresistible *aperçu*. Commenting on Werner Herzog's problematic *Heart of Glass,* he sardonically characterizes the experiment as Herzog's attempt to film the French rave reviews of his previous film.

Fassbinder's conversations and writings also elucidate the films directly. A remark of Fassbinder's to Renate Klett in a 1978 interview makes it clear that the ending of *The Marriage of Maria Braun*—which baffled Vincent Canby when he first reviewed the film in the *New York Times*—comments on the present as well as the past. Analyzing German television's decision to continue a program on soccer that included clips from various World Cup matches after pausing to report a shocking political murder, Fassbinder points up the link between the political realities of his own day and the era portrayed fictionally in his film. There the explosion of Maria Braun's house is juxtaposed with the radio broadcast of the 1954 World Cup match.

Fassbinder's essays and other writings commanded a degree of public attention rarely achieved by filmmakers in the United States. His articles appeared in major newspapers such as the *Frankfurter Rundschau* and *Die Zeit,* where they not only influenced the cultural scene but also intervened directly in the acrimonious debates on terrorism and anti-Semitism that stirred up West Germany in the late 1970s and early 1980s.

But Fassbinder's writings reveal more than just the impassioned social and political thinker. The more confessional pieces, such as his essay on Döblin's great city novel *Berlin Alexanderplatz* or the exposé for *In a Year of Thirteen Moons,* display an unusual but undeniable literary quality. The latter is arguably a minor masterpiece, succeeding, as do the best of Fassbinder's films, in lending exquisite form to a deformed existence.

On the occasion of this first American edition of Fassbinder's writings and interviews, it is appropriate to recall that Fassbinder loved American popular culture: everything from Hollywood melodramas to Janis Joplin songs provided raw material for his films. While he never made the cover of *Time* magazine—one of his many ambitions—he probably would have been delighted to learn he had been mentioned on *Miami Vice*. In an episode broadcast on May 1, 1987, an upstart young director proclaims from the stage of his experimental theater, "The German filmmaker Rainer Werner Fassbinder said, 'Film is the art of illiterates,' but I say that theater is the art of illiterates." Even though the statement attributed to Fassbinder was actually made by Werner Herzog, the aggressive stance and the gesture of sympathy for the disenfranchised might just as well have been Fassbinder's during his early "Action Theater" days in Munich.

The title of this volume is taken from a comment Fassbinder made during a call-in talk show focusing on the reactions, most of them hostile, to the television premiere of *Berlin Alexanderplatz*. In the context of the prevailing hysteria about terrorism, one caller's "Are you an anarchist?" was certainly intended as a political trick question. Fassbinder responded by asserting, "I'm for the anarchy of the imagination." This statement reaffirmed the director's commitment to an unconventional, sensual cinema, but it by no means signaled that he had abandoned his belief that anarchy could also prove productive in society and politics. The texts collected here reflect his sustained effort to, in the words of his fellow playwright and early critic Botho Strauss, "think about aesthetic and political events simultaneously." More effectively than any German dramatist-director since Brecht, Fassbinder transformed these simultaneous thoughts into the stuff of cinematic art.

Leo A. Lensing

Introduction

Rainer Werner Fassbinder was a director who gave a great deal of thought to his own work; the essays and interviews presented here prove that beyond a doubt. They mark stations along the way of this prolific filmmaker, whose work covers the gamut from socially critical films and sophisticated treatments of literary works to melodramas and self-tormenting confessional pieces, from low-budget productions to lavish Hollywood-style films. Fassbinder: "I would like to build a house with my films. Some are the cellar, others the walls, still others the windows. But I hope that in the end it will be a house." The texts collected in this volume provide approaches to this house, and to all its floors.

Whether Fassbinder is reflecting on his own work or writing about fellow filmmakers, whether he is describing his discovery of the actress Hanna Schygulla or vehemently speaking out in favor of the political film, he never hides behind safe, accepted opinions; he always takes a radical, subjective position. For that reason the essays in this volume are texts not just about films, but also about love, longing, dependency, repressed wishes, and dreams.

"His films liberate the mind"—we find this sentence in the essay on Douglas Sirk. Those characteristics Fassbinder prizes in Sirk help form the standard by which he criticizes Claude Chabrol, whom he once admired so much he dedicated his first film to him, *Love Is Colder Than Death* (1969). Six years later he finds Chabrol lacking in "tenderness for his characters" and accuses him of showing cynical contempt for his audience. To Fassbinder, the decisive factor is a film author's attitude toward his characters: he must confront the lifeless phantoms of a superficial, image-crazed world with real people, must develop commitment to, even love for, his characters and endow them with grandeur. Fassbinder finds arguments to support his position in the novelists Theodor Fontane and Alfred Döblin. What strikes him as admirable in the novel *Berlin Alexanderplatz* is that Döblin, the author, describes "with the greatest tenderness" "seemingly inconsequential, unimportant, insignificant individuals," "these characters reduced to mediocrity." Of Fassbinder, too, one may say that he never betrays his characters, no matter what wretched specimens of humanity they are.

In his essay on Döblin, Fassbinder formulates what he requires of art: the readers or viewers should be forced to analyze their own reality. Films should liberate the mind, not befuddle it. Through movies, viewers are brought up against new experiences. Film can distill truths from reality, which, "no matter how painful these insights may seem, bring our own lives closer to us." Through movies, viewers can also enter into new realms of feeling that are cordoned off in everyday life. Fassbinder in an interview: "When the lights go out in the movie theater, the dream begins, the subconscious takes over. I tell myself that anyone who goes to the movies knows pretty well what is in store for him, so I can expect more effort of him, and I can also expect him to enjoy the effort more. One should never pamper the audience, only challenge it."

Fassbinder was no theoretician. He liked to give his written reflections subtitles like "Disorganized Thoughts." He wrote only a few articles and essays; he preferred to seek out people to whom he could explicate his ideas on film theory and on aesthetic matters. The monologue did not suit his personality; the interview format made it easier for him to develop a position, in the give-and-take of discussion and argument.

Viewed all together, the essays, interviews, and notes collected here reveal an aesthetic of commitment that allows Fassbinder to react quickly and directly and does not suppress "radical emotions." The "anarchy of the imagination" was supposed to develop without constraint, free of any suffocating insistence on ideological legitimation or conformity to aesthetic dogma. Fassbinder did not hesitate to revise previous opinions, to contradict statements made earlier, to admit to past mistakes and make new ones. Such directness and honesty, his refusal to be wary and cover himself, carried the risk of his being misunderstood. The protests by homosexuals (directed against the film *Fox and His Friends*), the accusations of anti-Semitism (directed against the play *Garbage, the City, and Death*) prove, upon closer examination, to be unfounded, but they do confirm that Fassbinder ventured into taboo areas. He firmly believed that glossing over ugly truths was merely another form of defamation. He felt that one should not remain silent about the mistakes and negative behavior patterns of an oppressed minority; rather, these had to be described in such a way that they could be seen as the product of a specific social situation. In the interviews we hear the voice of the impassioned social critic who knew that films cannot change the world but believed they can release irritants that will continue to work in the mind of the viewer. "You can set up booby traps in such a way that the moviegoer, when he leaves the theater, does not discard prejudices he brought in with him, but maybe is scared by his own prejudices."

Fassbinder knew how—and that is what makes his work so fascinating—"to convert his sensibility, his fears, and his aggressions into film." What sets his work apart in a positive sense from the more intellectual, literary products of the German cinema on the one hand, and from the commercial products of the film industry on the other is that Fassbinder did not shun emotion or melodramatic scenes, but also never took refuge in a world of cinematic illusion. "I make my films out of personal involvement, and for no other reason," he confessed in a conversation. His films have been called a highly personal diary, in which despite—or perhaps precisely because of—their radical subjectivity, present-day German reality finds brilliant expression.

Michael Töteberg

On Translating
Rainer Werner Fassbinder

The style of Fassbinder's interviews, essays, and notes presents a challenge to the translator. Whether in the interviews or the essays and notes, much of the language captured on the page is essentially spoken language, full of colloquialisms, involuntary repetitions, filler words, pronouns whose antecedents are not quite clear, casual or almost deliberately inarticulate formulations, and sentences that trail off with "I don't know . . ." Sentence structure is often loose, following the twists and turns of Fassbinder's mind as he thinks on his feet. Sometimes he replies to a question so curtly one can almost hear him grunt.

Yet Fassbinder also uses, half-mockingly, half-seriously, "big" words—concepts from political science, from sociology, from psychology, from literary and cinematic criticism—the stock-in-trade of the German intellectual—and syntactical patterns to match.

This mix results in a curious effect: at times meaning emerges with almost startling clarity, while at other times the reader is left puzzled or confused. And one cannot establish an unambiguous correlation between either the colloquial or the intellectual mode and clarity of meaning or its opposite. Sometimes Fassbinder obviously intends to provoke the reader, as in his essay on *The Third Generation,* where he parodies German scholarly writing with wildly convoluted sentences and then interrupts himself to remark that "grammatically" at any rate the sentence in question is quite correct. One is tempted to speculate that this essay, at least, was written under the influence of cocaine.

Abrasive and antisentimental though he likes to appear, Fassbinder can also achieve pure poetry, as in this sentence, with its echoes of Virgil and Milton:

> Of this despair and the painful search for something in motion, and the courage to recognize a utopia and to open yourself up to it, however poor it may be—of these things I tell in this film. (p. 176)

In this translation I have tried to convey the full range of Fassbinder's style. Strategically placed contractions, jargon from various realms, slang, inconsistent levels of diction—all are employed in the interests of presenting Fassbinder as he might have spoken and written in English if he had settled in America. At the same time I have tried to keep a touch of strangeness, in the spirit of Brecht's *Verfremdungseffekt*, to remind us that in America, Germany, or France this willful master of the cinematic and the verbal image would always have thought, spoken, and written within the German cultural sphere from which he sprang.

Krishna Winston

Acknowledgments

We are indebted to Michael Töteberg, who allowed us to combine his two editions of Fassbinder's interviews and essays (see the Select Bibliography) and provided invaluable assistance with problems of interpretation and commentary. We would also like to thank Gerhard Ullmann, of the Munich Film Museum, and Jeanine Basinger, curator of the Cinema Archives at Wesleyan University, and her assistant, Leith Johnson, for helping us obtain photographs. For constant bibliographic support, we thank Steven Lebergott, head of Interlibrary Loan at Wesleyan University's Olin Library. We are especially grateful to our colleague, Arthur S. Wensinger, who gave us permission to adapt his and the late Richard H. Wood's translations of two of Fassbinder's texts, "Preliminary Remarks on *Querelle*" and "Hanna Schygulla."

L.A.L., K.W.

Part One

CINEMA BETWEEN
AUTOBIOGRAPHY AND
SOCIAL CRITICISM

"The kind of rage I feel"
A Conversation with Joachim von Mengershausen about *Love Is Colder than Death*

■ *Isn't it a little surprising, considering your plays, that the first film you made was of all things a crime film?*

I enjoy seeing crime films, and I think other people enjoy seeing crime films, too. Besides, I meant to send a message. I could always make a film that would have everything in it that this film has for me, but in a completely different form. That would be a problem film, I guess. I chose a crime plot because that kind of story is easy to tell. And I'm all for making simple things. But they have to be beautiful, too.

■ *But your film isn't all that simple.*

That does bother me. I see this problem in the work of other people, too; I think they're making films with pretty much the same thing in mind, that is, to do something that's just simple and beautiful, with something to it, but they just can't pull it off. One problem is, all those Hollywood movies are right smack in our way, and all we can do is react to them, primarily in terms of form. It so happens there really are a lot of beautiful films in the detective genre.

■ *Now of course your film doesn't exist in a vacuum, without any connection to your work in the theater. So my question is: Why a crime film?*

I felt I needed a simple plot for what I wanted to say. The first screenplay started from the premise that people are sitting in jail, are oppressed, and then try to make something of freedom. And that becomes a mirror image of society, if you want to call it that. They often do totally brutal things, because that's all that occurs to them, and also because people want them to be that way. I don't know, to me all stories are crime stories. To me the everyday oppression people experience is criminal. I could almost go so far as to say that you really can't make anything but crime films. Everything should be declared criminal. You read the paper, listen to the news, and you get madder

3

Fassbinder on the set of Love Is Colder than Death *(by permission of Ulrich Handl)*

and madder at what you hear, see, and read. I got to the point where I didn't feel like doing anything but portraying criminal situations.

■ *But if you take specific actions that the law defines as criminal and portray them as criminal, aren't you in fact obstructing the audience's view, so that it doesn't have a chance to reach the conclusion that "everything is criminal?"*

No, that's where form comes in, the narrative structure of the film; in fact, the so-called criminal actions aren't shown as criminal. I made the crime scenes, the murder scenes, as conventional as possible, so they would simply whisk by. That's supposed to show that criminality isn't muggings and murders, but rather people being raised in such a way that they have the kinds of relationships these people have, that they're simply incapable of getting their relationships straightened out.

What you're left with when you've seen this movie isn't that six people were murdered, that a few deaths occurred, but that these were poor people who didn't know what to do with themselves, who were simply plopped down as they were, and weren't given the option—no, let's not go too far here—who simply don't have any options. In my opinion, that's what you're left with. Because the other scenes, the ones without violence, are much, much longer. They take up about seventy minutes, as opposed to only ten minutes of actual killing. Think of the scene on the highway, when the three of them are just walking along for three minutes. I don't know, if nothing dawns on the audience when it sees those people just walking along ... I know if I'd seen a film like that at the age of twelve or fourteen, I would certainly have gotten something out of it.

■ *Of course there's always the danger that when you use the crime movie genre you may be preventing people from recognizing that any society that gives rise to criminal behavior is criminal. To be sure, in your film there's a series of scenes in which the acting and the photography are just plain strange, completely unusual for that genre.*

Sure, if I'd made a film that was narrated conventionally all the way through, it would have negated itself, and then it would have been like a film by Chabrol, at best. If I'd done it differently, without the crime plot, simply using alienation technique, that would have had the same result; it might have turned out like a Godard film. I should add that I don't think such films are really effective, if only because they never get to the right audience. I had to make my film the way I did, stylizing it in some parts, not in others. That seemed the only hope of getting the film to the right people; I want them to experience the kind of rage I feel, and then there was something else, too: it also had to be beautiful.

■ *You and Lommel make a very odd couple, not just in the way you look, but also in your acting styles. There's quite a discrepancy between yours and Lommel's, who seems a bit, and not just a bit, like Delon in* Le samourai.

First of all that has to do with the history of this particular film. I have to look cowering and beefy because I don't have any backup. See, this Franz I play wants to make it on his own. It starts out with a syndicate wanting him to come and work for it, and he doesn't want to, whereas Lommel does work for the syndicate. So Lommel can have a completely different walk and completely different reactions from mine, because he has this backup. He knows he isn't alone, while I'm completely on my own. And I want to be on my own, want to do my thing by myself. Lommel gets the nod when the guys from the syndicate aren't making any headway with their brutal methods. They send Lommel to cozy up to me. In the film it never does become clear whether Lommel is with the syndicate. They beat him up and drop him off. But that's a convention, too; that always happens to stool pigeons. Do you know *White Heat,* by Raoul Walsh? There you also have a stool pigeon who's beaten up and delivered to James Cagney. There's

Fassbinder and Ulli Lommel in Love Is Colder than Death *(by permission of Fassbinder-Foundation, Munich)*

also a homosexual component, much more obvious than with Hawks, for instance. Franz doesn't have any backup—he's a loner. Not like the great loners in the American flicks, though, where it's never really clear to me why they're loners. They're just heroes, I guess. Franz is no hero. He's primitive, just wants to work for himself, doesn't want to hand over any of what he earns.

■ *Why does he get involved with the other man?*

It's a question of friendship. He just likes him. But he never quite realizes that he likes the other guy. He tells him to come by his place sometime, and then the guy turns up, and then Franz even wants to have him sleep with his girl, simply because he likes him. He never thinks about it. He isn't even capable of that. Lommel doesn't think, either, just does what he's been told. And Hanna's the same.

Hanna's the key to everything. You can tell that the character she plays is totally bogged down in bourgeois values—much, much worse than all the others. That's what she wants to preserve, and that's the reason she betrays Lommel to the police, because she'd rather be alone than be part of a threesome; that she just can't handle.

■ *You use a kind of lighting that doesn't cast any shadows, that doesn't leave any dark corners, a set where no one has anywhere to hide.*

Right, everything's just there, the way it is. That alone makes my film different from all the others I'm familiar with. I really can't think of any, maybe very rarely one by Godard, and not even in them is it quite this way. There are always things that somehow veil everything and ruin it. That was what I was going to avoid in this film from the start. I would have liked to shoot this film against perfectly white walls, to make it unmistakably clear, so there'd be no chance to say: that can all be true. Yet you have to have some identification in this film, and that's why it can't just go ahead and bash all the emotions you've built up in the audience. It's perfectly all right for them to have emotions. But they should have them quite openly. That's why there are those incredibly long takes where you aren't given a chance—by cuts, for instance, that would suddenly make everything completely differ-ent—to miss the point, or get it all wrong.

■ *While watching this film I found myself wondering where the moviegoer's sympathies would lie. Probably least of all with your Franz, because he's so hostile and defensive.*

Well, actually the likable one is Franz. He becomes that, in spite of Lommel's incredible beauty. It often happens, of course, that people we don't like at first sight turn out to be the good ones. Anyway, only three characters really count. The moviegoer won't find it so easy to like me. But he has to think over everything he knows.

■ *Because of the ice-cold light, the film would seem to pretty much kill off any emotion ...*

You have a plot. Language. Sound and music, all of which create emotion. But the relationship between these three elements won't let the audience take the easy way out. In my opinion, it's really a film the audience won't have an easy time with, but actually quite a hard one. My film isn't supposed to let feelings people already have be neutral-ized or soaked up; instead, the film should create new feelings. That seems to me another thing that makes it different from the good Go-dard films, which are perfectly fine in themselves. I like them all, even *Two or Three Things I Know about Her.* It's an important question who you're working for.

■ *Fine. You gave a lot of thought to the audience you were film-ing for. That also implies you're aiming for something concrete, which the moviegoer can perceive as concrete. Yet there are some things in your film that can't so easily be translated into concrete terms, like the mysterious syndicate.*

Of course that's a form of camouflage, but then also a way of focus-ing on what matters to me. What matters is not that there are police-men in this world who beat up on students, and that sort of thing. That's a separate problem. It's all very interesting and important, and

something has to be done about it. But for me it's much more important that people are brought up to want to live as couples and have
kids, and that they're supposed to have such feelings. Even if they
don't have them, they have them anyway, and that's what I'm really
concerned with. I'm concerned with having the audience that sees
this film examine its own innermost feelings. Yes, that's what I'm primarily concerned with in this film, not with anything else. To me that's
more political, or politically more aggressive and active, than if I point
out the police as the great oppressors.

▪ *What influence did Jean-Marie Straub have on you guys?*

The Söhnlein family, who'd founded the Action Theater, asked
Straub, who had just made *Not Reconciled,* "Wouldn't you like to direct a play for us?" He didn't want to, but he said yes anyway. Then he
showed up one day. He found entirely different people there—it was
us. I showed him my short films right away, and he liked them. He said,
"I don't know anyone with this much violence in his films."

I started making this film when I met Lommel. We did a television
movie together. We really liked each other. Lommel had just made
Detectives with Rudolf Thome, and I had just done *The Bridegroom,
the Comedienne, and the Pimp* with Straub, and we said it would be
grand to do a film together.

▪ *Were you influenced by your work with Straub?*

Absolutely. First of all by the work itself. When he did *Sickness of
Youth* with us at the Action Theater and then this film, we all realized
filmmaking could be fun and interesting. From Straub I learned how
to develop a film stylistically, and from Straub I took over some theories. But at first I really didn't want to make films like Straub's.

▪ *A patron lent you money for this film?*

You can't really say "lent." She gave it to us and said, "If the movie
makes a profit, you can pay me back, and if it doesn't, never mind."
Otherwise it wouldn't have been possible. Even if I'd done all the
shooting in my apartment. You still have to pay up front for film, bulbs,
lamps. But for most things we just put down a deposit and got the rest
on credit. There are ways of handling these things. But of course you
have to buy the cans of film first. Then when you have the prints made,
you have to cough up some money. Otherwise they won't print a
single foot for you. Normally you have to come up with much more
than we did. It worked for us because we're called the "anti-theater,"
and that had some drawing power. Strangely enough, it worked with
almost all the vendors. But you have to have some money, otherwise
you can't do a thing. The cameraman got a fifty mark per-diem, and
some of the actors. But everything else was based on cost shares. Film

Fassbinder in Jean-Marie Straub's production of Sickness of Youth *(1968)*
(by permission of Cahiers du Cinéma, *Paris)*

is always done on a cost basis. That's how you work out the total amount: what the actual film costs, plus any contractual obligations. Let's say it comes to 152,000 marks. Out of that you pay the 70,000 or 80,000 marks you owe the various suppliers, and then the rest is divided up when money comes in. If more comes in than the film cost to make, then everybody gets a share in the profits. The film was made in such a way that the anti-theater wasn't really the producer, even though it was listed that way everywhere, but rather each individual involved in the film. That was the right way to go about it, for the simple reason, too, that people had an entirely different sense of participation than you usually get.

■ *The idea of doing it that way has been in existence for a long time. You appeal to the desire for profits, and that's how you make your people cooperative.*

From the beginning I said it was entirely possible we might not make any money. I informed each individual about that possibility, from the beginning. Everyone was aware of it. Even Lommel, who's really no child in these matters, came on the last day of shooting to ask about a contract, whether maybe we should draw one up, or not. I think everyone had fun being together for a while, and doing something productive. We already had a functioning collective, because in this case each one had very specific capabilities to put to work. After all, the cameraman and the actors can only do the things they can do. I didn't really direct the actors at all, or just a little, telling them where to stand, how to look. And the atmosphere helped make it come out the way I wanted it to.

■ *Well, the day I dropped in while you were shooting, the atmosphere didn't seem all that great. The cameraman was arguing about things like who was to blame and who wasn't.*

Yes, but less with me than with himself. Lohmann considers himself a brilliant cameraman. He certainly wouldn't defend himself to me—more likely to himself.

■ *Well, it's possible he was talking to himself, of course.*

I'm sure he was. I talk to myself, too. Sometimes I yell like a madman, but I don't mean anyone in particular. On the whole, the film turned out pretty much the way I had thought it might if everything went as well as possible.

May 1969

"At some point films have to stop being films"
A Conversation with Hans Günther Pflaum about *Fear Eats the Soul*

■ *Herr Fassbinder, in this film you've told a provocatively simple, simplified story. Is there a didactic program implied in your reduction of the conflicts to such a level?*

It seems to me that the simpler a story is, the truer it is. The common denominator for many stories is a story as simple as this. If we'd made the character of Ali more complicated, the audience would have had a harder time dealing with the story. If the character had been more complex, the childlike quality of the relationship between Ali and Emmi would have suffered—whereas now the story's as naive as the two people it's about. Though of course the relationships are much more complex, I realize that. But it's my opinion that each viewer has to flesh them out with his own reality. And he has an opportunity to do that when a story's very simple. I think people have to find their own opportunities for change—of course, you can go strictly by ideology, but for the larger audience I don't think that makes much sense.

■ *Couldn't the very simplicity of this film give the audience an excuse to dissociate themselves from the story, saying, "In reality nothing's that simple?"*

They have an excuse, or actually they're forced, to dissociate themselves from the story, not at the expense of the film, but rather in favor of their own reality—to me that's the crucial thing. At some point films have to stop being films, being stories, and have to begin to come alive, so that people will ask themselves: What about me and my life? I think this film forces people—because the love between the two comes across as so clear and pure—to examine their own relationships with darker-skinned and also older people. To me that's very important. You can't make it simple enough.

■ *On the other hand this simplicity can be incredibly provoking: for instance, when Ali's sitting in Emmi's apartment, and you*

11

*see the big, lonely, empty apartment and a little, lonely woman,
and he's describing his room, where six of them are crammed in
like sardines—the question just spontaneously occurs to you: Why
doesn't Ali simply move in with Emmi?*

Yes, we wanted to try to keep it so simple that people would keep
thinking: All sorts of things would be possible. I don't consider human
beings incapable of change. It's built into the structure of my film that
people begin to see, Yes, it *is* better if things are a bit different. And if
you think it out a little more, things can be even better. I'm not capable of providing a grand ideological scheme, and that's not my job,
either; other people are better trained and equipped for that. What
interests me are these little opportunities, because I know something
about them and find them stimulating.

■ *That must strike a responsive chord in a large segment of the
audience.*

Yes, that's what we discovered with the television series *Eight
Hours Are Not a Day:* the simpler the stories were, the more the viewers could do with them. The intellectuals and leftists charged that all
that wasn't true anymore, but they were wrong; it was still true for the
viewer, because he had a chance to translate everything into something that related to himself and his own reality. And if art, or whatever
you want to call it, seizes the opportunity to get discussion going
among people, it's achieved its maximum effect, I think.

■ *To what extent does* Fear Eats the Soul *incorporate your experiences with other films? I'm thinking primarily of the films of
Douglas Sirk, of course.*

Yes, actually ever since I saw his films and tried to write about
them, Sirk's been in everything I've done. Not Sirk himself, but what
I've learned from his work. Sirk told me what the studio bosses in
Hollywood told him: a film has to go over in Garmisch-Partenkirchen,
in Okinawa, and in Chicago—just try to think what the common denominator might be for people in all those places. To Sirk something
still mattered that most people in Hollywood don't care about anymore: making sure his work was in tune with himself, with his own
personality, that is, not just produced "for the public," like in those
films here in Germany that none of us like: those sex and entertainment films that the producers think the public likes, but they don't
like themselves. That's the difference between a production for the
masses by Sirk and one by Vohrer. Sirk hasn't done much that he's
ashamed of, and I'm impressed by that.

■ *The dramatic structure of the story of* Fear Eats the Soul *re-
minds me of Sirk: in the first half of the film the couple has to con-*

*tend with problems that come from the outside and tend to have a
stabilizing effect on their relationship. Not until this pressure from
the outside lessens do your protagonists (and the film itself) confront the internal conflicts, the problems the two of them are bound
to have with each other.*

Yes, but that's not Sirk, that's life. In the case of minorities, out-
siders, etc., it really is true that as long as they feel pressure from
outside they don't get around to their own problems, because they're
completely taken up with shielding themselves and assuring themselves of a kind of solidarity. As I was writing, it was hard for me to get
away from that; I wondered how to work it so people wouldn't be
putting so much pressure on the two of them anymore.

■ *What's the function of the final sequence, when Ali collapses
from a stomach ulcer, and the doctor at the hospital mentions that
that's a common diagnosis for guestworkers. Don't you have an
entirely different reality forcing its way into the picture at that
point?*

It's true to life. I heard about it from a doctor at a clinic. She described this scene to me in detail, and I could picture it perfectly. Here
you have this absolutely authentic bit of guestworker-reality breaking
in, and people have to deal with that, too ... Of course, the ending's
meant to take this private story, which I'm crazy about and also happen to think is very important, and give it a thrust into reality, including in the mind of the moviegoer.

■ *How long did it take you to shoot the film?*

We spent eighteen days shooting, so about four work weeks.

■ *Did your leading man identify with his role?*

Yes, to a large extent he did identify with it, and Brigitte Mira identified very strongly with her role, too, because in reality she has
a comparable relationship with a younger man. She can sense how
people react.

■ *Getting Brigitte Mira seems to me to be a real stroke of luck.
Why do your films, and some by your colleagues, too, suddenly
have so many actors who were really well known at one time?*

I had trouble with the younger actors. After about fifteen films,
Hanna Schygulla suddenly began to act so weird, expecting things of
her work that you just can't satisfy in work like this. Maybe you still
can in the theater, or in a long-term collaboration; but in the movies
it just can't be done—what with equal rights and so forth—you'd have
to invent films that didn't cost so much to make, I don't know. One
day I simply found myself longing for people who come in return for
pay, do decent work, and don't torment me. And then I discovered

that with certain people, like Karlheinz Böhm in *Martha,* for example, or now with Brigitte Mira, real personal relationships can develop, too. Relationships very similar to those with the old anti-theater and its superstars. Except that Böhm and Mira were much more down-to-earth in their work. I plan to continue this way.

■ *Has this changed your directing? The anti-theater had developed a certain speaking style, which Brigitte Mira, for example, can't slip into so easily. The family series you did still had that anti-theater sound.*

Finck still speaks that way, he hasn't changed a bit, and I fought and worked pretty hard with Luise Ulrich to get her to sound that way.

■ *With Brigitte Mira I had the impression you were onto something new again, this time with your actors.*

Yes, that also had to do with the relationship between Mira and me and the subject matter. Mira got involved for entirely personal reasons—but she's certainly not a person who thinks she has to feel involved in everything she does. She does many things that don't mean a thing to her, just for money. Here she really had something she could get involved in, regardless of pay and reputation. Because of that she became interesting to me, too, in a very strange way, and I've never worked with film actors the way I worked with those two in *Fear Eats the Soul.* I shot every take ten, fifteen, even twenty times, which I'd never done before; this time I really wanted to get the maximum out of every moment.

■ *Now that you're head of a theater, will you continue to make films?*

Of course. In any case, I wanted to cut back—two films a year, that should be plenty. One for television and one for the movies, that's my dream.

■ *What reciprocal relationships exist between film and theater in your work? Does working on a stage production change the film you do afterwards, and vice versa, does a film affect subsequent stage productions?*

In the beginning it was pretty extreme. In the theater I would stage things as though I was doing a film, and then I made a film as though it was on the stage; I was pretty pigheaded about that. But then I began to put my experiences to a different use. For me the most important thing about theater is getting along with people, and I do credit myself with being able to work with people better than many others. Instead of taking a break between films, I go to some theater and do a production for not much money. I learn all kinds of things in the process. For instance, it was wonderful working with Karlheinz Böhm when we were making *Martha.* We kept things moving and on target, and understood each other perfectly. Then we worked together in a theater for seven weeks, in Berlin, and abysses opened up between us. We suddenly discovered that we couldn't even speak to each other. For four weeks we'd worked every day from morning to night on a film, but not until we were in the theater did we find out how blocked we both are in our relationships. Actually we both really want to talk to each other. I do think experiences like that are very important.

■ *In the meantime you've made two more films,* Martha *and* Effi Briest. *Do you already have specific plans for 1974?*

Yes, first I'm going to do a film of *Hedda Gabler,* and then . . . oh, I want to do a film . . . I can't really explain what it'll be like.

■ *You're making me curious.*

It's hard to say. I want to try to do a film about myself: what it would be like if I weren't successful. I'm trying to find out what kind of person I'd have become. I would always have tried to earn my living from culture, but let's assume I hadn't had the chance to make films or do theater, then maybe I would have directed radio plays. That's what the film will be about: a young man who does radio plays. He'd probably have the same health problems I do, because they go back to an earlier time, and the psychic dislocations would probably all be about the same, they'd just express themselves differently. Or certain things would be real obstacles to him that aren't to me. I'm really excited about it now—I definitely want to make the film. "The Daily Moods of the Final Certainty"—that'll be the title.

February 1974

"I've changed along with the characters in my films"
A Discussion with Hella Schlumberger about Work and Love, the Exploitability of Feelings, and the Longing for Utopia

■ *You're always criticizing the "provincialism" of Germany, but you're not in America yet. Why not?*

You can't draw any conclusions from the fact that I'm still here. Besides, I'm in Paris most of the time. I think Germany's well on its way to being a nation where people become more and more alike. And that means that real individualists . . .

■ *Like you . . .*

You said it, not I . . . that people who react a little differently to reality have to ask themselves whether they can still afford to have opinions. Whether it's worth it. And that's where castration of the imagination begins.

■ *Could you see yourself being forced some day, like Günter Grass in Italy recently, to defend Germany against the charge of being a fascistic country?*

I couldn't bring myself to defend Germany the way Herr Grass does. Besides, they really should find a new word instead of "fascism."

■ *So what does keep you here in the Federal Republic?*

Obviously the language first of all, which I grew up with and work in. Then my upbringing, my childhood, which of course left their traces—actually those are the reasons why I didn't leave a long, long time ago.

■ *But you always emphasize that you hardly had an upbringing.*

I didn't have an organized, painful upbringing, the kind you'd have to rebel against later on. But afterwards no one could ever get me to go along with anything I didn't accept.

■ *Not even in school?*

No, not even in the Steiner school.

■ *People say you're authoritarian. Is that true?*

I used to be authoritarian, because I didn't have so many options.

Today I can afford to work without the authority that's usually reserved for a director. For that reason I prefer to work with professionals. Earlier, when people were trying to work nonhierarchically, the
group would always look for a Daddy or Mommy when the going got
tough. If I hadn't taken on that role, the group, I mean the various
groups, would have collapsed much sooner. But professionals don't
expect me to play a paternalistic role.

■ *Instead?*

They expect me to accept them as professionals, motivate them,
and acknowledge the significance they have within the production.
The better and more freely they can work, the less anxiety in the
atmosphere.

■ *Essentially you "dug up" some of the old professional
actors...*

That's not true. Colleagues like Karlheinz Böhm and Brigitte Mira
and Barbara Valentin were working all along. Karlheinz Böhm, for instance, regularly appeared on the stage; he had some big successes
there after his time in older German films. The fact that you work with
good stage actors in the cinema isn't particularly held against you elsewhere. And the film crews—apparently no one's interested in what
sort of human beings they are, how they live. People are only interested in the actors—how they live and sleep and that sort of thing.
But not even the left-liberal journalists are interested in the film crews.

■ *Well, what sort of people are they?*

From the beginning I've tried to line up film crews who know their
craft so well that they really enjoy learning new things. Not people
who are just learning the ropes, but those who enjoy trying out something new. It was similar with the actors: the more I had real professionals—the kind who could still be motivated—the less anxiety I felt,
and the more new forms could be tried out, because they had perfect
command of what was normally expected of them.

■ *What sort of anxiety do you mean, what about?*

About failing, about not being validated. It's only while you're still
learning your *métier* that you think you have to keep your eye on
everything. Not later on. A lighting man you can leave to handle the
job as he sees fit can do incredibly wonderful and important things for
a production. In the case of all the professionals who've got caught in
the wheels of television, you can see how their imagination's being
crushed, how they're being molded to perform on command. When
creativity's driven out and only routine performance is wanted, many
of them begin to drink, as a way of dealing with all the cringing they're
forced to do. And it seems to me that if you live your life in a cowardly

way, whatever you actually manage to do can't possibly be very courageous. But we happen to live in a country where that sort of thing's encouraged.

■ *Earlier on you spoke scornfully of the "left-liberal journalists"—what do you have against the leftists in the Federal Republic?*

Most of them aren't that at all, in my opinion. A left that's so little capable of organizing itself . . .

■ *Well, they're individualists, too.*

But if they really want to defend this individuality they should realize that some form of organization is needed. By the way, that's a sentence I don't find easy to say, because I'm basically against any form of organization myself. But how can we preserve individuality in a totally organized society, in a system that will soon be using computers to store information on each of our habits and preferences, if we don't fight it with halfway similar methods? As in fact the reactionaries are doing.

■ *You never say anything against them.*

Against the reactionaries? Just look at the films I make. Fundamentally I've never made movies for the reactionaries; they don't need to be told what I think of them.

■ *And where do you fit in politically in this country, if at all?*

Here I wouldn't categorize myself as "leftist." If I did, I'd have to ask myself which of these splinter groups I identify with, which one I'd want to work with to try to do something for freedom. I'm well aware of how depressingly ineffectual they are, and it seems to me you've got to find better ways to fight such terrifying things as that law that excludes political radicals from civil service professions. And soon you won't even be allowed to demonstrate against nuclear power plants. The fact that things could move at such a dizzying pace certainly shows that we don't have an effective left. And when this Italian professor asks in his seminar papers, "Why is there no opposition in the FRG?" people here smile at the question and say the man doesn't know much about the country, but I'm sorry to say he's right. There isn't any opposition.

■ *You don't expect to find similar horrors in American society?*

A society you haven't grown up in, which you can't see through as easily—well, obviously you'll be less critical toward it. In France you have a broad-based middle class whose life I would describe as more pleasant, and from the outset they're given more options than the Germans. People know they're allowed to have an opinion, and it's not held against you. So of course you enjoy forming one, you see?

■ *Is it still true, as we hear, that in Paris you go sit in a café,*
drink, play pinball, listen to music, and write your screenplays?

It's true, I've done that. In Munich, too, I always have the radio on;
I can get up, watch TV, and so on. I have to have an atmosphere where
I can switch to something else. These incredibly white sheets of paper
really have something terrifying, something paralyzing about them if I
tell myself they've got to be filled up with writing. For me writing isn't
a sacred act, to be carried out in absolute silence. I find writing strenuous, because you have to formulate in words something that already
happened a long time ago in your mind.

■ *And how do you react when people throw obstacles in your*
path when you're working on a project like Garbage, the City, and
Death, *when they charge you with being anti-Semitic?*

I didn't understand it; I found it infuriating. And then the reasons
they gave! That's the last taboo in Germany, this business with the
Jews. And clinging to this taboo, in my opinion, isn't a way of defending the Jews but a further form of discrimination. It stands to reason
that when you create a taboo you get a backlash. If you're not allowed
to talk about them, that simply means that someday they'll be the
scapegoats again. I can't explain it any other way.

■ *And those other taboos—homosexuality, prostitution, and*
transvestitism?

If you present the exotic side, the glamour, then of course they
don't treat these things as taboo, only if you show the societal context.
That's the case with all minorities. Earlier, when I was still making films
where the representatives of the minorities were good and the others
were bad, society really lapped up my films. But when I came up with
the much truer idea of showing the minorities the way society has
made them, with all their twisted behavior, then suddenly people
didn't like my films anymore.

■ *Do you yourself belong to a minority?*

Yes, to several.

■ *To which ones?*

Well, to the minority that can afford to leave this country. Then,
since I have the concrete utopia of anarchy in my head, I'm an extreme proponent of democracy, and that's a minority, too. That's
something you hardly dare mention anymore, this business about anarchy, because we've learned from our media that anarchy and terrorism are synonymous. See, on the one hand you have a utopian ideal of
a form of government that would function without hierarchies, without fear, without aggression, and on the other hand you have a concrete social situation in which utopias are suppressed. The fact that

terrorism could develop here means that the utopian ideal was suppressed far too long. So a few people flipped out, understandably. And a certain ruling class actually wanted that, perhaps even unconsciously, in order to be able to constitute itself more definitively.

■ *What do you do when you're not working? What do you do for fun?*

Don't know. I enjoy going for a drive. Not really looking for adventure, the way other people do, younger people. Nope, in countries and cities where there's a different culture, where I don't even bother to try to get a handle on the social inequities. Just driving around. I might even describe it as tourism.

■ *You go alone?*

I'm trying more and more to learn how to be alone.

■ *The things we often read, about your being a "misogynist" and so on—are they true?*

Somehow it's really idiotic to always have to be saying, "I'm not a misogynist, I'm not an anti-Semite." This is where I think this misogynist business comes from: I take women more seriously than most directors do. To me women aren't just there to get men going; they don't have that role as object. In general, that's an attitude in the movies that I despise. And I simply show that women are forced more than men to use some pretty revolting methods to escape from this role as object.

■ *And how about you personally?*

I have pretty much the same relationship with men and with women. When needs become compulsions, when something that was once fun degenerates into a demand, I always react aggressively and negatively. With Ingrid Caven, the woman I was married to at one time, I still have my most important elective affinity.

■ *Didn't you use to be fairly jealous?*

I still am.

■ *At the moment do you have a, shall we say, happy relationship with anyone?*

Nope, I don't. For three and a half years I've been living with Armin Meier, and that's a particularly difficult relationship. Then, as I said, the important relationship with Ingrid, which now that we're divorced has actually gone back to what it used to be. The fact that someone's simply there, you understand, something you don't have to use all the time or use out of habit. Then I have a very complicated relationship with my mother. I finally came to understand her as my mother at a time when she was very ill. On the one hand that brought out pity in me, on the other hand guilt, because in my egocentrism—as a child I was terribly egocentric, because I didn't have any authority figure who could have put me in my place—I saw her illness as my fault, which then brought out hostility in me. That seemed to me the only way to endure this guilt, no matter how ludicrous and imaginary it was. I'm certain we'll never get over these complications completely, but in the meantime we've become capable of developing something we couldn't have earlier, a friendship. So those are three; the fourth of my happiness-producing or non-happiness-producing relationships is the one with Michael Ballhaus . . .

■ *The cameraman?*

Yes, as a director you really need a cameraman. It goes so far that your two independent private lives actually come to be dependent on each other—that became clear to us the longer we worked together. How important my cameraman is to me is a relatively recent insight. Earlier I would have denied it.

■ *And all these relationships you regard as "material" to be used in your work. Can you really still live spontaneously?*

Viewed quite soberly, no. On the other hand, I think that by going through extreme situations involving despair and pain, even when they're used as "material," you can arrive at a new spontaneity. That seems to offer a better chance of achieving a new naiveté of experience than repression.

■ *That sounds pretty fragmented, pretty negative. Isn't there any positive realm for you?*

Not for me. It seems to me the society I live in is shaped not by happiness and freedom but rather by oppression, fear, and guilt. In my opinion, what we're taught to experience as happiness is a pretext that a society shaped by various forms of compulsion offers the individual. And I'm not about to accept that offer.

■ *Well, where do you get the strength to go on working?*

From my utopian ideal, from my perfectly concrete yearning for this utopia. If this yearning is driven out of me, I'll come to a dead stop; that's why I have this feeling I'm being murdered as a creative person in Germany, and please don't take that for paranoia. In my opinion, this witchhunt we've been going through, which I think is only the tip of the iceberg, was staged to destroy individuals' utopias. And also to cause my fears and guilt to become overwhelming. When it's reached the point where my fears are greater than my yearning for something beautiful, I'll have to put an end to it. Not only to my work.

■ *To your life?*

Yes, sure. There's no reason to exist when you don't have a goal anymore.

■ *But you are trying to realize parts of this utopia in your own life, aren't you?*

Yes. Of course you try it first in human relationships. But I'd say that I've been more successful at driving away fears through work, through work done jointly with others. And then there are moments of great happiness that validate me in what I'm doing, and not only me, the whole team.

■ *Could you imagine falling madly in love, going away somewhere and not working at all?*

Funny, when I've fallen madly in love it's always resulted on the contrary in a craze for work. I want to work with the person in question, because for me it all goes together.

■ *You're working right now on your new project,* Berlin Alexanderplatz. *How far along is it?*

It's a complicated project: a television series that runs thirteen and a half hours and—with another cast and a different format—a film. It's an attempt to film the novel in two fundamentally different narrative styles.

■ *This project was so important to you that for the time being you gave up going to America.*

In many of the films I've made, there are quotes from Döblin's novel. Actually it's not the character Franz Biberkopf, but the constellation of how, because of a certain incompetence that people get from their upbringing, they mess up their lives. The main point of the novel is that people mess up because they don't dare to admit to their needs and desires, and as a result their souls atrophy, and they aren't capable of living a so-called normal life anymore.

■ *In the script for the television series or for the film are there passages that are completely different from the novel, or did you stick close to the book?*

In the final analysis, of course, everything's different. The television series is an attempt to encourage the reader to read, even though he's offered visual gratification. The film works entirely differently: first of all, it narrates a story in concentrated form, which achieves its effect only retroactively, when the moviegoer's consciousness and imagination kick in. You might say I've stuck close to the book. You might just as well say I've made some crucial changes.

■ *Why?*

In favor of the women, I should point out. In Döblin the women are narrated with considerably less specific identity than the men. I've tried, to the extent it was at all possible within this narrative framework, to describe the women as just as valuable as the men. That's one very definite change from Döblin. For him, women, as in the eighteenth-century novel, are more objects that a man takes advantage of when the mood or the need strikes. In my opinion, Döblin was bogged down in this tradition. That's the most crucial and important change I made. And then in Döblin there are lots of interior monologues. For those I wanted to and had to find visual images, strings of images that would set in motion the same interior monologue in the viewer that Döblin portrayed with literary means, and on approximately the same literary level.

■ *Have you already picked the actors for the two versions?*

Yes, the most important roles are already fairly well set. In the television version Klaus Löwitsch will play Franz Biberkopf, Eva Mattes will be Mieze, and I'll play Reinhold. Andrea Ferréol will play Eva; Franz Buchrieser, an Austrian writer and actor, will play Meck— those are the big parts. In the film Gérard Depardieu is Franz Biberkopf, Klaus Löwitsch is Reinhold, Isabelle Adjani is Mieze, Jeanne Moreau is Eva, Charles Aznavour is Meck, and that's it.

■ *Will they speak Berlin dialect in the film?*

Nope, no way. I want a kind of synthetic language to be invented, and each actor should do that for himself. It's not supposed to be a uniform Berlin dialect, but rather a fairly consistent synthetic language that has some connection with the native dialect of each actor who's speaking and acting, which grows out of it.

■ *What other "local color" will there be? Will you be shooting on Alexanderplatz?*

For me, and I think this was the case with Döblin, too, Alexanderplatz isn't the important thing. The important thing for me are the refuges, the places people go to hide. They tell me more about the external world, about the elements of fear and danger lurking in external life, than the real external world. I think whatever fears are at work inside people can be recognized from the places they flee to; how they settle in—these places provide the opportunity for such a recognition. Do you understand what I'm saying?

■ *What's the function of this synthetic language? A language that isn't spoken anywhere, by anyone?*

I find it awful when a person in a film talks the way people talk in real life. In my opinion that robs a thought of its general strength. It eliminates the general state of fearfulness. How should I put it? It reduces everything to something the moviegoer can reject, simply because he doesn't happen to speak this dialect, doesn't move this particular way in real life. In my opinion artificiality offers the only possibility for giving a broad spectrum of moviegoers access to the specific world of an artistic work.

■ *How do you feel in Paris—in comparison with Munich?*

Better, because in Paris there are many more opportunities to do the things you want to, but also the freedom not to do them. I don't have to clutter up my mind with things I'd like to do but can't, the way I do in Munich.

■ *What sort of things?*

Cultural, personal, sexual, whatever.

■ *You couldn't conceive of living out in the country?*

No.

■ *What sort of a relationship do you have to nature, if any?*

I don't find nature any more human than human beings.

■ *Just as cruel?*

Yes.

■ *Is there one recurrent dream you have?*

Yes. There's a dream in which I've committed a murder. Sometimes I know whom I've murdered, and sometimes I just know that I've murdered someone, and sometimes I don't even know whether I've murdered someone, but I'm living under suspicion or on the run.

■ *Along with the feeling of being pursued, do you also have a sense that you're guilty?*

That's the problem I'm always turning over in my mind. I don't believe that being pursued is the crucial thing in these dreams, but rather the idea that there's something that gives me this sense of guilt or wants to make me aware of some kind of guilt through the dream. That's more important than the part about being pursued, which is just very uncomfortable. And that part is probably only there to make me experience the guilt, or whatever it is, in a more concrete way.

■ *Is there ever a time when you're cheerful?*

Always—for instance I'm cheerful right now.

■ *Aha. But it doesn't show.*

It doesn't have to. Cheerfulness that's characterized as cheerfulness by the usual signs usually isn't the real thing. I'm cheerful in a certain way, and it's for myself. Expressing it—that's something I can't do.

■ *You don't want to, either.*

I probably can't do it because I don't want to. If I'm so cheerful that people notice, they'll be totally nonplused and say, "He must be mentally deranged," or something like that. As much as possible I want to avoid replaying my life. Do you understand what I mean?

■ *No.*

Well, I don't want to trot my feelings out all over again, the way it happens in a film or on television or in the theater, where you would stage it so others could see what was happening inside you.

■ *Is that too simplistic for you, too crude?*

That's neither too simplistic nor too crude for me. It would just take an effort that would destroy the feeling for me.

■ *Yet other people's feelings don't matter to you.*

No, I experience other people's joy just the same as mine. I don't have to be told about it.

■ *Haven't you ever heard from others that your presence doesn't exactly encourage people to be open, because you always have this air of artificiality about you?*

I'd think it would be just the opposite. But when a person who's eating feels it's necessary to keep saying, "Oh, what a marvelous piece of meat!" or "This sauce is incredibly delicious!" I have a strange feeling that for some reason he has to talk himself into believing it. Or if you're out for a walk and the other person keeps saying how lovely it is to go walking with you and look at the sunset. Then I say, "No way, thanks a lot." Up to here and no farther. Someone who always feels the necessity to say what he may or may not be feeling—he must have to talk himself into it. There's a wonderful film about this, which I saw when I was very young and which had a big influence on me: *Le bonheur,* by Agnès Varda. The film says that for people who are objectively happy but who feel they have to keep asserting it, happiness is incredibly interchangeable. The man has a wife and two children, and they always find everything just beautiful. Then the woman kills herself, yes, she does, and then he goes on to the next one, and everything just continues as before, because there's no real emotion behind it. That's how I would see the problem on the whole. In principle I'm not against expressing something now and then; on the contrary—language is a significant means of getting things across, after all. But I just think it shouldn't be a constant thing. Especially when it comes to feelings, I really react critically.

■ *Are you sometimes afraid of seeming banal to yourself?*

No, I wouldn't say that. No.

■ *For instance, can you say, "I love you?"*

I can, for instance. There comes a moment when I can't do anything but say it. I've even got myself to the point where I don't tell myself how dumb it sounds. In the beginning I would say, "I love you," but make it ironic. In the meantime I've taught myself not to, and when the moment comes, I simply say it. Which doesn't mean that I'm not standing back and watching myself at the same time. But this business of always checking to see if my experiences can be used as material is another question.

■ *So you do use these love scenes as material, don't you?*

That's true. On the one hand I use what I've experienced as material; on the other hand I allow my film characters much more leeway than I give myself. For instance, I reached the point much earlier with the characters in my films where I could give them a chance to express their feelings directly.

■ *So through your film characters . . .*

With my film characters . . .

■ *Through and along with your film characters you yourself have changed?*

Yes. If you look at my first ten films one after the other, you'll notice that these characters really had a chance to react incredibly directly in situations. Basically they're not very talkative, right? And suddenly . . . yes, in the first ten films the expression, "Wow, that's crazy!" occurs at least fifty times, simply because someone experiences a situation as so powerful, as so complex, that that's all he can say. That can mean anything and everything, terrible or terrific. At that time I wouldn't have allowed myself to say something like that. But today I would.

■ *What sort of relationship do you have to sex?*

Hm, hm, hm, that question's too general.

■ *In your films, at any rate, sex always plays a very big role. Could you picture yourself as a hermit off writing somewhere in a mountain hut?*

I couldn't do that. When I write, I consider my work a substantially more satisfying sexual act than with another person. Certainly I'm not a hermit off in the wilderness somewhere, but I have substantially more sexual contact with my work.

■ *In your case do work and love contradict or complement each other?*

I don't follow a fixed pattern, if that's what you mean—one day of living, one day of writing. Rather, I've lived a few weeks during which a project took concrete shape in my mind, and then there's nothing but work for a few days, a few weeks, it depends, and that's really the sexual contact with the work process; it turns me on. It's no accident that there have been people in my life who became jealous of a typewriter, a writing pad, a tape recorder, or a camera, even more jealous than they would have been of another human being.

■ *Are you capable of, how shall I put it, surrendering to another person?*

Once I had a relationship in which I came pretty much to the verge of self-surrender. That happened to me once, but it won't happen again.

■ *You're sure?*

Absolutely sure.

■ *Self-protection?*

Yes. From that relationship I learned never to let a relationship get that way again.

■ *And an equal relationship between two people who are equally strong?*

That would be desirable, sure. In practice ... well, you can only hope, let's put it that way.

■ *So theoretically you could live alone.*

You're asking why I don't forgo my relationships? I guess I still need them for some reason. Unfortunately.

■ *Unfortunately?*

Yes, unfortunately. I'm at a point where I would actually be very glad if I could live without steady relationships. Probably I'd be happier. To what extent I'd succeed in achieving that is another question.

■ *What do you actually have besides work, love, smoking, and drinking?*

Not a thing. What I do gives me pleasure. Even the pressures I occasionally subject myself to—deadline pressures and the like—aren't stressful for me.

■ *But when you express it that way, it doesn't really sound convincing.*

Yes, yes, because it's changed a little, because I have to recognize that I subject myself to fewer pressures than I used to. But I can't work for the desk drawer, that I can't do. Writing or directing a play in the theater, making a film—there the external structure provided by deadlines really meets my needs.

■ *You've never been tempted to write stories or a novel, without time pressure and without a commission from a publisher?*

No. I guess I'm too extroverted. The thought of not being certain that later on it ...

■ *Might become a bestseller?*

No, not at all. Will at least get published and have a chance to reach a person I'm writing for. I can't write for myself, that's not necessary.

■ *How would you define yourself if you had to? What are your weaknesses?*

It's fairly hard to answer that. As I see it, and as I live, I don't have any weaknesses. I've set things up so that objectively I won't have any, but can simply live my life subjectively, the best way I can conceive of. I know that's a luxury. Maybe that's my weakness, that I do it. But I'd answer your question this way: I don't have any weaknesses so long as I'm still working to do something about the things I consider wrong. They only become weaknesses when they become rigid, become final stages.

■ *So you'd picture the ideal partner as being just like you, without weaknesses?*

That would be my ideal, yes.

■ *Yes?*

Hm.

■ *You haven't found anyone like that yet?*

No, hardly.

■ *So the people you were together with were more like your opposites?*

Up to now I've picked people to live with for a longer time who didn't present an intellectual challenge for me. More psychological, practical challenges, if at all. Maybe that's a weakness. But then I've had so many important experiences that I couldn't have had with people I could only interact with intellectually. I'd really like to be involved with someone with whom everything is possible. Where sex, eroticism, consciousness, everything is in constant dialogue. And that in one person—that would be great. Except I don't believe anymore that it's possible.

■ *Have the themes of your films, the general tenor, changed markedly in the last ten years?*

No, the tenor, if you will, hasn't changed. The theme's remained the same, and always will remain the same: the manipulability, the exploitability of feelings within the system that we live in, and that at least one generation or more after us will certainly have to live in. What's changed is the workmanship, the form, where I always try to get beyond what I've already mastered. In contrast to other artists, I've given up the purist notion about art that I once had: that art has to be very direct and very simple. For me that always had to do with the level of my technical skill. For me it would have been a mistake to stick with these theories once they were developed. For others that may be perfectly all right.

■ *In your films death appears often. You've said that there were situations in your life when you played with the idea of killing yourself. How do you feel about that at the moment?*

Life doesn't become manageable and accessible until the moment when death is accepted as the true aspect of existence. As long as death is treated as a taboo, life remains uninteresting. A society based on the exploitation of human beings has to treat death as a taboo. In my life there came an important moment when my body suddenly realized it was mortal. Since then life's been much more fun for me. Even if it doesn't always appear that way, as you've remarked a couple of times. It was the business with the pain in my heart. It got to the point where I couldn't breathe, where I said to myself, Okay, now you're going to swallow all the pills. It wasn't until the doctor examined me and said that physically there was nothing wrong with me that the symptoms stopped. Within three days. The body really is terrifying.

■ *Why?*

This difference between the body, which gets you in the end, and the spirit, which is actually immortal—that's really a terrible discrepancy. A spirit which, existentially speaking, can move about freely, and a body with intestines—ugh!

■ *It sounds as though you don't have a particularly affectionate relationship with your body.*

That's where you're completely mistaken. I have great affection for the opportunities for fun, for pleasure, for everything my body's capable of producing. No doubt about it. Still, not for one moment does the body lose the repulsive feature that it can refuse to meet the needs of my spirit. The spirit's there, and in a different body it would certainly be different, too. Of course the spirit has to make do with the specific body through which it experiences things.

■ *Do you actually want to be someone entirely different, or are you satisfied with who you are?*

No, no. Well, maybe way back, when I was between fifteen and twenty and had really bad acne. Otherwise, never. I'm much too content with myself. Really, I'm so satisfied with myself that it borders on lunacy.

■ *Certainly there are some people making films that you would have liked to make yourself.*

I'd like to have made *Amarcord,* by Fellini, *The Damned* by Visconti, five or six films that Douglas Sirk's made, *Le diable probablement* by Bresson, twenty or thirty American films . . . Maybe I couldn't have done it, either, but that's not my problem.

■ *You didn't mention any German directors.*

Yes, I did. Douglas Sirk is German.

■ *But how about the young filmmakers?*

There are a few—*Eika Katappa* by Werner Schroeter, *48 Hours to Acapulco* by Klaus Lemke, *Yesterday Girl* by Dr. Alexander Kluge —those are the most important. *A Degree of Murder* by Volker Schlöndorff.

■ *Is there any sort of contact, exchange of ideas, collaboration among the German directors?*

Only very sporadically, and nothing organized. I have connections with filmmakers, but they're entirely personal in nature: with Werner Schroeter, Daniel Schmid, Walter Bockmayer. I have relationships with directors like Ulf Miehe, Uwe Brandner, Hark Bohm. In a rather complicated way, too, with Wim Wenders and Werner Herzog. From my end, and maybe also from his, I have a very strong relationship with the "little doctor," Alexander Kluge.

■ *How about Herbert Achternbusch?*

I've met him once or twice, but he's not someone I could develop a strong personal relationship with. His art may be interesting from the outside, but not from the inside.

■ *In your opinion, what effect can films have on society? What can a filmmaker do for society?*

He can do a lot. Entertain. Tell stories in such a way that the moviegoer is entertained and afterwards is no stupider; he can make various things clear to him or make him want to get various things straight for himself, he can express fears. For others. If no one does that, we'd withdraw into the kind of silence in which sooner or later you become a moron. Film can give the moviegoer the courage to continue expressing things, taking a position on them, and making it known. I do feel that film as a medium can be effective in all sorts of ways. And it's always a means of entertainment, and should remain that, too. Like literature, which is also supposed to be fun, or music, quite aside from the effect it can have.

■ *If you were to do an interview with yourself, what further questions would you have?*

I don't have any other questions, I don't know. This was your interview, after all.

1977

"This is the only way we can do films here: by making them without worrying about losing money"
A Conversation with Wolfram Schütte about *The Third Generation*, Cinematic Politics, and a Strategy against Resignation

■ *Now that you've finished shooting* The Third Generation, *I'd like to hear whether you still stand behind what you wrote in a foreword to the screenplay. Is it true, as you claim there, that the time is past when people here were reluctant to make the kind of film that's simultaneously political and commercial, comparable to those of Rosi, Damiani, or Cayatte?*

In spite of all I've experienced, and particularly the problems I had working on *The Third Generation*, what I said is not even that far from the truth. If you take a film like *Knife in the Head*, for instance—I'm not talking about quality here—there you certainly have a film that deals in its own way with political questions or brings them up for discussion, and yet that film's been very successful.

■ *But it was your hope, in respect to your film* The Third Generation *as well, that state subsidies would be available for treating current political material like that.*

I thought that, but at least in my case it didn't turn out to be true. Maybe because the underlying theme is a little harder to grasp than in *Knife in the Head;* but I'm thinking in general more of films that aren't as extreme in their politics (without being "extremist") as my most recent one. What I'm thinking of are films that react promptly and directly to something that's still going on. The fact that people always want to have screenplays before they invest any money, that an idea for a treatment, a subject, isn't good enough for them—that's a real obstacle. The moment I sit down to write a screenplay, I'm going to be more cautious, I'm going to give some thought to what so-and-so or so-and-so will have to say about it. Then I'm already in the meat grinder, and time goes by, during which all my radical emotions fizzle. Because of this, maybe what I said in my Foreword was   31 too optimistic; maybe other people should do this, too. Maybe they should confront the situation of occasionally making a film without all these obstacles.

■ *But what you're talking about is very individualistic. Your examples from Italy come from a specific tradition, a regular film industry, no matter how much it's come down in the world. Here we have nothing like that anymore.*

Should you sit around waiting until something's become a tradition, or shouldn't you rather roll up your sleeves and get to work developing one? All you can do is try to get a bandwagon going that lots of other people will jump on.

■ *But apparently we don't feel such a pressing need for that sort of thing. Since the collective film* Germany in Autumn—*where you had a whole bunch of people "on board"—nothing remotely comparable has been done.*

For my part I've tried to carry on with what I understood the production of *Germany in Autumn* to be all about: with *In a Year of Thirteen Moons* and *The Third Generation.* At the time Kluge and I said: If we have to wait till a plane's hijacked to have a reason for making such films, the whole thing is ridiculous.

■ *Of course you're in a fortunate position: you can write your own screenplays (and very fast, too).*

Well, it's the same with Kluge, for instance. After *Germany in Autumn* we wanted to do a film together, but then Kluge's been involved in these ongoing battles over cinematic politics for twenty years, so even though he was euphoric over *Germany in Autumn,* he still thought you really should have a written script. But I'm sure he can get over that. The bad thing about written scripts is the pressure to conform to the wishes of the television editor or the funding agencies. So the screenplays end up having a different structure from what you would have given them. As a result, from the word "go" the film is headed in a direction that militates against spontaneity and subjectivity. I certainly don't consider it a disadvantage when a person can write his own screenplays, but the killer is that you don't write screenplays for making a film but for getting funded. Maybe that's a small distinction, but it's a crucial one.

■ *Well, what demands would you make, in light of the situation in filmmaking here?*

That an industry be established . . .

■ *But how could that be done?*

You can do it by saying, for instance, Okay, now we've made the film *Germany in Autumn,* and it brought in money. And our demand was that the money be used to make other movies like it—by us or others. And without censorship before the fact. But those people in the Filmverlag have already begun to practice censorship by saying, We're the Filmverlag, we financed *Germany in Autumn*. We made it possible, so we have to see what else we're going to make possible. That's the same kind of censorship or noncensorship as in television. For instance, I wanted to make a film with Kluge and Wolfgang Berndt on *The Marriages of Our Parents,* and the Filmverlag people were giving us funny looks. Well, that didn't bother me, but Kluge and Berndt got depressed right away. And I can't maintain enough euphoria for the three of us, it's hard enough to keep up my own. So that's what did in the project: the way they looked at us—"Ummm, is that *really* such an important subject . . . " A funny look, a head cocked to one side, did in the whole project.

■ *Isn't it true that people in the industry here don't really believe in cinematic successes and therefore dole out their energy only in cautious little doses?*

That's true. It must have something to do with their reluctance, their fear. Theo Hinz from the Filmverlag said to me at the time, "Why don't we do a sex film, with several directors?" So I said, "Okay, why not?" If he'd just made the suggestion and then kept his hands off, the film we would have made about sex—if we'd approached it the way we did *Germany in Autumn*—wouldn't have been nonpolitical and wouldn't have been a sex film like the rest of them. But when he started to pick and choose, to tell me which directors he thought had a "feel for eroticism," it made me sick, and I thought to myself, this isn't going to work. It's been my experience that these people who run companies apparently can't take any kind of criticism they don't consider "constructive."

■ *But when you say we really should make films that are political and commercial at the same time, it turns out that that's been possible only in a few individual cases. And then all we have in the way of a potential coproducer and distributor is the Filmverlag; television either blocks you, or you have to tailor what you write to its wishes. But then what other possibilities are there?*

Well, there's the possibility of simply making films.

■ *But why aren't they being made anymore?*

That's a trick question. I've made them, after all.

■ *Yes, that's why I'm asking you specifically.*

I can only guess that the others don't make them because of all the problems, and that's how it should be. If people capitulate on films that are "critical of the system" because of the problems others create for them, well, they probably don't really want to make those films anyway. That may sound mean . . .

■ *Yes, in a sense that's a devastating judgment . . .*

That may be. All I can say is that if I think I really have to do something, nothing in the world's going to stop me—well, hardly anything. I'll do it anyway, somehow, sometime. And if more people were that way, we wouldn't have only *Katharina Blum, The Second Awakening of Christa Klages, Germany in Autumn, Knife in the Head*—we'd have lots of other films.

■ *But if so many projects have been rejected or got hung up or were abandoned for one reason or another, where is that pile of screenplays that never made it?*

Well, there's a version of *Knife in the Head* that was rejected. Clearly for political reasons. Then there's *The Earth Is Uninhabitable Like the Moon*, which couldn't be made. Then there's certainly some project or other of Kluge's that he has in a drawer somewhere, and probably some by the Berlin crowd.

■ *You say "probably."*

Well, it's hard to talk about screenplays you don't know. After all, people don't run around with big smiles on their faces and screenplays tucked under their arms that they can't get any funding for.

■ *Yes, but why doesn't this become known?*

That's a good question. Because it would look like failure.

■ *But apparently they're also scared . . .*

They certainly are.

■ *But unless two or three overcome this fear, how's the situation ever supposed to change?*

It hardly can. But look, when the *Frankfurter Rundschau* prints my foreword to *The Third Generation*, I certainly don't make a lot of friends that way. So other people should also go around saying: I'd like to make a film about such-and-such, but I don't dare to, I don't even dare to write a script, because no one will finance it anyhow. That would at least be something.

■ *But of course they're all so cut off from one another . . .*

Yes, we have to talk about organizing now. But people prefer to have less to do with each other rather than more.

■ *And how do you feel about that?*

Well, when we founded the filmmakers' syndicate I considered it more a coalition of directors who could really discuss what they ought to make in the way of films and how to put them across. But very quickly it degenerated into an association that dealt only with legal issues. Whenever you brought up subject matter, they'd say, We'll be stuck here for three days. Well, we probably would have. You're asking me to tell you something I don't know myself: how you get people to come together.

■ *But you're the only one who's working all the time. The question is whether the others can't or don't want to . . .*

I think they can't. They won't get involved in all the things you have to get involved in if you want to keep working all the time. I don't know . . .

■ *Do you actually have any contact with the younger ones? After all, there's a new generation coming along . . .*

There certainly is, but I know them only from the film academy in Munich. The few I do know really have entirely different interests.

■ *What sort of different interests?*

They're not interested in making political films. They love to watch the hits from the fifties, and that's the kind of thing they'd like to be making, too.

■ *Do you have the impression that's a general trend?*

I have the feeling it's a trend. It doesn't mean a thing to those young people to make a film about here and now. For instance, all those things that play on television and pretend to be concerned with reality are incredibly pathetic, at least in part. They'd never make you want to do anything like that. If you look at the documentaries we've had, you really wouldn't want to be in the same boat. I can understand that very well. Even Caterina Valente movies are more fun.

■ *Do you still believe it's possible—the distributors, movie-theater owners, and their organizations dispute this—that West German films can pay for themselves in their own country?*

Yes, I believe it is. I don't "still" believe it, but I do believe it can come to be the case again, though only if you make such films without worrying about losing money—as we all did at one time. I'm thinking of political films. That sounds so dry—that's not what I mean. They should certainly be films that have some glamour, but also have something to do with the city where they're made, or with the country or the people used in them. It may be that the pressure to make films was considerably greater on those who began in 1966/67. They'd been sitting around for ten years without being able to do anything. Maybe this pressure doesn't exist to such a degree anymore. I'm happy to hear that the young ones are writing a manifesto, but what if it stops there? It was different with people like Schroeter or Bockmayer. When they began, they already had ten eight-millimeter films lying around, and it may turn out that it was the best work they ever did.

■ *Back to* The Third Generation *again. You wanted to make the*

*film here in Berlin with money from the Berlin Senate and with
funding from WDR, didn't you? That didn't pan out.*

That didn't pan out. WDR finally withdrew for what were obviously political reasons. The producer in charge told me the movie
represented a point of view he didn't share and also didn't dare to
have his broadcasting company represent. The representative of the
Berlin Senate first spontaneously said yes, but then he pulled out too
when we got around to discussing the topic. In addition there was a
very strange letter from Berlin's police commissioner, who refused us
permission—we needed permission from him—to film in a Berlin
bank. Maybe I should have told them I was doing an entirely different
movie—something like a "love story in divided Berlin"—and then
gone ahead and made the one I had in mind. Then I would have gotten
money. But you can only get away with something like that once, and
I don't think that's the right way.

■ *But now you've made the film. And what changes resulted
from the situation?*

Nothing about the film was changed. The acceptances sounded so
firm and actually were, too, that I couldn't change anything. When the
support was withdrawn, we were already into our first week of shooting. What did change is that I'm maybe 300,000 marks more in debt.
I shot the film the way I would have if I'd had 500,000 marks more.
It's a question of courage, or of craziness. I could have stopped at that
point, and my debts would have been smaller, but I wouldn't have had
the film; that was never a real option for me. Maybe that's something
you can't ask of other people.

■ *Doesn't that weigh on you? All the debts?*

Only as far as my work's concerned. Debts I can repay. But you
can't ask that of other people—I mean, I would of course ask it of
them, unfair as I am. Why can't you folks do it if I can? But if I think it
over calmly, I just can't ask that of anyone: that the main thing should
be the film, and then a heap of debts, and the other person doesn't
know how he's supposed to pay them. But that's the only way the kind
of films could get made that might result in an industry some day. I
can't picture it any other way. Because what I wouldn't find so good
would be an industry that involved selection committees and lobby-
ing; then you'd have to make so many compromises. You just have to
do it the capitalist way, accepting the suspicion and the risk. If I make
a handbag, I don't know either whether I'll be able to sell it. First I
produce it, then I try to market it. I'd rather try to sell a film than go
around peddling a screenplay or an idea. At least a film is done,
whereas an idea can still be done in.

■ *If you compare* The Third Generation *with* In a Year of Thirteen Moons, *which is a very complex, complicated film after all . . .*

Well, the new one's very simple, because it has one theme, one central question, one starting point in the imagination: that is, that in the last analysis terrorism is an idea generated by capitalism to justify better defense measures to safeguard capitalism. The idea itself is fairly complicated, so I told myself I'd make the film fairly easy. Here the basic idea was supposed to be told as colorfully as possible, as strikingly as possible, so that the moviegoer could get somewhere with this basic idea.

■ *In your foreword you talked about how this third generation of terrorists lacked any real political motivation.*

Which is true, yes. I think this is a generation of terrorists who have no more goals, no utopia; the others at least had the despair they'd experienced. The third generation doesn't throw a bomb in order to put something else in place of what's destroyed. It just hurls a bomb. That's it. But that's not the main problem the film's about. The main problem, rather, is that it's precisely those people who don't have any reasons, any motivation, any despair, any utopia, who can easily be used by others. That's the idea I wanted to get across by making the film. It doesn't matter, for instance, whether there ever really was an entrepreneur who set up terrorist cells in order to increase sales of his computers. There doesn't have to have been. It's quite sufficient for me if I say, The rebels in Northern Ireland are playing into the hands of England, which wants to keep that area under its thumb. The idea's the same.

■ *But there is a difference, because there you have a causal connection.*

But you can say, If it weren't that way, you'd have to invent it. Of course the whole thing isn't a documentary about terrorism; I don't know whether that's what people see in it. But what was the effect of the things that have happened in this country over the last few years? Well, laws have been pushed through which they (the politicians) apparently would have liked to have anyway. I mean, when the federal chancellor says, I'm grateful to the lawyers that they didn't examine the whole Mogadishu business from the constitutional point of view, it's wonderful, it's so nice, I just love it, because he's saying exactly what I've been trying to point out.

■ *Well, what do you think of the "German Model"?*

There's no way around it: the model's a democracy, as pretty as you please, but what kind of democracy defends itself by appealing to values that you're not allowed to criticize? Where you can't even say anymore, What kind of values are these on which everything's based? When even a question like that is forbidden? When real democracy would mean keeping democracy alive by constant questioning and criticizing. But over the course of time it's turned out that democracy here is handled in such an authoritarian way that you couldn't do any better in an authoritarian state. At least I wouldn't say that the "German Model" is one for the entire Western world.

■ *Is there any connection with the fact that in the epilogue to* The Marriage of Maria Braun *you show the pictures of the German postwar chancellors, but significantly not the picture of Willy Brandt?*

Yes, I have the impression that the period under Willy Brandt was an exception, that Brandt actually encouraged self-questioning, which Wehner apparently didn't want, to be specific, keeping the elements that support the state open to criticism. I just have the feeling that what Brandt did was something not everybody was happy with. I understand democracy as something that functions like a kaleidoscope, that is, not permanent revolution, but permanent movement, permanent questioning by every generation. When I see the fuss being made over *Holocaust,* I wonder why they have to make such a fuss; have they really repressed and forgotten all of that? They can't have forgotten it; they must have had it on their minds when they were creating their new state. If a thing of so much significance could be forgotten or repressed, then something must be pretty wrong with this democracy and this "German Model."

■ *But why did it have to be an American television film that got people talking about the subject again? Why wasn't something like that made here?*

I did want to do something. I wanted to do it with *Debit and Credit,* which wouldn't have stopped with the Bismarck period. But what scared people off was precisely that I wanted to continue the story into the present day, and logically I would have gotten to the Third Reich and this republic we have now. And for some people that was pretty scary.

■ *You dedicated your film* The Marriage of Maria Braun, *which was finished last summer, after* Despair, *but only now introduced at the Berlin Film Festival, to Peter Zadek. What meaning do such dedications have for you?*

I don't do my dedications in such a way that I say, This film has a lot to do with so-and-so, who it's dedicated to, but in this case, for instance, I want to say that Zadek is one of those who shattered the ossified way of life that *The Marriage of Maria Braun* describes. From a certain point on, Zadek was also very important to me, as a person, as someone to talk to. It liberated me a bit to know there was someone around who was over fifty and completely set in his ways and then changed himself so totally. I find something very positive and hopeful in that. Five years ago he was a major figure just as he was, and then he changed himself totally.

■ *When you speak of encouraging things, was Zadek the only one who gave you hope?*

In the last few years I've seen eight or nine films that meant a lot to me, and two theater productions and a few musicals that contained more hope and utopia than a thousand encounters. I'm thinking of *Solares* [by A. Tarkovski], then *Le diable probablement* [by Robert Bresson], Zadek's two most recent productions of *Othello* and *A Winter's Tale*; then there's a film by Maurice Pialat with the title *We Won't Grow Old Together;* then I've seen Visconti's *The Damned* thirty times. *Le diable probablement* is certainly the film of an old man, but no one can deny that the film is incredibly young in spirit—whether it's a glorification of suicide or an acceptance of it, or, as I think, the opposite, that is, that Bresson says: You have more opportunities to live your life if you accept death. It's simply incredibly beautiful, even just from the point of view of form, when you see that someone who's so old, and had already reached an end with *Lancelot,* didn't simply churn out an "old man's film" with *Le diable probablement.* Because that isn't an old man's film but a young film.

■ *Well, that's something we see more often nowadays, a radicalism of age, the radicalism of the elderly, which you just don't find in younger people.*

No, you do find it, though not very often. Kluge has, or might have, something like that. He's just too smart to become completely stupid, he can't do it somehow, at least I always hope he can't. Then there's Horst Laube, who really amazed me incredibly. When he was the dramaturg at the Frankfurt Theater you couldn't even talk with him. Then he took himself out of the whole theater racket—he still does something here and there to earn some money—but he started to write all over again. It's not a matter of what he turns out, but what impresses me and appeals to me is that there are people who can find their way out of the dead-end street where they'd gotten bogged down. Of course when you look at those who find their way out, you realize how many others there are who never make it.

■ *Have you read Bernward Vesper's book* The Journey?

Yes, I've read it.

■ *And didn't that stimulate you, give you ideas?*

Stimulate, yes, but that's the kind of book I live with, and something from it certainly flowed into the things I've done most recently, *In a Year of Thirteen Moons* or *The Third Generation*. But there are a few things, books, which I live with more. There's a whole series of projects I haven't filmed. Among them are Unica Zürn's *The Man in Jasmine*, a book that impressed me the most this past year. But when I think of it, it's more works of art than people that have impressed me. But also people: Zadek, Kluge, and Laube.

February 1979

"Reacting to What You Experience"
Ernst Burkel Talks with Douglas Sirk and Rainer Werner Fassbinder

■ *Herr Fassbinder, in your films it's noticeable that you always place yourself clearly at the center.*

FASSBINDER: I've always done that. But in hindsight that was also true of the so-called Hollywood studio directors. When you look at films made by them, those films can only be by a certain director. That it's more personal in our case has to do with the fact that we don't have that studio system, and therefore can insert our own personality more freely and easily. But even with the studio system, where there was always something in the way, you can see clearly that this film can only be by Douglas Sirk, say, or this other one only by Raoul Walsh. In spite of the studios, in spite of the fact that they had to work at least part of the time with actors they didn't want to work with, you still get a very personal view of the world.

■ *Is that what constitutes your concept of the cinema?*

F: I tell what I experience, and anything I pass on truthfully has to be valid for other people, because my way of seeing things may have a different setting from other people's, but ultimately they're the same experiences. That's why I think that if I tell a story very personally, it'll be valid for more people than if I try to tell it in universal terms. But even within this "film land" he [Sirk] was in, the personal way of seeing was so important that individual bodies of work were created. The only difficulty is figuring out what the personal, the specific, element is in these people's films. A sentence by Jean Paul can always be recognized as a sentence by Jean Paul, but then a Douglas Sirk sequence can also always be recognized as a Douglas Sirk sequence, in spite of the industry and the conditions it imposes. The fact that we're a bit more personal now has to do with the fact that we can afford to be that way—at the moment. That may change. Perhaps some day I'll get to work in another system, but in the system we have now we'll always focus on the personal element. And that's what I saw concretely for   41 the first time in Douglas Sirk: that apparently under the conditions of a completely different system, where everything revolves around money, you can still come up with something very individual and personal.

SIRK: Rainer's hit the nail on the head. The most important thing for a filmmaker should be an image of his reality. When I see a Max Beckmann, for instance, I know it can only be Beckmann; an Emil Nolde is Nolde, and with Rainer I know it's Rainer. He has an unforgettable signature, an unmistakable signature.

F: Mine is hard to mistake. There actually are people who imitate things, simply try to copy something just because they like it, rather than adapt it. After I'd seen Sirk's films, when I made my next film—that was *The Merchant of Four Seasons*—I was in danger of copying *All That Heaven Allows*, too. Later I tried to do a remake of what I'd seen in it. That was *Fear Eats the Soul*. But you mustn't simply do something over again, just because you like it; you should try to tell your own story, using your film experience. That's why the scene in *Fear Eats the Soul* where the television's kicked in is different from the one in *All That Heaven Allows* where the children decide to give a television set for Christmas in place of the guy. My story is set in a coarser, more brutal world; the same story in Sirk's film unfolds in small-town America, where it works better. Yet the process of giving a television set instead of a man appears much more brutal against this background than the brutal act in my film. These are the sorts of little details where you can't just imitate; you have to do an adaptation to fit the setting.

S: Rainer, you're absolutely right. My wife and I saw *Fear Eats the Soul* together and think it's one of your best and most beautiful films, which unmistakably carries your signature. My wife, who certainly knows my films, too, never thought at the time that there was any affinity with *All That Heaven Allows* as far as the material was concerned.

F: My way of making films is different. He was surrounded by the system, and had a specific amount of time for making a film. With my films I react to what I'm experiencing, how I feel. That doesn't mean, though, that there has to be a difference in that respect. Perhaps the difference is that I'll make a hundred films, and he's made thirty-nine. That doesn't mean anything; it just means that in a different situation I've been able to make films that were more direct and radical, that I've reacted differently and more spontaneously to reality than he did. He had the entire system looking over his shoulder. In view of that, it's all the more admirable that a person could manage to create a whole personal world, in spite of that stick-in-the-mud American studio system. Not many people have pulled that off—many of them have gone under, have made generic films, have latched onto success, have sold themselves to their very depths. To sell yourself isn't so bad; it happens all the time. But to sell yourself to the depths, down to your emotional cells—so many people have done that that I'm terribly grateful for these few people, these few bodies of work from America where I learn something about a life and time, about thoughts, about ways of thinking, about ways of feeling, about ways of telling stories. And Douglas Sirk belongs to that handful of directors, and because he's a German he's also very close to me personally.

He was entirely different from the way I'd pictured a Hollywood director up to then. He was the way I hoped he'd be. I hoped someone who made Hollywood films wouldn't just read Mickey Mouse comics and chew gum, but would be able to discuss Arnolt Bronnen and Brecht. Sirk succeeded in meeting the demands of the system and nevertheless making personal films. After I'd made ten films that were very personal, the moment came when we said we had to find an opportunity to make films for the public—and then came my encounter with his films and with Douglas Sirk himself. That was incredibly important for me. And as far as the alleged father-son relationship is concerned—this was, and is, altogether different, because father-son relationships are usually a struggle. I've found someone who does art in such a way that I've realized what I have to change in myself. I'm doing things now which may show him that what he set out to do is being carried on. And now we meet here to make the film *Bourbon Street Blues* together and find that wonderful. But there's too little time, and the film's too small, or maybe any film wouldn't be enough. But I believe he's learned more about me from my films and I've learned more about him from his than through this collaboration.

S: The big difference is that he's making films and I'm not making them anymore ... Before I met Rainer I sensed something, and then when I saw him I recognized, with that eye every filmmaker has to have, a personality of great originality.

■ *Herr Fassbinder, can you imagine reaching a point where you wouldn't make films anymore?*

F: I don't know yet. Probably I'll always make films, at least that's how I see it today—but it might turn out entirely differently. I can't imagine the point where I wouldn't be able to make films; actually I'm just beginning. In fact, films are just beginning to be seen as something of intellectual value.

I have to try to create connections, to protect myself from drowning in connections made by other people. I have to try to be on guard against these purist undertakings that I'd be completely vulnerable to otherwise. Art? With the things you do, you try to sensitize your audience in a certain way to life and the world around them. That's a sensitizing process which you've put yourself through and now have to transfer to your audience—that's all it is.

S: When we were talking about his role in this academy production, I told Rainer: Just imagine you suddenly couldn't make films anymore, for some reason. In the same way this person here can't write anymore. Rainer understood that immediately: he has to make films. I can't imagine him not being able to make films anymore. I have the feeling that he's just at the beginning of another, even greater career.

F: It doesn't matter a bit whether a person really writes or only does it in his imagination, like Chekhov in the Tennessee Williams play whose role I have. If he can summon up enough strength in his imagination to be successful in his imagination, to have a presence as someone who writes, then it's no different from someone who's really successful. Thomas Mann said, "I would rather participate in life than write a hundred stories." You don't exactly know what's more important. Participating—there I feel very inhibited. It should be possible to participate in life indirectly—only as a mediator. You can't say either that it's a choice between making films and living, or what have you—that's going too far. Why shouldn't I live for people and still do my work? Of course filmmaking takes energy, but at least I'm not doing alienated labor. When you do alienated labor, maybe you use less energy and live ten or twenty years longer, but they're sad years. To me it's better to make films and live differently—even if it's more strenuous.

March 1979

"I make films out of personal involvement, and for no other reason"
A Discussion with Hans Günther Pflaum about *Berlin Alexanderplatz* and *Lili Marleen*

■ The Marriage of Maria Braun, Berlin Alexanderplatz, *and now also the project* Lili Marleen—*those are all films which in their setting at least have more to do with the past. After such radical and consistent films about the present like* In a Year of Thirteen Moons *and* The Third Generation, *where does this striking interest in the past come from?*

It was always there—it's nothing new, I'd say. It so happens that we Germans have learned so little about German history that we—or I—but certainly also a good part of my generation, whether they be moviegoers or moviemakers—have to do quite a bit of catching up on basic information. And as a filmmaker you can use this information as the basis for the story you tell the audience. All that means is making reality easier to grasp.

■ *Well, in the last few years in this country we've had a whole slew of films based on literature, and they reveal two different possible attitudes: on the one hand, you can tell about the past as if the whole thing were an allegory; that is, you mean the present, or at least try to imply it. For instance, Bernhard Sinkel wanted to see* The Good-for-Nothing *as a film relevant to the present. The other possibility is to tell about the past and about the documented past in such a way that it remains the past and doesn't mean the present, or at most one of the roots of the present. Probably those are two very different approaches.*

Yes, they certainly are. My relationship to Döblin works this way: Döblin wrote the novel at a time when he couldn't and didn't anticipate the Third Reich on the scale it actually assumed. So he wasn't "prescient," let's say, to the degree that others maybe were; but by focusing on various behavioral patterns he offered a precise characterization of the twenties; for anyone who knows what came of all that, it's fairly easy to recognize the reasons that made the average German 45 capable of embracing his National Socialism. That, I'd say, would be the overt political element. Of course you can also say that there are parallels between the Weimar Republic and today's—but only maybe.

■ *But you're not interested only in parallels—you're interested in the past itself?*

First of all, I'm interested in showing how the Germans—well, I said "the average German," but actually I know the Germans best— how the Germans are predisposed in such a way that the idea of fascism, which you can argue about, I'd still say, can lead them to something like National Socialism, which you can't argue about anymore.

■ *Now the novel* Berlin Alexanderplatz *appeared in 1929, and in later editions there are notes by Döblin and statements about his work; in them you always find antitheses like "construction and decay," "order and dissolution" as characterizations of that period. Maybe that really does have a lot to do with our times after all.*

It certainly does. I mean, the fact that I've thought so much about the novel, maybe not continuously over the years, but very specifically and intensely in recent times, to the point that I also wanted to make a film out of it—that certainly has to do with my seeing so many things nowadays that frighten me again. I see citizens who'd rather have peace, order, and discipline again, and this in a society that in many respects is falling apart, in a negative way, not a productive way. There's a way of falling apart that can be productive, you know. There are sudden ruptures that result in new impulses. But you can also have a breakdown of imagination and individuality, and what you end up with—it only sounds simplistic—is scared people.

■ *That brings up something that your earlier films point to, even the names in your earlier films, where this Franz Biberkopf is already present very early on as a character or just as a name. That is, along with your political interest in the film there's also a very private, personal interest in this particular character that motivates you.*

There is a private interest, of course, no doubt about it; but the moment you set out to make a television film, knowing that four million people may be watching every week, you can't separate the two anymore. Even your private interest gets converted into an objective one. I mean, the private interest is still there, of course, but that's not what you focus on when you're making the film.

■ *The older we get, the more clearly we probably recognize that we're all very ambivalent types—mightn't this Franz Biberkopf be a character you identify with? Would that be a part you'd like to play?*

On the one hand, certainly, yes; on the other hand, this is a character, a person who wants to believe, beyond all possible and conceivable limits, that people can be good, even in the society he lives in. That people, whom he considers fundamentally good, which I do, too, could be good even in this society, which I consider bad, but he doesn't exactly, or not so explicitly; now *that* I don't believe. To that extent Franz Biberkopf isn't a character I identify with. In this case I'd say instead that I can learn from him to express my attitude toward reality more precisely.

■ *Well,* Effi Briest, *for instance, has both a historical and a contemporary meaning, but it's set in a milieu or a space which in a certain sense can only be created artificially nowadays when you film this story. In the case of* Berlin Alexanderplatz *there seem to be other possibilities, because the settings are much more concrete. And there are still people around who know how this world, or rather, this setting, looked. Does that make for problems with filming the story?*

No, I see the situation as more similar to *Effi Briest.* You can't recreate it exactly, either. I'm not even interested in trying to do something that maybe could be done if you had lots of financial backing. Or even with less, I don't know; actually, I never gave it any thought, because I immediately decided to do it the other way, I mean not reproducing exactly an authentic setting out on the street; instead it seemed to me that you could tell how it really would look out on the streets better from the kinds of refuges people created for themselves, what kinds of bars they went to, how they lived in their apartments, and so on. So I concentrated more on interiors. I even think I would have had enough money to reconstruct Alexanderplatz and to act as though we had original material, but that wouldn't have been very interesting. I'm not interested in how a person looks crossing Alexanderplatz today. I'd be more interested in how someone looks crossing the Kurfürstendamm.

■ *In Döblin's novel the most exciting part isn't necessarily the plot. Does that interfere with turning it into a film?*

It's pretty exciting, I'd say; that is, at first it doesn't seem exciting. For quite a while all you get is an introduction to a person, until eventually a story involving two men begins to jell. But then what happens between the two, and how the two in turn interact with others, how the two of them end up on a collision course, that's plenty exciting, I'd say.

■ *You misunderstood me, or my question wasn't very clear. I mean, you could do a plot summary for the novel that would be completely arbitrary and wouldn't convey the special quality of the novel at all.*

Yes, that's true of all good novels, I'd say. I think a good novel is always one that becomes completely arbitrary when you reduce it to an intentionally mediocre plot summary. Novels with a really neat, exciting story aren't good novels, I think. I think things that have a touch of arbitrariness about them are more accurate for the time they were written for, and then historically for people who read them later; the seemingly arbitrary novels contain more truth than the ones that are skillfully laid out.

■ *How do things stand with your planned cinema version of* Berlin Alexanderplatz?

That's a story in itself. Separately from the television screenplay, which is about three thousand pages, I wrote a special version for the cinema. Because I think if you have three hours rather than fifteen, you have to tell the story differently. That's why I'm opposed to the idea of taking what we've already filmed and cutting it down to get this other version; the shooting would have been done differently, with different dynamics. But the screenplay exists, and some day, when the legal situation with regard to this work is more favorable, I'll do the film, that's certain. And it doesn't bother me a bit that there already is a film and my television series—I don't give a damn. It didn't bother me with *Effi Briest* at the time, either. I mean, if a film's good, it has a strength all its own.

■ *What do you think of the old film version by Piel Jutzi, which was completed only two years after the book appeared?*

As a film it's not bad. It just seems to me that the film doesn't have much to do with the book. Not much is an understatement, I should say nothing at all. It used the book as a pretext for telling a story. Maybe it's a story that can be found in the book, if you want to. But I'd say it was a mistake to call it a film version of the book. So I think Jutzi's work is good only as a film.

■ *How long will the television series run?*

Fifteen hours.

■ *How long did the shooting take you?*

We spent 150 days shooting.

■ *For this television version, was a kind of "series dramaturgy" also necessary or important? Or does one segment simply break off, to be followed by the next on the following day?*

You can't just stop and start at random. That's no good. But Döblin already had his novel divided into ten chapters with main chapters, subchapters, what have you. And because of his collage technique it isn't particularly hard to divide the story cinematically into chapters. You could also have taken and found entirely different points that would have served as beginnings and endings. There are many possibilities. It isn't that it doesn't have beginnings and endings, but it isn't made according to Durbridge dramaturgy, either. So it doesn't stop with a suspenseful situation that'll make people tune in for the next segment to find out how the story continues. That I certainly don't want.

■ *Now, Döblin's novel has such explosive power that it's hard to imagine a German television company's warming to it. Does that mean the novel had to be defused, or were there conflicts in this area?*

No, I was fortunate that on the one hand I had good connections with WDR and on the other hand they'd just suppressed two things of mine. So they couldn't really suppress this, or make it impossible. The editorial staff wanted it anyway, and at the very top they must have said, "All right, now we've had these three things . . ." I don't know how they talk, but I'd say, "Now we've done in his other two projects, and at least *Berlin Alexanderplatz* has so much literary merit that we can always justify doing it."

■ *Well, at least as far as printings go, it was by far the most successful of Alfred Döblin's novels; but he also didn't make nearly so many enemies with any other novel. Might we be in for a repeat?*

That's hard to say. I don't think so. It's my opinion that quite a few things have changed after all, so far as the reception of literature or, more recently, films based on literature, is concerned, what was new and shocking in Döblin's novel no longer shocks people. I don't think the film language in which I try to tell the story is shocking either, in that sense. The last book, that is, the last film in the series, certainly has a very idiosyncratic film language, which certainly can or will give rise to controversy. That's the part in the novel where Franz Biberkopf's in the insane asylum and more or less reviews his entire life before he recovers, coming out of it a mediocre person. This part will certainly stir up some controversy or other.

■ *When you lose some of the provocative effect, is something important gone for good? That was the question I asked myself in connection with the film version of* The Tin Drum. *When the book appeared, people called Grass a "Kashubian warthog" and all sorts of other unflattering things. But for the film premiere the so-called dignitaries turn out in tuxedos and flock to a banquet in honor of the author; perhaps that makes it legitimate to ask whether in the process of filming the novel a bomb wasn't defused.*

In principle I wouldn't say that. The fact is that between the publication of *The Tin Drum* and the premiere of the film things changed in people's attitude toward art. Quite independently of whether Schlöndorff's film version defuses the novel or not. Let's leave that aside for now. But you can't be angry with the film for not having the same shock effect the novel once had. To do so, it would have had to work with devices that would be as shocking today as those the novel used back then—but then it wouldn't be the same novel. So I don't know whether that's a valid argument. I myself would prefer it if the moviegoer watched the movie with less hostility and with more opportunity to be conscious of what's taking place before his eyes and what it can mean to him personally; that's better than if he's shocked into rejecting the whole thing at first sight, no matter how the shock may later work in his subconscious to achieve a positive effect. That can happen, too. But with a television series it's like this: if the viewers are shocked, they'll stop watching. Then we've gained nothing. I'd rather have them watch and at least come away with the idea of the story that's being told—and why it should be told.

■ *I recall from earlier conversations that for a long time now you've consciously made a distinction between movies and television and see the two tasks facing you as quite different.*

That's right. I've always said you have a different kind of responsibility. With a movie I would argue much more for shock effects, because I agree with Kracauer when he says that when the lights go out in the movie theater it's as if a dream were beginning; in other words, that a movie works through the subconscious. The movie version I've written really is entirely different.

■ *How does it differ from the other, leaving aside the differences dictated by the much shorter length?*

It's not only not nearly so epic in style, but also not nearly so positive in its portrayal of Franz Biberkopf; rather it underscores the contradictions and the craziness of the character more than the television version. Here it's more that people will understand it and it won't scare them away, that they can grasp it directly while watching it. To consider the audience you're working for is as legitimate, I believe, as it used to be, say ten years ago. People say, all right, the television viewers are people who're sitting at home while something comes into their living room . . . And there are incredibly many of them, that's another factor, unbelievably many, far more than at the movies. And I have a different mission with them.

■ *I think that's right. And splendid, because many filmmakers approach the question from precisely the opposite direction. They*

*say they're making something for television, so they really don't
care about a lot of things, because it's being paid for, after all, or
rather, financed. When they make something for the cinema, then
they say, "Now we have to consider the audience, because people
are supposed to go to see it, buy tickets, pay."*

Yes, but that's not the case with me. You can see that from many
films I've made. And specifically from the films I actually financed entirely on my own and without any public monies, like *In a Year of
Thirteen Moons* or *The Third Generation.* They're much more uncompromising; I wouldn't have made them for television. I tell myself
that someone who goes to the movies pretty much knows what awaits
him. So I can demand more effort of him. Do you understand? And I
can also expect him to get more pleasure out of the effort. The argument that used to be cited, that the viewer wants to be entertained or
something in the evening, no longer applies to the movies since we've
had television. On television you have such a varied entertainment
program that people who want to be entertained can certainly find
something every night. For that they don't need to go to the movies, I
think. People really go to the movies in order to have new experiences—and quite consciously to have new experiences. That means I
have an audience I can push and challenge to the utmost. But I'm also
aware that many people see it differently.

■ *And the fact that many people see it differently could mean
the paralysis or even the death of the new German cinema.*

I don't want to see the new German cinema die, but it's in danger,
that's for sure. The standard discussion of this problem doesn't usually
go nearly as far as I do when I say there simply has to be a greater
sense of responsibility; others, when they make films for the cinema,
think they have to make them more palatable. That's something I
wouldn't say even for my television films. It has nothing to do with
pleasing the audience, but simply with using narrative methods that
don't scare it off right away. It has to do with creating a consensus
between oneself, the work—or nonwork—and the audience. What
takes place on the basis of this consensus is another question. I don't
think I've ever tried to "please," even in my work for television.

■ *Will the television viewer have a chance to identify with this
Franz Biberkopf now and then? In all his ambivalence?*

Certainly. The television version's long enough for that, by all
means. And you go through too many stages with this character not to
find yourself identifying with him in some parts. I set up the role that
way, too. I had two ideas about how to set up the role. One would
have been to make it highly stylized, the other to open it up so you

could identify with the character. I chose the latter because the script I'd written was already literary enough; I don't need to have it stylized still further by the actors. What Günter Lamprecht, Gottfried John, and Barbara Sukowa in the three main parts play in the film has a lot to do with opportunities for identification. I hope it turns out that you're jolted out of this identification time and again, that you have those moments of clarity in viewing the characters that are necessary to keep you from drowning in the story.

■ *When you read the novel, there are parts where you have an awful lot of trouble with Franz Biberkopf.*

You have a lot of trouble, but there are also many moments when you feel compassion for him. Well, compassion may be an exaggeration. A lot of sympathy, and then there are moments when you say, Oh boy, another debacle! When you're ready to say: That's just like my own life; whenever something really shitty happens to me, it's followed right away by something just as bad.

■ *That's why these things are painful, and irritating, too. If you stopped caring for this character, none of it would hurt.*

Then it wouldn't hurt at all, no. That's why I find Lamprecht so ideal for the part, because with him you have someone who immediately evokes a lot of sympathy; so the viewer will really be irritated by the bad breaks he gets in life.

■ *Does that mean that in a possible film version a different actor could or should play Franz Biberkopf?*

That's what I'd planned. When I was still intending to do both versions simultaneously—for reasons of economy, by the way, because of the sets—we could have used the same sets—I actually wanted to have an entirely different cast, not use the same actors at all. That has to do with having an entirely different narrative method, depending on whether you're presenting a story in fifteen hours or only three. And Lamprecht, it seems to me, is someone who has such a broad range of expression that it can easily cover fifteen hours, but he lacks the intensity—and I don't mean to belittle his skill as an actor—that I'd be interested in having for a two-and-a-half-hour version. For that I'd want someone whose acting was just more intense.

■ *Literary scholars have gone to great lengths to prove that Alfred Döblin was influenced by James Joyce. It's also been established that while Döblin was working on* Berlin Alexanderplatz *he read Joyce for the first time—but by then he'd already written part of the novel. Döblin himself admitted that from that point on there might be some influence. Does that have any stylistic implications for filming the novel—a need to shift the action inward, into the mind?*

No. To me this kind of debate over whether he'd read *Ulysses* or not is pretty pointless. Because you don't really see it in the novel. So even if it were the case that he'd read *Ulysses* while he was writing, you don't see any change in the style. I'd say instead that maybe, if it was that way—you don't really know—maybe he found confirmation for his own way of telling the story. But not that he changed his narrative style; certainly not. While writing the screenplay I was really deeply involved with the novel, and I can't say that I discovered any sort of stylistic break.

■ *How long did it take you to write the screenplay?*

You can't really measure how long it took me. The "original version" was about three thousand pages, and it took me an insanely short time. But it wasn't your usual work pattern, either. I'd work for four days, then sleep for twenty-four hours, then work for four days, without interruption. Of course that puts you in a different rhythm. If you go at it the usual way, writing some in the morning and some in the afternoon, you have to gear up again every time to get back into the material. So I didn't have that, except briefly every four days. So writing for about a hundred hours straight and only having to gear up once meant that I could write a lot faster. It's certainly not a healthy way of writing and not one I'd recommend to anybody. But that's what made it possible to do it in such a short time, which was how it had to be. The screenplay had to be finished by a certain time because shooting was supposed to start for *The Marriage of Maria Braun,* and all of that had to be planned out. I had only so much time, and no one believed it could be done. I wasn't absolutely sure myself that I could do it, but I tried it this way, and it worked.

■ *What got written first, the television or the cinema version?*

I wrote the television version first and then took a long time—the hardest work was actually done in my mind—to figure out how to approach the cinema version. Once I knew, it went fine; but it didn't come to me for three whole months, at least three months. I was pretty much in despair, too, because I didn't know how to do it.

■ *We were talking before about writing the screenplay for the television version. I'm trying to remember the novel, and it occurs to me that Döblin uses a lot of biblical motifs. Are they there in the film?*

They're still there in the film, yes, maybe somewhat different from the way they are in Döblin, to whom they may have been more important, personally as well. To me they're important for society.

■ *Do you also see the story of Franz Biberkopf as a passion play?*

It's that, too, of course. Though more in Franz Biberkopf's imagination than in the narrative. He's invented a character who experiences his own life as a passion play in his imagination. But I think among the few motifs you carry over from childhood are powerful religious motifs, for example. On the other hand, Döblin says nothing about Franz Biberkopf's parents—they're just not there; they aren't mentioned. Döblin thought he could get around Freudian psychoanalysis that way—which on the other hand he couldn't do, because this obtrusive subconscious has something tremendously Freudian about it, even without father and mother.

■ *In the novel there are many things that go on in the mind and were maybe not so easy to portray with the camera. Does that mean that even in writing the screenplay you have to put in things of your own invention?*

I didn't have the feeling that I had to invent a lot of things. In the novel there are various motifs that sometimes jump out and grab you; I just tried to adapt those in different ways. Sometimes into dialogue, sometimes into visual images. But that wasn't a huge problem.

■ *Are there characters in the film that don't occur in the novel?*

Yes, there's one character in the film that doesn't occur in the novel; it's sort of his alter ego, which knows more about life than he's willing to admit to himself. In the novel you just have scraps of narrative coming out of the subconscious; I turned those into a character. That's the only new one.

■ *How do you go about telling a story like that with our present-day awareness? You can't think away our knowledge of what followed the twenties—which Döblin didn't have when he was writing. Does our modern consciousness make itself felt in the production?*

No, I tried to follow Döblin's narrative as unobtrusively as possible, and specifically not to work in this consciousness after-the-fact, not to work in the Third Reich like a good little academic. In the film there are about as many or as few allusions to the possibility of a Third Reich or National Socialism as in the novel, where tendencies in that direction are pretty clear. Döblin didn't like the Nazis much, even then. Though he also didn't take them very seriously—but I should add that the Nazis themselves aren't the most important thing. What's more important, ultimately, are all those people who played along with them.

■ *Now, films like* Effi Briest *or* Despair—A Journey into Light *were at one and the same time real film versions of literature and*

unmistakably "Fassbinder films." Will the same be true of Berlin
Alexanderplatz *and . . .*
      . . . that'll certainly be the case . . .
      ■ *. . . and not only in style, but also in the attitude toward the*
characters?
      Also in the attitude, certainly, because I don't just film literature,
but have actually always—with one exception, I don't know—filmed
literature with which or toward which I had a different relationship
than just knowing that it existed and that it was good, or that it seemed
to lend itself well to filming. They were all books I had a personal,
intense, and exciting relationship with.
      ■ *Now, in the German cinema, and not only there, experience*
seems to show that the bigger the budget for films, the more imper-
sonal they become. There are many examples of this. A counter-
example, one of very few I see in this country, would be The Marriage of Maria Braun. *Is that a question of skill—being able to still*
make personal films on such a grand scale, or is it a question of
attitude and morality?
      It's both, no question about it. It's certainly a moral position I have
that I can never approach my characters any other way. No matter
how big a budget I have at my disposal. On the other hand it's also a
question of skill that I could do so much and in so many types of
production. With some of the television productions I've made, I've
had a lot of money at my disposal, you know. So I've made some films
where I had no money at all, and others where I had a lot, and some
where I had just about enough. A big budget can make a lot of things
easier; certain films you shouldn't even attempt on too small a budget.
But there are enough stories to tell, or stories I think it would be
worthwhile for me to tell, that can be done with a smaller budget.
      ■ *The projects you've set aside—those are stories you shouldn't*
do with a smaller budget?
      Yes, otherwise I would have done them. The Frankfurt film *The*
Earth Is Uninhabitable Like the Moon shouldn't be done cheaply,
because otherwise it'd be just what they predicted. The characters
would be grubby and weird, and that's just what they mustn't be. It
has to be a splendid big movie, preferably in CinemaScope and with a
great cast, and that's the reason that film hasn't been made yet. Of
course I could have done it cheaply, but that seemed wrong to me.
The Frankfurt B-picture, or whatever, is something else again—in
black and white, and shot very quickly. That would be possible; you
can do it that way. But it's not the way this screenplay's structured; it's

structured so that impoverishment of the people grows out of luxury. The B-picture itself is a luxury. And it's not just a B-picture situation where everything's wretched; rather, it's so luxurious and on the other hand so soulless that the people who live there just go to pieces in a certain way. I wanted to trace this process precisely, showing how I think it evolves, not just showing the result as a sort of documentary event—which isn't my job, either, or at least wasn't at that time. If I want to do a documentary, I'd prefer to do something else.

■ *Will you make the film at some point?*

There's no question I'll make the film. The screenplay's done, and it's not getting worse day by day; it'll retain its good features. Someday it'll be possible for me to do this film on the scale I want without outside help.

■ *How do things look for the cinema version of* Berlin Alexanderplatz? *What's happening with the legal problems you mentioned?*

The legal problems arose because the exclusive rights for cinema and television were bought first by Albatros, and Bavaria only bought the television rights from Albatros.

■ *So there are no problems with the original holders of the rights?*

No, except that at the moment Albatros holds the rights; but that won't be the case forever. And if Albatros manages—in spite of the fact that this series has been done just now—after five years it's still "just now"—to make a movie, I don't care. I'll make mine anyhow.

■ *Your next project is shooting* Lili Marleen. *Hearing that causes a little irritation at first, because it looks as though maybe for the first time in your life you've taken on an assignment just to direct a film.*

You can't say that.

■ *Has the situation been misrepresented?*

No, nothing's been represented; there was just a simple announcement. Certainly that's how it looks. But the fact is that between me and the decision to do the film lay a screenplay. And this screenplay must have turned me on. Otherwise I wouldn't have agreed to get involved. So it has something to do with me, somehow. What specifically it has to do with me doesn't really seem all that interesting, objectively speaking. But then there's the second point, that I was given a chance to have a lot of influence on the script, or on the story, or on the way the story's filmed, so that in the end it would become more and more my story. I have the right to rewrite the dialogue to fit the actors or the locales, as I did with *The Marriage of Maria Braun* or the others. In Luggi Waldleitner I have a producer who has something I find terrific: he's just crazy about movies. The fact that he wants to make money I even see as an advantage.

■ *And what's the advantage?*

I've often said that the advantage of the American studios is that they offered their directors more leeway because they wanted something that would sell. They didn't want to make money on producing, but on distribution. And Waldleitner's also a person who, I've always had the feeling—and I don't think much will change there—wants to make his money not by skimping on production costs but rather by marketing what gets produced. I find that perfectly legitimate; two interests come together here: my interest in having the maximum leeway for a film, and his in getting the maximum ticket sales, which I for my part don't mind a bit; it's terrific when a whole lot of people see a film.

■ *Luggi Waldleitner certainly is one of those who plow any money that's earned right back into films, rather than going out and buying apartment houses or something like that with it. But how do you manage to collaborate with the scriptwriter Manfred Purzer, who, and I can say this without being judgmental at all, isn't exactly on your wavelength? After all, there was a massive conflict between him and you even just over the subsidy for the film.*

Yes, that's a tricky subject. When I met Waldleitner for the first time, I was pretty sure ahead of time that he would offer me *Lili Marleen*. But I didn't know who the script was by; the morning of that same day someone told me, in confidence. So it was a big decision for me whether I should go at all. Then I said to myself, Okay, what's the big deal? I can read it, and if I don't like it, I still have the right to say no. To be honest, I did start reading it with the hope it'd be bad. All right, for various reasons it turned me on. I said, Okay, this is something I can really get into. Waldleitner also knew about the problems I have with this scriptwriter, and I told him straight out over lunch. He answered that in that case we'd simply have to look for another scriptwriter who could revise it in line with my ideas. Then it turned out that after three days I said to myself, What's the big deal? Purzer's the one who's had the most to do with the project up to now; you can't get him completely out of the story, out of the film, anymore. That being the case, maybe the best thing would be for me to sit down with him. So I jumped over my own shadow, something that a year ago I wouldn't have thought I could do. Just like that. An additional factor was that two people—one of them was Günther Rohrbach—told me that when it came to film dramaturgy Purzer was the only one of all the people involved in the project you could really talk to. If you don't get into politics, you can have really productive discussions about cinematic issues with him. So after three days I told Waldleitner that he shouldn't bother looking for another scriptwriter; I wanted Purzer to keep on writing. That is, I wanted to meet him first and tell him my ideas and see whether he could do anything with them. We had a meeting, and in many respects everything went very well as far as the script was concerned—and other than that I didn't have any dealings with him.

■ *How great is the danger that it might become somehow a synthetic story? Years ago Luggi Waldleitner told me he had a* Lili Marleen *project; at first he probably just had the title, or the song, and then I suppose the story was worked out afterward to go with it.*

No, the story wasn't worked out afterward. There was already the life story of Lale Andersen, a person who did have a very exciting life. On the one hand, only one love story in her entire life; on the other hand, a really big career in the Third Reich. Something I wouldn't reject a person for out of hand. I can certainly picture how such a thing comes about. There are two factors: the need to survive, and then for the artist the need to have a career. There are other examples of people who had big careers in the Third Reich.

■ *So, how and when was the screenplay written?*

Well, if Luggi Waldleitner's supposed to have had only the title *Lili Marleen* and the song in the beginning, the life of Lale Andersen added something to that, in fact three things: first of all, a love story involving two people, which is the love of both their lives precisely because it isn't consummated, can never be consummated, because the two are separated. He's a Swiss Jew and works for the Haganah, and she's a singer in Nazi Germany. So this love only works because it isn't consummated, and that's something that interests me in any case. The second element is the phenomenon of someone within the Nazi regime, or any such regime, wherever it may be, who wants to survive in a way that isn't simply a matter of collaborating. She just very consciously wants to survive. The third is that you have someone who thinks she's an artist and wants to be a success, even under such a regime. Never mind whether it's the Third Reich or not. Those are all things that have enough to do with what I've done before that you can't say it's completely alien to me, a total departure; that was enough for me to be able to say, Yes, I'll do it.

■ *Is there a written biography of Lale Andersen?*

Yes, there is.

■ *And how much bearing does it have on the film? How much is research, how much invention?*

Manfred Purzer has built up a huge archive—he spent four years on it. The basis of the story is certainly the biography of Lale Andersen, who, by the way, really made her way through all the requisite beds, that was certainly the starting point. But biographies are usually prettied up. In addition there were many, many other stories that weren't told, just hinted at and which inspired Purzer—and other writers were involved, too—to come up with certain stories.

■ *Who else worked on it?*

Someone from England and an American. The story of the screenplay itself is quite an adventure—I don't know all the details. Purzer tried to tell me the story of how it got written.

■ *And when you became involved, was there already a finished screenplay?*

There was a finished screenplay, but it was clear to everyone that it was by no means the final one. That might have been what Niklaus Gessner would have filmed, maybe. To me the story would have been too slick. I tried to make the distinction between good and evil and so on less simplistic, to situate them in the characters, giving them both positive and negative traits. But the screenplay was already at a stage where all that wasn't so hard to do. It would even have been possible, except for a few scenes, to make those changes during shooting.

■ *So you came into a project that was already pretty far along?*

What you can say is that something was offered to me—and this wasn't the first time—which I got caught up in and then took on. I didn't do other things that were offered to me for many other reasons, because they didn't have much to do with me. But I stand behind whatever comes of *Lili Marleen,* or the work, among other reasons because it entails a degree of risk that I find very exciting, because it could really turn into a disaster.

■ *Is this film going to be expensive to make?*

It certainly will be an expensive film, but that's not my concern. For me it's exciting to see whether I can succeed in making a film that tells its story in such an expensive and expansive way, that is, tells it in such an audience-effective way, and in spite of that conveys all the inconsistency of human beings that I see in them. But if in the end it turns out just to be big and successful, I'd consider it a failure. But that's precisely the exciting part, and it's one of the factors that made me feel I just had to try. It's a story which you can also fail completely with.

■ *To what extent does a "big" film like this depend on stars?*

Xaver Schwarzenberger, Fassbinder, and Hark Bohm on the set of Lili
Marleen *(courtesy Deutsche Kinemathek, Berlin)*

The main part's played by Hanna Schygulla, and she fits the part
like ... I don't know, you couldn't have come up with anything better
for her. Depend on stars, well, that's a good question. I can only quote
someone or other: The good thing about stars is that often they actually are better than the others. There are certainly lots of unrecog-
nized stars, but just as certainly there's a large number of so-called
stars who aside from that really are very good.

■ *How free are you with the casting? How free will you be with
the work altogether?*

Completely. Freer than I'd be with any young German producer,
that's absolutely certain. I can remember things with Michael Fengler
where it was a question of casting, for instance, when I wanted Bernadette Lafont for a part in the film version of *Berlin Alexanderplatz*.
I told him to call her and ask if she had time, and then he gave me the
message that everything was all set. I knew Bernadette Lafont, and I'd
told her once that I'd like to work with her someday. Then I ran into
her in Paris and said, "See, I don't make empty promises." So she said,
"What?" And I said, "What do you mean? Didn't he call and say we
were doing something together?" And she said, "No." And that's something that doesn't happen with Waldleitner. It's a small point, but it's

important, and it makes me feel good. If someone objects, as some of my friends do, that you shouldn't make films with the money of rightists, all I can say is that Visconti made almost all his films with money from rightists. And always justified it with similar arguments: that they gave him more leeway than the leftists.

May 1980

"Why these problems with Franz Biberkopf?"

A Discussion with Klaus Eder about the Reactions to *Berlin Alexanderplatz* and about Film Treatments of the Third Reich

■ *Did you expect the violent and controversial reactions to this film?*

Of course I didn't expect them to take this form, but then, too, the discussion's been pushed in a certain direction by certain interests, especially the Springer press. Never mind why.

■ *Might it have something to do with your signing the declaration vowing not to work for the Springer newspapers anymore?*

I was the first of the fifty-two people who signed it. I really had no idea they would take revenge so quickly. It was almost like a hate campaign, such as I've never really experienced in this country. Aside from the fact that I didn't expect it, I find it somewhat sad that as a result of all this the viewer can't really work out his own conflict with the film as I'd hoped, but instead has to work out the conflict as posed by these other media—so it's not a conflict with the film but a conflict against the film. It was clear to me from the start that this was no easily digested television film that would let people would sit back and enjoy it like an American miniseries; it was my intention to have the audience confront it, but with it, not against it.

■ *Isn't there the additional factor that the film's shown over a long period of time, divided into fourteen installments?*

That would have to be looked into, whether the viewer is capable of handling this kind of series, where each part isn't self-contained, where you really need to know what went before in order to deal with what's being shown at present—whether the viewer isn't capable of learning this, whether this doesn't offer possibilities. It is hard, you know, to show a fifteen-and-a-half-hour film at one sitting. You just can't do it. Maybe it could have been shown in two- or three-hour segments; that would certainly have been better.

■ *The film cost twelve or thirteen million marks, which is actu-*

ally not only not expensive for a fifteen-hour film—you might even call that cheap.

It's very cheap; a lot of people played games with the numbers, even though they knew better, mentioning only the total figure without saying that the price per minute is way below your usual production costs in television. If they want to slander a person, nobody can stop them, obviously.

■ *A second problem is the darkness of the film on the screen. What's the idea of drenching the screen in blackness?*

That's not quite the way it is. There's a scene which is, and is supposed to be, very dark: the scene where the two Jews get Franz Biberkopf on his feet again. That's supposed to be so dark that in fact you can only make out hands or the outlines of faces, and of course the German television viewer isn't used to that. He's used to a television aesthetic that's more or less an extension of the *Tagesschau*, where everything is bright and moves quickly and so on. My technique contradicts the viewer's expectations completely; people have to look a long time, just as with Rembrandt's pictures, where you really have to look a long time before you figure out from the contours what Rembrandt was trying to do; here, too, it takes a while for them to see what's important about the image or images. They just don't have the patience. I guess the viewers fiddled with the knobs on their TV sets and tried to make the picture brighter, and of course that didn't help. But that, too, was just used as evidence that the film was sloppily made. Everyone who knows anything about filmmaking knows that the darker you make something, in other words, the more you work with the kind of lighting we used in *Alexanderplatz,* the more light you need. And it's more complicated to deal with. On the other hand, I'm surprised people accept it in Hitchcock's films, for instance; he also does a lot with having you see the faces of the actors only in outline. They saw *Alexanderplatz* as a television film, I suppose. To me it seems obvious that you have to use the same aesthetic techniques for television as for the cinema.

■ *I wouldn't want to blame it all on the viewers. I guess the television screen has a smaller range of contrast than the cinema, and I guess the cinema is also way ahead of television in its aesthetics, and much richer.*

Technically something certainly does get lost in television, that's obvious. But the main thing is that the viewer has been taught a television aesthetic, and that's certainly not his fault. But when he keeps being exposed to it, he gets used to having these television movies, most of which are shown right after the news, be no different from the news in their aesthetic and narrative technique. Anything else scares people off, simply because they're not used to it. So their first reaction is anger. But aside from that one scene, which is supposed to be dark, all the others have the usual dark-light contrasts, which like other feature films do lose something on television, but should certainly be acceptable.

■ *In this film you have a historical setting, Alexanderplatz, which people can visualize; yet it doesn't appear in your film. Your film is transposed into interior settings. Why is that?*

Because Alexanderplatz doesn't exist anymore, there were only two possibilities: to reconstruct it, to rebuild it; and that was something that I wouldn't have liked, because it would have been a set. So I said to myself, What Alexanderplatz really was can be shown just as well in other ways, through the places which the people who are otherwise on Alexanderplatz or on the streets of Berlin flee to. How they hide, how they seek protection from this metropolis that's just growing too fast. That works very well for me; I think the square is very much present, even if you don't see it. For me the square is there. Another viewer might say Alexanderplatz is only there if he can see it. You can argue about that, or not, as the case may be. I could picture a film treatment of Alexanderplatz in an adaptation, where you could use the Place de Pigalle or Forty-second Street in New York, because those are still places like what Alexanderplatz was in the twenties. But in Germany there just isn't any one central square anymore where everything comes together and the whole sociological structure of the population can be found.

■ *What actually interested you about the figure of Franz Biberkopf?*

That gets harder and harder for me to say. In the beginning it was easy. I always said, This is a person who goes around for much too long trying to believe in goodness in this world, in this system he lives in, though he actually knows better. Maybe he hopes that if he sees it this way, it will be this way, and people are, people can be good. Not until very late does he accept the idea that in this system people just can't be any different from the way they are, and he can't be either. But he could afford to go through the world in this anarchistic way only because he wasn't a worker, but just lived on the margin of the working world. For that reason it isn't a worker's novel. It's a novel that takes place on the margin of the normal working world, but for that very reason says a lot about the working world, I think. When I talk about the unemployed or about those who behave like the unemployed or those who refuse to work, I'm also saying something about workers. When Hermann Peter Piwitt writes in *Konkret* that Döblin was an "impersonator of working-class voices"—other films can be made; nothing stands in the way of that.

■ *It seems to me you of all people can't complain about the critics' response to your film.*

I'm not complaining. I'm only complaining because these are people whose political ideas I usually find a lot more congenial than those of the gentlemen from the Springer media. In itself, the reviews that saw the film as a complete whole really did see it as it is. And no one can claim the film is a great departure from Döblin. Clearly it's the film version of my particular reading of Döblin, and that certainly comes closer to Döblin than any attempt to film him "objectively." That would certainly result in something pretty sterile.

■ *What fascinates me about this film is that it isn't Fassbinder or Döblin but actually both. With some scenes you have the impression they must be Fassbinder inventions, and then you check in the novel and there they are.*

I can only confirm that. A subjective treatment of literary material does more justice to the literary material than an objective one. To me that notion is very exciting.

■ *Franz Biberkopf occupies the central position, of course. And you said he was a man who originally just wanted to find goodness, or not to go astray, and who's robbed of his life by the system. Of course this system becomes very clear in the film. If you pay close attention, you can see at the very beginning, when he's leaving prison, the bellowing SA hordes marching in the background. So the film takes place in the time before the war; it's a film that shows the period before 1933.*

It deals with the fears and worries you have yourself. To what extent can the system do you in? You wonder whether maybe you might simply decide to join the parade rather than struggling all your life to maintain a critical attitude, a strenuous, vigilant attitude. I think dealing with material like Döblin's can really help you steer clear of the path Franz Biberkopf takes—he'll probably vote for the Nazis later on. To that extent it's really a substantial piece of objective life support, and yet the treatment's subjective.

■ *Thank God the film's subjective! I think its fascination lies to a large extent in the fact that you bring yourself into the film, with your experiences in the Federal Republic. Of course that's what raised so many hackles.*

It doesn't have to raise hackles. My hope is that what makes many people nervous at first will sensitize them in the end to what German history is. That's necessary, even essential. Because if German history gets repressed once more, something'll start to stir in the depths again. These questions weren't all settled by the Third Reich.

■ *Lili Marleen is your next film. It describes the period of the Third Reich. The Döblin film described the time leading up to that. The postwar period's portrayed in* The Marriage of Maria Braun. *Should these three films be viewed as a trilogy?*

Ultimately, it'll be a mosaic. I hope to make films about other aspects of the history of this period, too. I'm trying to open up the Third Reich to criticism by first showing it through one person who's experienced it fairly consistently. I think it's possible to say something about National Socialism, which is specifically German, simply by showing what was appealing about it. The parades had a certain aesthetic of their own that appealed to people. The swastika had a certain aesthetic appeal. The slogans about community and *Volk* and so on all had their appeal.

■ *Would you go as far as someone like Hans Jürgen Syberberg and see the Third Reich and fascism as a spectacle, as an aesthetic event?*

No, not exclusively. In its self-portrayal the Third Reich did have a lot to do with spectacle. But for me the Third Reich wasn't just an "accident." It was a predictable development in German history. But its "impact" has a great deal to do with the aesthetics of staging. Yet the moment you say there were also concepts like solidarity, like Volk (without "one Reich, one Führer" this time), you have to say that all this can also result in something positive. When people cooperate but remain critical toward each other or toward the things they're doing, sticking together is wonderful. I still think that: that simply cooperating with others must be wonderful, or more wonderful than being alone. But on the other hand you can exploit that, as it was exploited in the Third Reich.

December 1980

"I'm a romantic anarchist"
A Discussion with Frank Ripploh about *Veronika Voss* and *Querelle*

■ Veronika Voss *is your third film about the fifties in the Federal Republic, after* Lola *and* The Marriage of Maria Braun. *Sad films. Yet the postwar years were also characterized by a hopeful euphoria. When and why do you think things began to go wrong?*

I happen to think there was no real euphoria; I think people kept themselves going with all sorts of external things, but didn't actually live those times. Or somehow they got through them by keeping busy, but they didn't—how shall I put it?—really experience them intellectually and psychically.

■ *In your most recent films,* Lili Marleen *and* Veronika Voss, *you reveal those kinds of contradictions through female characters. Is it easier with "heroines?"*

I find it easier. Men in this society are under a lot more pressure than women to play their roles. Of course women also have their roles, but they can break out a lot easier, or step out of line. With men that's immediately interpreted as dropping out or something. Men are expected to conform. To that extent they're more boring, on the whole. When women venture outside of society, they don't immediately fit into that nineteenth-century stereotype of the woman of the night.

■ *In the film a woman journalist says, "People are interesting to me when they're losing. When they've lost, they stop being interesting to me." How are we supposed to interpret that?*

She means that from her newspaper perspective. You always find this attitude in people in the media; it's their job to watch other people smash up. They need stories.

■ *Do you like to stand back and watch, too?*

Yes, sure, I do.

■ *Is it titillating?*

Maybe titillating, too. I don't expect the journalist in the film to   67 think it through. As for me, I hope to understand at least, I try to understand why people smash up.

■ *What does the "longing" of Veronika Voss consist of?*

You know that better than I, I'd say. Longing consists of being identical with herself, of recovering the identity she lost temporarily as a result of circumstances.

■ *With the death scene, including the way it's staged, I had the impression she accepts her death, even though her "suicide" was cold-bloodedly planned. A voluntary death, or murder?*

She accepts it completely because she knows in any case that the game is played out, there won't be any more variations—that's how I'd interpret it—no major opportunities for variations, and then a person can simply accept the end; there isn't anything left that interests her much.

■ *Some time ago I saw a rough cut of the film. But it still had a part where she wants to get away, and holds up a slip of paper to the window, on which she's written "Help!" She wanted to live.*

That wasn't supposed to mean wanting help . . . But it didn't come out quite right, and that's why that scene isn't in there anymore . . .

■ *In the film the Katz woman says, "Maybe instead of morphine I should give you a prescription for a person to love you."*

That just means Katz knows that would be a possible surrogate. To me, she's not merely a bad person; she's quite aware that she's playing along with the circumstances under which she lives when she prescribes morphine. Maybe she also does it because she makes money on it.

■ *In your film, Veronika Voss tells the doctor, "You've given me a great deal of happiness." Dr. Katz replies, "No, I've sold it to you." What about this idea that happiness is for sale, and do you think what you call happiness really has to do with money?*

Yes, I don't think anything's possible without venality. Some aspect of venality forms part of every opportunity to be happy.

■ *How do you buy your happiness?*

Not much differently from other people.

■ *Recently the paper* Die Zeit *ran a long, gossipy report by Rosa von Praunheim that dragged you and Werner Schroeter through the mire by telling all sorts of inside stories on you. According to him, you wave five-hundred-mark bills at male prostitutes, you get other people dependent on you, etc. What goes through your mind when a "colleague" spews out that sort of thing about you?*

Nothing goes through my mind. I know Rosa's just running amok; he knows himself it's not true. And what am I supposed to do? He knows it's not true, it isn't true, and if readers believe it, I can't convince them, so I keep my mouth shut. If someone wants to believe it, he will, and he might just as well; it isn't in my power to change that.

■ *But on the subject of "power": here you are, Germany's most successful director, and that puts you in a certain position of power. Is it easy to handle that?*

It was hard for me, because for a while you have the feeling everything's just great. And you can use that, but you have to be self-critical, as I said.

■ *Have you run into any exciting new talents recently?*

Nope. For a while I was intensely interested in the work of Walter Bockmayer. The opportunities offered by the German film-subsidy system, and also the films that get subsidized, gave him a taste for things that were all wrong. In this country talent is more endangered than encouraged. Subsidies carry a lot of risk. That has a lot to do with the fact that nowadays film itself is more expensive, much more expensive than ten years ago. Ten years ago you really could make a perfectly decent film for—I don't know—one hundred thousand marks. Today that's not possible. If you go to the subsidy people today and haven't already scraped together two million, your project is underfinanced. And then you have to gross two million. That's a burden for the director, and quite a cloud over a career that's just beginning.

■ *Recently you mentioned in an interview that there are plenty of people just waiting for you to fall apart. Who were you thinking of?*

No one specific. That's like the time when the Oberhausen people were saying, The only people left around here really have no right to be in this field; and at the time that was true. Back then, in the sixties, there were no German films. Nowadays when the new generation of directors complains that everything goes to Fassbinder, Herzog, Schlöndorff, that's a little different, because we're really doing something. I can understand someone being bitter if he does something and has trouble getting support. But I did many things without subsidies, completely at my own risk, even going into debt. I can't really understand the young people who say they have to have subsidies to make films. I always say—I've already told you this—just go ahead and do it, go into debt, and either it'll pan out, in which case you can pay the money back, or if not, you declare bankruptcy—basta. But to sit there and wait till you have your million, and all this bitching about other people getting it—that's idiotic. I don't know who would have subsidized my first films, because when I began I wasn't capable of submitting a normal screenplay. And it wasn't in my own interest to make opportunistic films based on screenplays. I could only manage in my kind of chaos, and there's nowhere I would have found support for that.

■ *How do you see your personal financial situation now? If you don't get a subsidy, can you just go ahead and make a film about something that's important to you, out of your own pocket?*

I could make a film; I could probably get a relatively cheap film off the ground.

■ *What would be a "cheap" film for you?*

Well, I could do a film that cost half a million without going into debt. Anything over that I'd have to do on credit, and because I'm not incorporated, but am my own company, I'd have to sign for it myself.

■ *In* Veronika Voss *you don't treat actors very kindly. Let me quote: "Actors are dishonest, stupid, and vain. If they don't get parts, they turn to the bottle." What other laws of nature have you observed in human beings?*

Oh, there are lots of laws of nature. Actors aren't necessarily stupid and vain, but when they stop getting parts, it's a law of nature, I think, that they turn to the bottle. That has to do with all the waiting around. Actors wait around a lot, and what are you going to do with the time? You drink . . .

■ *Do directors drink a lot, too?*

There's a horde of directors who drink and are really at risk, who are alcoholics. There's a lot of drinking in the industry, it's much worse than with other drugs in the industry. To me, alcohol's the most dangerous drug for artists, because it ends up really making you stupid.

■ *That was your fortieth film. I have the feeling many people see you as a hamster in an exercise wheel, constantly under pressure to produce. Do you see it that way, too?*

Well, there are two factors here. First, I don't work more than other people, more than someone stamping out cans in a factory, or the like. I just work all year long; I don't take as many vacations as the others in the industry. That's one side of it. The other side is that I really have a drive that's hard to explain—it makes me have to do things, and I'm actually only happy when I'm doing things, and that's my drug, if you will.

■ *Do you believe in an equal love relationship between two men?*

I can't say; I haven't experienced it yet. I've always had relationships with people who were strong in themselves but in terms of their profession were in a weaker position, because if they'd continued to work in their profession, the misunderstanding would have been incredible. I mean, what does a butcher earn? What do I earn?

■ *You're very cautious when it comes to love affairs?*

I wasn't always, which was stupid of me, and that's why I had the experience two or three times that relationships I'd entered into euphorically ended in disaster. But as I said, those are experiences you have to have had, even if that sounds cynical.

■ *Are your many films a sort of love substitute?*

When I was very small I already knew I was supposed to make many films. I can only tell you that when I shot my first take it was more fantastic than the most fantastic orgasm I ever had. That was a feeling, indescribable.

■ *The next film will be based on Genet's* Querelle ...

That's really a difficult story; it can easily turn out corny or fascistoid; I hope I can keep to the fine line where it's neither.

■ *Fascistoid—what do you mean by that?*

When you read it, it reads like a glorification of violence, of murder, of betrayal, simply because Genet says human existence is actually consummated only when you've descended to the worst, the lowest level possible in this society. But, it has to be absolutely clear that this pertains to this particular society. If you don't function perfectly in this society, you have to become a traitor, a murderer, you have to be violent.

■ *Is violence something that fascinates you?*

To the extent it's steerable and predictable, it's something that fascinates me. As soon as it isn't those things, it also doesn't interest me anymore, that is, it still interests me as a phenomenon, but I don't like to have anything to do with it; it's like I said before about people who've drunk alcohol and then get to a stage where you can't have a sensible conversation with them anymore. The way they suddenly change their attitude, their views radically, and then don't remember a thing about it the next day.

■ *Well, we know that people who have to lick boots all day to keep their job or whatever also need a "boss" in sexual relationships and accept "violence" in sex. That's how it also is in professions that put people under pressure. People in managerial positions who bark at their employees and so on like to turn the situation around with domineering prostitutes and are starved for surrender and submission.*

Absolutely.

■ *How is it with you? Do you like sadomasochistic sex games?*

Yes, so long as they're within limits that let me control them. No matter who plays which role, it has to be controllable in every respect. I've been with people who I knew had a tremendous urge to be done in, and there I have to keep myself under control so I know I don't want to do them in. I don't think there's any such thing as a plain sadomurderer; well, of course there is, but those are the exceptions, which you have everywhere. But there isn't a sadistic murderer per se; people always have to have the feeling that the other person wants it, and then there could be dangerous situations. I haven't had those yet.

■ *Do you never seek out such situations?*

Nope, otherwise I would have found them. I think I've been in enough places in the world where that was possible, but instead I've always run into people who wanted that from me. I've had some moments where I had to say, Rainer Werner, it's time to stop.

■ *What are you afraid of?*

Death.

■ *Everyone's afraid of that.*

Nope, most people are afraid of dying and not of death itself; it's the suffering leading up to death, long or brief illnesses, nope, I'm afraid of simply not being here. And that's childish or not childish—what do I know—up to now I haven't been able to do anything about it. So I'm always trying to portray attitudes like that of Veronika Voss, to try them out for myself, to see whether they're possible, whether I could manage to develop such an attitude, to get rid of this fear.

■ *When does it come over you particularly?*

Oh, I can't tell you. It comes over me when I'm writing, when I'm fucking; or during breakfast suddenly I feel afraid.

■ *What do you see as your strong points, your weak points?*

Oh, it's so hard to say such things about yourself, but my strengths and weaknesses are certainly the same thing; there's this strange compulsion to work, which is certainly a strength and a weakness at the same time.

■ *What does it enable you to get through?*

Oh, certainly those dead moments, those empty moments you have in life can be more easily gotten through that way.

■ *Do such moments result from disappointments?*

Oh, I don't think so. I'd say I'm manic-depressive, and I just try to be depressive as seldom as possible. Incredible amounts of work help to bridge the gap.

■ *A person can categorize himself as a democrat, a tyrant, a Christian, a resister, an anarchist, a liberal, a conservative. How do you describe yourself?*
I'm a romantic anarchist.

March 1982

Part Two

FELLOW FILMMAKERS
PRO AND CON

Imitation of Life
On the Films of Douglas Sirk

"Film is a battleground," said Samuel Fuller—who once wrote a screen-play for Douglas Sirk—in a film by Jean-Luc Godard, who, shortly be-fore he shot *Breathless,* wrote a hymn in praise of Douglas Sirk's *A Time to Love and a Time to Die.* Whether it be Godard or Fuller, someone else or me—none of us can hold a candle to him. Sirk has said that film is blood, tears, violence, hate, death, and love. And Sirk has made films, films with blood, with tears, with violence, hate, films with death and films with life. Sirk has said you can't make films about something, you can only make films with something, with people, with light, with flowers, with mirrors, with blood, with all these crazy things that make it worthwhile. Sirk has also said that lighting and camera angles constitute the philosophy of the director. And Sirk has made the most tender ones I know, films by a man who loves human beings and doesn't despise them as we do. Darryl F. Zanuck told Sirk one time, "The film has to fly in Kansas City and in Singapore." That's crazy, isn't it—America!

Douglas Sirk had a grandmother who wrote poetry and had black hair. Douglas was still called Detlef then, and lived in Denmark. And it happened that around 1910 the Scandinavian countries had their own film industry, which produced primarily big human dramas. And so little Detlef and his poetry-writing grandmother went to the tiny Dan-ish moviehouse, and both of them wept again and again at the tragic death of Asta Nielsen and many other wonderfully beautiful girls with white-powdered faces. They had to do this in secret, because Douglas Sirk was supposed to become a cultivated man in the great German tradition, humanistically educated, and so one day he gave up his love for Asta Nielsen so that he could love Clytemnestra. In Germany he did theater, in Bremen, in Chemnitz, Hamburg, and Leipzig; he became educated and cultivated. He counted Max Brod among his friends, met 77

Kafka, etc. A career began to take shape that might have ended with him as general manager of the Munich Residenztheater. But no, in 1937, after he had already made a few films in Germany for UFA, Detlef Sierck emigrated to America, became Douglas Sirk, and made films that people in Germany with his level of education would have smirked at.

All That Heaven Allows

That's how it happens that in Lugano, Switzerland, you can run into a man who is more alert, brighter than anyone else I've met, and who can say with a very small, happy smile, "I must say, sometimes I've really loved the things I've done." What he loved was, for instance, *All That Heaven Allows* (1956). Jane Wyman is a rich widow, and Rock Hudson is pruning her trees. In Jane's garden is a "love tree," which only blooms where love is present, and so Jane's and Rock's chance encounter becomes a great love. But Rock is fifteen years younger than Jane, and Jane is completely integrated into the social life of an American small town. Rock is a primitive type, and Jane has a lot to lose—her girlfriends, the good reputation she owes to her deceased husband, her children. In the beginning Rock loves nature, and Jane at first doesn't love anything, because she has everything.

That's a pretty shitty starting point for a great love. Her, him, and the world around them. But basically that's how it looks. She has the motherly touch; she gives the impression she could completely melt at the right moment. You can understand why Rock is wild about her. He's the tree trunk. He's perfectly right when he wants to be with this woman. The world around them is evil. The women all have large mouths. There aren't any other men in the film besides Rock; the easy chairs are more important, or the drinking glasses. To judge by this film, an American small town is the last place I'd want to go. Finally Jane tells Rock she's leaving him, because of the idiotic children and so on. Rock doesn't put up much of a fight—he has nature, after all. And Jane sits there on Christmas Eve; the children are going to leave her, and have given her a television set. At that point everyone in the moviehouse breaks down. They suddenly understand something about the world and what it does to people. Then later Jane goes back to Rock, because she keeps having headaches, which happens to all of us if we don't fuck often enough. But when she's back, it isn't a happy ending, even though they're together, the two of them. A person who creates so many problems in love won't be able to be happy later on.

A still from All That Heaven Allows *(courtesy Museum of Modern Art, New York, Film Stills Archive)*

That's what he makes films about, Douglas Sirk. Human beings can't be alone, but they can't be together either. They're full of despair, these films. *All That Heaven Allows* begins with a long shot of the small town, over which the credits appear. It looks dreary. Then the crane shot swings down toward Jane's house, where a girlfriend is just arriving, returning some dishes she borrowed. You can't get much more dreary! A traveling shot past the two of them, and in the background

Rock Hudson and Jane Wyman in All That Heaven Allows *(courtesy Museum of Modern Art, New York, Film Stills Archive)*

stands Rock Hudson, as an extra would stand there in a Hollywood film. And because the friend can't stay for a cup of coffee with Jane, Jane has coffee with the extra. Even now all the close-ups are of Jane. Rock still doesn't have any real significance. When he does, there are also close-ups of him. That's so simple and beautiful. And everybody gets the point.

Douglas Sirk's films are descriptive films. Very few close-ups. Even in shot/countershot sequences, the partner is always partly visible in the frame. The moviegoer's intense emotion doesn't come from identification but from the montage and the music. That's why you leave these films feeling somehow dissatisfied. You've glimpsed something of other people. And you can voluntarily recognize or have fun grasping what's important for you in the film. Jane's children are nuts. An old guy turns up, to whom they are superior in every respect—youth, knowledge, and so on—and they think he would be just the right partner for their mother. Then Rock comes along, who's not much older than they are, more handsome, and not even all that dumb, either. And they react with scare tactics. That's wild. Jane's son fixes a cocktail for each of them, Rock and the old guy. Both of them praise the cocktail. Both times the same shot. With the old guy, the children are totally at ease. With Rock the atmosphere in the room is on the verge of an explosion. Both times the same shot.

Sirk knows how to deal with actors—it's staggering. If you look at the last films of Fritz Lang, made around the same time, where the worst sort of incompetence manifests itself, you know what you have when you have Douglas Sirk in your head, right? In Douglas Sirk's movies the women think. I haven't noticed that with any other director. With any. Usually the women just react, do the things women do, and here they actually think. That's something you've got to see. It's wonderful to see a woman thinking. That gives you hope. Honest.

And then the people in Sirk's films are all situated in settings that are shaped to an extreme degree by their social situation. The sets are extraordinarily accurate. In Jane's house you can only move a certain way. Only certain sentences occur to you when you want to say something, and certain gestures when you want to express something. If Jane entered another house, Rock's, for instance, would she be able to adjust? That would be something to hope for. Or has she been so molded and messed up that in Rock's house she would miss the style that's hers, after all. That's more likely. That's why the happy ending isn't a real one. Jane fits into her own house better than into Rock's.

Written on the Wind

Written on the Wind (1957) is the story of a super-rich family. Robert Stack is the son, who was always worse in everything than his friend Rock Hudson. Robert Stack really knows how to spend money—he flies planes, boozes, picks up girls, and Rock Hudson is always right there with him. But they aren't happy. What's missing is love. Then they meet Lauren Bacall. She's different from all the other women, of course. She's a simple woman, who works for a living, and she's gentle and understanding. And yet she chooses Robert, the bad guy, though Rock, the good guy, would suit her much better. He also has to work in order to live, and has a big heart like her. She picks the one things simply can't work out with in the long run. When Lauren Bacall meets Robert's father for the first time, she asks him to please give Robert the benefit of the doubt. It's so disgusting when this good-hearted woman sucks up to the good guy so he'll smooth things out for the bad guy. Oh, yes, of course everything has to go wrong. Or let's hope it does. The sister, Dorothy Malone, is the only one who loves the right person, namely Rock Hudson, and she stands by her love, which is ridiculous, of course. It has to be ridiculous when, among all these people who take their compensatory actions for the real thing, it becomes absolutely clear that she does what she does because she can't have the real thing. Lauren Bacall is a substitute for Robert Stack, because he must realize that he won't ever be able to love her, and vice versa. And because Lauren picks Robert, Rock loves her all the more, because he won't ever be able to have her. And the father has a model oil-drilling rig in his hand that looks like a penis substitute. And at the end, when Dorothy Malone, as the last remnant of the family, has this penis in her hand, that's at least as mean as the television set Jane Wyman was given for Christmas. That was just as much a substitute for the fucking her children didn't want to let her have as the oil empire that Dorothy now heads is her substitute for Rock Hudson. I hope she doesn't make it, and goes crazy, like Marianne Koch in *Interlude*. Insanity represents a form of hope in Douglas Sirk's work, I think.

Rock Hudson in *Written on the Wind* is the most stubborn pig in the world. He must sense some of the longing Dorothy Malone is feeling. She throws herself at him, she carries on in public with guys who resemble him somehow, to make him get the message. All he can say is, "I would never be able to satisfy you." But he would, God knows. While Dorothy is dancing in her room, the dance of a dead woman—that may be the beginning of madness—her father dies. He dies because he's guilty. He always reminded his children that the other one, Rock, was the better man, until he really was. Because Rock's father, who hasn't earned any money and can go hunting when he feels like it, was always the better man in the eyes of the father, who could never do the things he wanted to. The children are the poor wretches. Probably he realizes his guilt and drops dead of it. In any case the moviegoer realizes it. His death isn't horrible.

Because Robert doesn't love Lauren, he wants a child by her. Or because Robert doesn't have any prospects of accomplishing anything, he wants to beget a child, at least. Courage detects a weakness. Robert begins to drink again. Now it becomes clear that Lauren Bacall doesn't have anything to offer her husband. Instead of going out drinking with him and showing some understanding for his pain, she just becomes more and more noble and pure, more and more nauseating, and you see more and more clearly how well she would suit Rock Hudson, who's also nauseating and noble. These people who were raised for a specific purpose and have their heads full of manipulated dreams are

Rock Hudson and Dorothy Malone in Written on the Wind *(courtesy Museum of Modern Art, New York, Film Stills Archive)*

totally screwed up. If Lauren Bacall had lived with Robert Stack instead of living next to, off of, and for him, he would have been able to believe that the child she bears was really his. He wouldn't have had to groan. But this way his child is really more Rock Hudson's, even though Rock never did it with Lauren.

Dorothy does something evil—she makes her brother suspicious of Lauren and Rock. Yet even so, I love her as I've seldom loved a person in a movie. As a viewer I'm with Douglas Sirk on the trail of human despair. In *Written on the Wind* everything good and "normal" and "beautiful" is always very disgusting, and everything evil, weak, and confused makes you feel sympathy. Even for those who manipulate the good people.

And then the house where all this takes place. Dominated, people say, by the grand staircase. And mirrors. And always flowers. And gold. And coldness. The sort of house you build for a lot of money. A house with all the fancy doodads you get when you have money, and among which you don't feel comfortable. It's like at the Oktoberfest, where everything is animated and colorful, and you're lonely like them. In this house, which Douglas Sirk had built for the Hedleys, feelings must put forth the weirdest blossoms. The light in Sirk's films is always as unnaturalistic as possible. Shadows where there shouldn't be any help to render plausible emotions that you would prefer to keep at arm's length. The same with the camera angles in *Written on the Wind*—mostly oblique, mostly from below: chosen so that the strangeness of the story doesn't manifest itself in the mind of the viewer but on the screen. Douglas Sirk's films liberate the mind.

Interlude

Interlude (1957) is a film that's hard to get into. At first everything seems false. The film takes place in Munich, and it isn't the city as we know it. The Munich in *Interlude* consists of grand buildings. Königsplatz, Nymphenburg Palace, the Hercules Hall. Then later you realize that this is Munich as an American might see it. June Allyson comes to Munich to experience Europe. What she experiences is a great love, the love of her life. It's Rossano Brazzi, who plays a conductor of the Herbert von Karajan type. June Allyson stands out somewhat among Douglas Sirk's characters. She strikes me as too natural, too healthy. Too fresh, although she does become very ill, in the end. Rossano Brazzi is a conductor through and through, even in the tenderest whisperings of love. The way he moves, eternally posturing, putting on a show for others, even when he means what he says completely seriously; it's a masterpiece of directing. The way Brazzi plays that is the way Wedekind's *Music* would have to be performed.

Brazzi has a wife, Marianne Koch. And this is the character who is perhaps the most important for an understanding of Douglas Sirk's view of the world. Marianne Koch loves Rossano Brazzi. He married her, and she was always happy with him, and her love was her undoing. She went insane. All of Sirk's characters are pursuing some kind of longing. The only one who has experienced fulfillment is done in by it. Can one interpret this to mean that in our society a person is only okay in the eyes of society if he goes panting after something, like a dog with his tongue hanging out? As long as he does, he'll adhere to the norms that allow him to remain useful. In Douglas Sirk's films, love seems to be the best, most sneaky and effective instrument of social oppression. June Allyson goes back to the United States with a minor love she's met. They won't be happy together. She'll always dream of her conductor, and the man will sense his wife's discontent. They'll concentrate all the more on their work, which will then be exploited by others. Okay.

The Tarnished Angels

The Tarnished Angels (1958) is the only black-and-white film of Douglas Sirk's that I've had a chance to see. It is the film in which he had the most freedom. An exceptionally pessimistic film. It's based on a story by Faulkner, which I don't know, unfortunately. It seems Sirk desecrated it, which was good for it.

This film, like *La Strada,* shows a dying profession, but not in such a gruesomely highbrow way. Robert Stack was a pilot in World War I. He never wanted to do anything but fly, so now he flies around pylons at air shows. His wife is Dorothy Malone, who does parachute demonstrations. They can barely live on what they make. Robert is brave, but he doesn't understand a thing about the plane. Then there's the other member of the threesome, Jiggs, who's a mechanic and loves Dorothy. Robert and Dorothy have a son, who, when Rock Hudson first meets him, is being teased by other soldiers: "So which one's your father? Jiggs or . . . " Rock Hudson is a journalist who wants to write something fantastic about these gypsies, who instead of blood have motor oil in their veins. At the moment the Shumans have nowhere to stay, and Rock Hudson invites them to his place. During the night Dorothy and Rock get to know each other. You can sense that the two might have a lot to say to each other. Rock loses his job, a pilot crashes during a race, and Dorothy is supposed to sell herself to get a plane, because Robert's is on the fritz. Rock and Dorothy don't have so much to say to each other after all. Jiggs fixes the broken-down plane, Robert takes off and dies. Dorothy leaves. Rock gets his job back.

Nothing but defeats. This film is nothing but a collection of defeats. Dorothy loves Robert, Robert loves flying. Jiggs also loves Robert, or maybe Dorothy and Robert? Rock doesn't love Dorothy, and Dorothy doesn't love Rock. At most it's a lie, even if the film sometimes makes the whole thing believable, just as the two of them think for a few seconds that maybe . . . Just before the end Robert tells Dorothy he's going to give up flying after this flight. And then of course he dies doing it. It would be inconceivable for Robert to pay real attention to Dorothy instead of flirting with death.

In this film the camera is constantly in motion, acting like the people the film's about, as if something were actually going on. In reality, in the end they could all lie down and let themselves be buried. And the traveling shots in the film, the crane shots, the pans! Douglas Sirk shows these dead souls with such tenderness and with such a light that you say to yourself that they're all in such a shitty situation and yet so lovable that something must be to blame for it. What is to blame is loneliness and fear. I've seldom felt loneliness and fear the way I do in this film. The moviegoer sits there in the cinema like the Shumans' son in the merry-go-round when his father crashes. You realize what's wrong, want to run and help too, but when you think about it, what can a little boy do against a crashing plane? They're all to blame for Robert's death. That's why Dorothy Malone is so hysterical afterward. Because she knew. And Rock Hudson, who wanted a sensational story. When he finally has one, he blames his colleagues. And Jiggs, who was wrong to repair the plane, sits there and asks himself, Where are you all? It's bad enough he never realized before that no one was there. These films tell about the illusions people can construct for themselves. And why people need to construct illusions. Dorothy saw a picture of Robert, a poster of him as a proud pilot, and fell in love with him. Robert wasn't anything like the picture, of course. What to do? Create an illusion. Be my guest. Nobody's forcing her, you say to yourself, and you want to tell her that her love for Robert wasn't real love. What good would that do her? With an illusion in your head you can stand the loneliness better. Be my guest. I think this film shows that that isn't true. Sirk made a film where there's constant action, in which something's always going on, where the camera moves frequently, and where you learn so much about loneliness and how it makes us lie. And how wrong it is that we lie, and how stupid.

A Time to Love and a Time to Die

A Time to Love and a Time to Die (1958). John Gavin comes home to Berlin on leave from the Eastern Front in 1945. His parents' house is destroyed. He runs into Liselotte Pulver, whom he knew when they were both small. And because they're so desperate and alone, they begin to love each other. The film is quite properly called "A Time to Love and a Time to Die." The time is the war. That's obvious: it is a time to die. And where you have death and bombs and cold and tears, love can flourish in Douglas Sirk's world. Liselotte Pulver has planted a little flower outside her window, the only speck of life amidst the ruins. John Gavin will die in the end, that's clear from the outset. And somehow all this doesn't have anything to do with the war after all. A film about the war would have to be different. It's actually about the situation. War as a situation and as nourishing soil for an emotion. The same types, Liselotte Pulver and John Gavin, if they met in 1971, you'd have a smile, a "how are you," "well, look at that," and that's it. In 1945 it can turn into a great love. This is quite right. Love doesn't have any problems here. The problems are all going on outside. Inside two people can be tender to one another.

For the first time in a work by Douglas Sirk a small love, unprepossessing people. With big, incredulous eyes they stare at what's happening around them. It's all unfathomable to them, the bombs, the Gestapo, the madness. Under the circumstances love is the simplest thing, something you can hang onto. And so you cling to it. But I wouldn't like to be forced to imagine what would happen to the two of them if John survived the war. The war and its horrors are only the backdrop. You can't make a film about war. How wars come about—that would be important, and what effect they have on people or leave behind. This isn't a pacifist film, either, because you never for a minute say to yourself, Without this gruesome war everything would be so beautiful or whatever. Remarque's novel, *A Time to Live and a Time to Die,* is pacifist. Remarque says that without war this would be an eternal love; Sirk says that without war there wouldn't be any love here.

Imitation of Life

Imitation of Life (1959) is Douglas Sirk's last film. A big, crazy film about life and death. And a film about America. The first great moment: Annie tells Lana Turner that Sarah Jane is her daughter. Annie is black and Sarah Jane almost white. Lana Turner hesitates, understands, still hesitates, and then quickly acts as though it were the most natural thing in the world for a black woman to have a white daughter. But nothing is natural. Never. Not throughout the entire film. And yet everyone tries compulsively to consider his thoughts or his wishes his own. Sarah Jane wants to be white, not because white is a prettier color than black but because you can live better as a white person. Lana Turner wants to be an actress, not because it's nice for her but because when you're successful you have a better position in the world. And Annie wants a grand funeral not because it will benefit her—she'll be dead, after all—but because she wants to display to the world an importance she was not allowed to have in life. Not one of the protagonists realizes that all these things—thoughts, wishes, dreams—grow directly out of their social reality or are manipulated by it. I don't know any other film that shows this phenomenon so clearly and so despairingly. Once, toward the end of the film, Annie tells Lana Turner that she has many friends. Lana is amazed. Annie has friends? The two women have been living together for ten years, and

Lana doesn't know a thing about Annie. Lana Turner is surprised. And when her daughter reproaches her for always leaving her alone, Lana Turner is also surprised, and when Sarah Jane suddenly rebels against the white goddess, and when she has problems and wants to be taken seriously, there, too, Lana Turner can only be surprised. And she's surprised when Annie dies. You can't just go and die like that. That's not right, to be confronted with life so suddenly. Throughout the entire second part of the film all Lana can do is be surprised. The result is that in the future she'll play dramatic roles. Suffering, death, tears—you have to put them to some good use. The problem Lana faces becomes the problem of the filmmaker. Lana is an actress, possibly even a good one. That you never find out exactly. In the beginning Lana has to earn money for herself and her daughter. Or does she want to have a successful career? The death of her husband seems not to have affected her much. She knows he was a good director. I think Lana wants a successful career. Money comes second, after success. After that comes John Gavin. John loves Lana; for her sake, in order to support her, he has put aside his own artistic ambitions and taken a job as a photographer with an advertising firm. Lana simply can't understand that—his denying his ambitions out of love. Yes, I'm quite certain Lana doesn't want to make money; she wants a career. And John is stupid, too; he confronts Lana with the choice between marriage and a career. Lana finds that exciting and dramatic, and decides in favor of her career.

That's how it goes throughout the film. They're always making plans based on happiness, on tenderness, and then the telephone rings, a new offer, and Lana perks up. The woman is hopeless. And John Gavin, too. He really should have seen after a while that it wouldn't work out. And yet he hitches his life to this woman. Whenever things won't work, they pursue them doggedly, these people. Then Lana's daughter falls in love with John; she's the type John would like, but she's not Lana. That's understandable. Except that Sandra Dee doesn't understand it. Maybe a person who's in love understands less. Annie loves her daughter, too, and doesn't understand her at all. When Sarah Jane is still little, it rains one time, and Annie brings her an umbrella to school. Sarah Jane has been passing for white in her class. When her mother brings the umbrella, the lie comes out. Sarah Jane will never forget that. And when Annie is dying and wants to see Sarah Jane and goes to visit her in a bar in Las Vegas, Annie is still so full of love that she doesn't understand. To her it's a sin that Sarah Jane wants to pass for white. That's what makes this scene so terrible: the cruel one is Sarah Jane, and the poor, pitiable one is her mother. But, in fact, it's

exactly the opposite. The mother who wants to possess her child because she loves her is brutal. And Sarah Jane is defending herself
against her mother's terrorism, the world's terrorism. That's cruel; you
can understand both of them, and both of them are right, and no one
will ever be able to help either of them. Unless, of course, we change
the world. We all cried over the movie. Because it's so hard to change
the world. Then at Annie's funeral everybody comes together again,
and for a few moments they act as though everything was all right.
And this occasional "acting as though" permits them to go on making
the same mess of things, because they do sense what they're longing
for, actually, and then they lose sight of it again.

   Imitation of Life begins like a film about the character played by
Lana Turner, and then imperceptibly it becomes a film about the Ne-
gro Annie. In the end the director set his own concern aside—the
relevance of the theme to his own work—and looked for the decep-
tion of life in Annie, where he found a much crueler situation than he
could have discovered in Lana Turner or himself. Even fewer opportunities. Even greater despair.

I've tried to write about six films by Douglas Sirk, and in the process
I've discovered how hard it is to write about films that have something
to do with life, that aren't literature. I've left out a lot of things that
might be important. I've said too little about the lighting, how carefully it's handled, or how it helps Sirk transform the stories he had to
tell. And that besides him only Josef von Sternberg uses light so well.
And I've said too little about the sets that Douglas Sirk had built for
the films. How incredibly accurate they are. I've not analyzed sufficiently the importance of flowers and mirrors, and what they mean to
the stories Sirk tells us. I've not stressed sufficiently that Sirk is a director who gets the most out of his actors. That under Sirk's direction
chatterboxes like Marianne Koch or Liselotte Pulver become human
beings you can and want to believe in. And then I've seen far too few
of his films. I'd like to see all thirty-nine of them. Then maybe I'd be
farther along, with myself, with my life, with my friends. I've seen six
films by Douglas Sirk. Among them were the most beautiful in the
world.

February 1971

. . . Shadows, to be Sure, and no Pity
A Few Random Thoughts on the Films of Claude Chabrol

> There is nothing finer than siding with the oppressed; the true aesthetic consists in defending the weak and the disadvantaged.
>
> — GERHARD ZWERENZ

> For all guilt is avenged on earth, even that of passing off apparitions or semi-apparitions as human beings.
>
> — THEODOR FONTANE

It begins the way it continues. And ultimately hasn't changed to this day. For when François passes through Sardent, his birthplace, which he hasn't visited for a long time, Marie tells him with rare perspicacity that he's looking at all the people as though they were insects. That was in 1957 in *Le beau Serge*. And Chabrol, who identified with François, is lying when he ends the film with the character's spiritual transformation. Chabrol himself has undergone no such transformation; on the contrary. Otherwise his future work would have taken up where *Le beau Serge* ended, with François's recognition that you have to do something to help. And then—honestly—he might have become a great filmmaker. Now, in retrospect, the ending of *Le beau Serge* looks pasted on, a self-conscious Christian pose. And he didn't become a great filmmaker, even though there are lots of things that are pretty and nicely done in his work, and even a few great films. Chabrol's eye is not that of an entomologist, as is often claimed, but that of a child who keeps a number of insects in a glass jar and observes the strange behavior of his little creatures with a mixture of amazement, horror, and pleasure. Depending entirely on how he's feeling, and that may be determined by how well he's slept, whether he's eaten well or badly, he alters his attitude toward the animals. So he has a shifting attitude. He doesn't do research with them. Otherwise he could, and would have to, discover reasons for their brutal behavior, and convey these to us. Never mind that there have to be some little creatures who are less colorful than the others, less showy, but the vast majority of them are completely colorless creatures that provide the basis for the existence of the more beautiful ones. But these are completely overlooked by the child, who doesn't do scientific observation but only looks, allowing himself to be dazzled by the glittering, special ones; he overlooks them, and therefore can't really understand the behavior of his favorites. The child becomes more and more blind, and out of anger and despair at his own blindness—for he does sense his own inadequacy—this child will some day make a film with his creatures, and will call it *Nada*—"nothing."

Again and again it's fate that strikes, chance that intervenes and allows the story to continue. Why does Paul shoot his cousin Charles? Well, it's fate. And an accidental fate to boot. It could have happened differently: the bullet could have hit Paul when Charles fired at him in the dark. Then at least the idiocy that pervades the story would have been pulled up short. As it is, it just persists all the way to the end, this idiocy that's actually stupidity. And what's significant about consistent stupidity? The consistency or the stupidity? What of it, the plot just speaks all the more to the heart of the undiscriminating moviegoer, whom one despises anyway. What's the real story on fascism in France in 1958? *Les cousins* is a period document without a period and without documentary value; fascism in France in 1958 can't simply be Wagner and a Jew who people yell "Gestapo!" at. True, a dark-skinned student is twice made the butt of stupid remarks, that one must admit. And it's very courageous of Chabrol to have shown that. But what about the hundreds of thousands of North Africans who are exploited and discriminated against in Paris? But of course you can't reproach someone for something he didn't do, can you? Though it seems to me that precisely the things you don't find in Chabrol are the most crucial. True, there's the hatred between Thérèse and Henri Marcoins. After a long marriage, hatred is what's left in *A double tour.* That's something, anyway. More, at any rate, than Paul's speechless scorn for Charles in *Les cousins,* which in fact doesn't "result in the long run in a different confusion, a collective one this time: in fascism" (*Cahiers du Cinéma,* 1960). My God, it takes more to produce fascism than the contempt a clever young man feels for his sluggish cousin.

So the hatred in *A double tour,* marriage, which destroys the human being because it is actually inhumane, the raising of children in marriages, and what must then become of these children, unavoidably—that would be a good topic. Even as a fairy tale, certainly; a film doesn't have to be a piece of reality caught in a trap. But as a lie? Chabrol is right: you can tell all the lies you like about a small segment of society to which hardly anyone has access, like the upper middle class. Or isn't it possible after all for the audience to rethink the lies in terms of its own reality? Doesn't all this have something to do with our parents' marriages? The hypocrisy that surrounds possessiveness? But the fact that our parents are possessive this way isn't really their fault; it's the fault of their upbringing, and the reason they were brought up that way has to do . . .

Chabrol doesn't see it that way. Chabrol is indubitably a proponent of marriage, as his later films prove. And marriage is primarily an institution that sustains the state. But Chabrol is opposed to hypocrisy in marriage, opposed to possessiveness, instead of being against marriage. It's all so cheap, the feelings and the needs, too. No interest in the real needs and the real feelings. No indication that the needs people consider their very own are actually only the needs they're told to have. Everything seems to be in perfect order. In Chabrol the disorder that occurs is irrational, not inevitable, as is actually the case in this society. Richard Marcoux (in *A double tour*), a son who was brought up wrong and a murderer, doesn't become a murderer because he was brought up wrong, but because he's also retarded. And that's Chabrol's lie, which takes away from the audience the opportunity to rethink the fairy tale in terms of its own reality. But then why make a film? Only to make money? Well, it's an industry, after all, the film industry. And making money is an honorable motive, to be sure, but is it the only one? And how about the fact that such films are dangerous because they make people stupid, take away their courage instead of giving it back to them, blur their vision instead of sharpening it? It's just art, after all, and what harm can art do? Maybe . . .

Chabrol must have sensed the cul-de-sac into which he'd maneuvered himself with *A double tour* and where he would later settle in so comfortably. He did make *Les bonnes femmes*. And had bad luck with it. *Les bonnes femmes* is the only one of Chabrol's films in which there are mostly real human beings, not shadowy figures. Finally Chabrol shows a touch of tenderness for his characters, a tenderness that he could muster later only very rarely and only for certain characters, for instance, those played by Michel Bouquet. Here he follows his characters into the most ugly and disgusting situations, but he sticks by them; the child pokes his hand into the glass container with the insects. Of course it gets bitten. And it will be a long time before he'll poke his hand in again, putting it at the mercy of the creatures. At least he hasn't dared to do it yet. True, he fished out certain insects, particularly brilliant ones, and cautiously stroked them. But it didn't go beyond that. The critics gave Chabrol a good slap in the face. And the audience followed the critics. And yet, strangely enough, the critics took the side of the characters whom, for once, Chabrol actually loved in this film. I think the critics and the audience despised the good women and punished Chabrol for showing them how and what they despise. And in addition, *Les bonnes femmes* is a revolutionary film, because it really does provoke rage against a system that lets people go under this way. It's a film that makes it very clear that something must be done. Unfortunately, Chabrol's method of work forced him to make large-budget films; otherwise, he could have made cheaper films with less money and learned to do perfect work even on a small budget. Exactly the opposite occurred. He learned to make sloppy films on a large budget. That's one way to do it.

At first Chabrol tried after *Les bonnes femmes* to make something like B-flicks, but they obviously suffered from too little action and a bit too much art. At least the audience didn't like *Les godelureaux, L'oeil du malin, Ophélia* and *Landru.* From this period, Chabrol's second, I'm familiar only with *Landru*—a strange monstrosity. Newsreel clips from the First World War are juxtaposed with theatrical tableaux. Landru, who appears in the story not as a monster, but as someone who behaves cruelly in a cruel time, is played by Charles Denner, under Chabrol's direction, with such extreme exaggeration that you don't want to believe the story. Everything is so contradictory that in the end you've seen "nothing," experienced nothing. The enjoyment you generally have as a viewer because you're a few steps ahead of the characters is canceled out because Chabrol takes such pleasure in anything disgusting, a pleasure he surrenders to until it becomes a mania, a mania that's just plain boring, boring to the point where the entire film becomes boring, because it is really nothing but itself, the film, and the images—all beautiful, by the way—become hostile images. That may mean that at this time Chabrol saw the audience as his enemy, more drastically than later on, and well, of course, why should you do anything nice for your enemy?

Between 1957 and 1962 Chabrol was able to shoot at least one, if not two, long feature films. In 1963 he had enough funds only for an eighteen-minute sketch, so the ensuing third period in his work can also be explained by his need to earn money. But only "also." There's a certain consistency in the fact that with his two "Tiger" films he was making spy films supportive of the government, with hardly any attempt to subvert the genre; on the contrary, he was trying to satisfy its requirements. But that's done much better by someone like Terence Young, for example. Chabrol has nothing original to add to the genre. He even has a good deal of trouble imitating; everything comes out a few sizes too small, including the pleasure you might get from these films. What remains is the pact between Chabrol and his republic. In Chabrol, France doesn't have a critic, a Balzac of the twentieth century, which is what he likes to think of himself as; at least that's what these films prove. Rather, France has in Chabrol a cynic within the system, a cynic with a great longing for naiveté, for a lost identity. And this strange combination produces films like *Marie-Chantal contre Dr. Kha, La ligne de démarcation,* and *La route de Corinthe.* Seemingly naive spy flicks with naive heroes. That's still acceptable in the two spy films, *Marie-Chantal* and *La route de Corinthe,* because the spy movie is a naive genre, but it becomes a complete farce in *La ligne de démarcation,* which can be measured against reality. It's no accident that Chabrol of all people had Colonel Rémy write a screenplay for him. After all, the former Resistance people later became the most reactionary representatives of a dubious nationalistic morality. Chabrol was completely taken in by him, with his clean, neat storyline. Nothing but good Frenchmen, enough to make your hair stand on end, and even the cowardly aristocrat, who throughout the film considers it ridiculous to resist the Germans from the underground, is allowed to die with his soul cleansed in the end. And the good Frenchmen briefly strike up the "Internationale," only to conclude with the "Marseillaise" after all. At that point, a self-conscious pan to the swastika banner doesn't help; by then any hint of the question of what became of liberated France has already floated away down the romantic Rhine. The two other films with the accidental heroines, Marie-Chantal and Shanny, are pretty, to be sure, as pretty in fact as Marie Laforet and Jean Seberg. There's not much more to it, although some people may lose themselves in deep metaphysical speculation as to what message Chabrol may be trying to convey when he gives the petty-bourgeois Chantal power over all mankind. All power to the petty bourgeoisie or something like that? Who knows?

Chabrol was not able to shoot the announced sequel to *Marie-Chantal* after all. A good thing, too. I'm not really inclined to believe Chabrol's earnest assurances that in this period he was working strictly to earn money. After all, there are five films and two planned sequels over a stretch of four years; at that rate, a person has to know what he's up to. And he also knows what he might have done; every genre has already been subverted to the point that you can do everything in such a way that its effect turns it into the opposite. Just look at the pasted-on happy endings in Hollywood films; you could do them one way or the other. Chabrol chose the easy path of affirmation, and I'll say it again: I think he knew what he was up to.

With *Le scandale,* even though it was made before *La route de Corinthe,* Chabrol entered his fourth period, the one usually associated with the name Chabrol. Brought down to a common denominator, you could say that in this phase Chabrol has been working to check out bourgeois values. The question is, is he checking them out in order to transcend them, or to preserve them? I think the latter. Well, Chabrol seems sad that things are no longer so orderly and clear, sad that human beings are so bad. Chabrol is still not interested in the circumstances and the systems that make people what they are, but in the result, so long as it's picturesque enough. And that's inhuman. Chabrol's films from this last period are inhuman because they're fatalistic, cynical, and misanthropic. And the exceptions confirm the rule. Strangely enough, in contrast to earlier, the stories that are irreal from the outset, like *Les biches* and *La rupture,* are more bearable. And *Le boucher* is a great film in spite of everything; there Chabrol develops for the first and only time a story out of real people. Oh, it's the only time he develops anything at all. The only film that doesn't throw everything at the viewer as ultimately meaningless and immutable, no matter what. That's what he does in all his other films. He hits his audience over the head, and with such perfect form that you can hardly resist. And that's what makes him so dangerous. The universe he portrays does make sense on its own terms. But it has nothing to do with the lives of those who finance these films by buying tickets, though you can't see that, except in *Les biches* and *La rupture.* Both of them are films that are so perfectly smooth that they open up somewhat, and it doesn't matter either that there are no people to be seen, only shadows. Shadows, to be sure, that have an ineffable glamour. Shadows with which a story is nicely told. Probably Chabrol is the director who has the most complete mastery of his way of telling a story. Even if the films are becoming sloppier and sloppier in form. Sometimes you think Chabrol has just discovered the zoom, the most pathetic of all film techniques. In every film one or two incredibly beautiful traveling shots; otherwise, nothing doing—flat, slick images with no attention to the lighting or to the colors. And two really awful films: *Docteur Popaul* and *Nada.* That's pure fascism there. Absolutely obvious. But all that was there earlier as a predisposition, and then one day it just emerged.

Chabrol's disdain for his audience becomes very clear in his four television movies. You just can't work as mindlessly and heedlessly for so many people as Chabrol does here. Instead of recognizing television as a challenge, maybe the greatest for a filmmaker, he sees it as a nuisance. But there's a certain logic to that.

1975

The German Cinema Is Being Enriched
A Few Thoughts about a Wonderful Film, *Jane Is Jane Forever,* by Walter Bockmayer

In the process of working up the problems of underprivileged marginal groups, artists one fine day stumbled upon "the elderly." As it turned out, this was a lucky and advantageous find for the makers of art. It relieves them of the risky preoccupation with homosexuals, Jews, communists (real ones), workers, women/children, and much else that you get precious little comfort from taking seriously within the German culture industry; said industry has proved increasingly successful at engendering fear, and has produced a situation that consolidates fear in such a subtle way that almost every creative person has fled into a sort of inner emigration, while simultaneously practicing inner censorship. Many of them are already so far gone that they actually mistake the results of this self-censorship, conducted with delicate brutality, for what they actually intended to produce. But that leads us too far afield. And some of them are left with the problems of the elderly, so you can't accuse them of lacking courage, since they do show a society that mistreats its old people, and you've really shown it to a society like that when you've shown that, right?

No, not right. Since we've had *Jane Is Jane Forever,* by Walter Bockmayer, you can understand why the culture industry reacted in such a friendly way to all the plays, television shows, and films about elderly people. All these works, of varying quality, confirm the system they claim to criticize: German artists have developed a sort of criticism from within the system that makes one sad and fearful. The end result will be a German art that is dead, incapable of taking cognizance of anything but itself. The few who try to stay alert must count on being hit in the face sooner or later. Those who will do the hitting firmly expect, and probably rightly so, that those who have been hit will sing songs with their new gold teeth, songs that sing of love. For the last holdouts who refuse to lie to themselves, our society has various little devices in reserve. Drugs, for instance, or foreign countries, and then of course one can also take one's own life. Peace will rule in the land.

Smack in the middle of this situation Walter Bockmayer has made a revolutionary film. How much of it is sheer naiveté doesn't matter; the "revolutionary" in art, with its intellectual substructure, is usually no longer revolutionary, but rather, because of its faith in institutions, usually counterrevolutionary. Otherwise how could the German theater, which is on the one hand decidedly and perfectly oriented toward Marxian ideas, on the other hand fulfill "most gratifyingly" the requirements and norms of the bourgeois theater?

Bockmayer, however, didn't choose the safe course. Possibly he didn't even know the statistics about old-age homes or the sociological makeup of their populations when he set out to make his film about old age; or rather, *Jane Is Jane Forever* is actually not a film about old age but rather a film expressing the fears about old age of an artist who is endowed with a great, specific sensibility. This film doesn't whip up cheap pity or momentary impulses of the "one really should ... " variety; the 80 percent of moviegoers who are between twenty and thirty (that's a statistical fact) aren't provoked to exchange meaningless winks with the cunning old heroes; no pat solutions are offered, no poor, lovable old folks are exploited, begging with innocent, honest dumb-doggy eyes for public monies—*Jane Is Jane Forever* makes palpable, vivid, unforgettable, the fear of old age felt by those who made the film.

But no melancholy opens up the heart so far that the brain doesn't get any air and suffocates. None of those favorite fortuitous sadnesses is called upon to produce those famous tears of which one needn't be ashamed. We aren't allowed to hide from rage at the fact that we live in a society that makes us afraid of growing old. We're forced to think things through. We're forced to ask whether fear of being old can exist in us without fear of simply being, today and tomorrow. This film liberates us to the point that we can ask, Why is there so much fear in us? Who gains from it? Must it be this way? And shouldn't we think again about what we must change, and by what means, and how quickly?

In many respects *Jane Is Jane Forever* is an exemplary film. Produced with the resources of the wonderful "Kamerafilm" department of Second German Television, where filmmakers are given just enough money to work with to make them feel morally obligated to come up with something of feature quality, which usually results in their waking up on a mountain of debt, which makes them (I dare to write this again) fearful and manipulable and harmless. Bockmayer managed to rack up fewer debts than most and didn't try to cover up the skimpy production conditions. Time and again the film itself lets us glimpse the niggardliness of the sponsoring television network, which in the end will take credit for making this production possible at all—that's how it goes. Bockmayer also doesn't conceal his own limitations, admitting in areas where he's still learning that he is still learning.

Thus, confessed poverty and (temporary) directorial limitations that for once are not skillfully covered up combine to produce a richness rare in the German cinema. A richness that can help to formulate what people have suffered and to liberate minds.

April 1977

Chin-up, Handstand, Salto Mortale—Firm Footing
On the Film Director Werner Schroeter, Who Achieved What Few Achieve, with *Kingdom of Naples*

For more than a decade, which is a long time, almost too long, Werner Schroeter was the most important, exciting, decisive as well as de-cided director of alternative films, films generally referred to as *underground films,* a term that well-meaningly limits and prettifies this sort of film, eventually suffocating it in a tender embrace.

In reality there is no such thing as *underground* film. It exists only for people who know how to make neat distinctions between Up Here, Down There, and Way over There. In reality there are only films, and they are smack in the middle of the whole, which is neither black nor white but gray. And then there are the people who make these films. And just as these people and their films differ from one another, the urgency they feel to make films also differs. And some refuse to hold off on making a film till they have some silly certification or other in hand, attesting that they're "professionals"; they make films with a devil-may-care attitude, in 35-millimeter or 8-millimeter, it really doesn't much matter.

But the culture industry, which in some respects is more powerful here than elsewhere, has settled on a simple distinction between film-makers it calls "professionals" and those who are "underground," and watches sternly to make sure this neat division is respected. Once someone has been labeled an "underground" director, for the sake of simplicity he should remain one, preferably forever. Thus hardly any director in the Federal Republic ever succeeds in breaking out of the ghetto to which he has been consigned, where things are made more or less comfortable for him, let that be said. And that can easily make a person lazy or cowardly, as the case may be.

On the other hand, if a director tries to climb out of the "under-ground" into the "mainstream cinema," the resistance he will encoun-ter in the German culture industry is remarkably tough and unani-mous; it robs many of their courage and certainly destroys a whole heap of talent.

Werner Schroeter will one day have a place in the history of film that I would describe in literature as somewhere between Novalis, Lautréamont, and Louis-Ferdinand Céline; he was an "underground" director for ten years, and they didn't want to let him slip out of this role. Werner Schroeter's grand cinematic scheme of the world was confined, repressed, and at the same time ruthlessly exploited. His films were given the convenient label of "underground," which transformed them in a flash into beautiful but exotic plants that bloomed so unusually and so far away that basically one couldn't be bothered with them, and therefore obviously wasn't supposed to bother with them. And that's precisely as easy as it is wrong and stupid. For Werner Schroeter's films are not far away; they're beautiful, but not exotic. On the contrary.

This director Werner Schroeter, whom they try to belittle, whom they try to shove into tiny, stupid pigeonholes, and whose films— I keep saying this—they call "underground" films, and the underground—well, there are some important things, but down there, you know, and besides, these films are too cheap to impress those very people who wouldn't give any money for them—this Werner Schroeter has been endowed with a clearer, more comprehensive view of this ball we call the earth than anyone else doing art, of whatever kind. And strange, wondrous secrets of the universe it seems to me reveal themselves a bit to this lucky, privileged man.

In case it's not obvious, let me insert here that this good luck and this greatness I have just described of course in no way mean that this person, as a living being, as a body, is above it all and satisfied. On the contrary. I know of no one else, besides myself, who is so desperately intent on chasing after a shamelessly utopian and probably infantile vision of something like love (these words, ladies and gentlemen, unmask themselves in any case, don't they?) and stands there helpless in the face of ever-gray-green experience. But: experience makes you dumb. Both of us will probably continue as before.

Back to the topic: the director Werner Schroeter, it was asserted at the very beginning, has achieved something that hardly anyone achieves. Well, what is it? Ten years in the "underground," viewed by the "Kamerafilm" department at Second German Television as a reliable fool, who almost as reliably as beer brought in hymns of praise from viewers in and outside of Germany, which may have raised the self-esteem of these presumed midwives, but at the same time blinded them to the fact that each of Werner Schroeter's films cost a good deal more than Schroeter was getting from them. But for a long time that didn't inspire them to generous new thoughts, and why should it have—a person with debts has no choice; he's almost dependent, so he'll continue to behave. And he's cheap. And anyway. Werner Schroeter stayed in this vicious circle longer than most, of course always filled with a strong, indestructible hope of being able to break out some day. To make films for the cinema, films for people, the more, the better. But it just didn't want to happen.

After a while there were only a few people with an opportunity to make films who hadn't learned their trade from observing Werner Schroeter at work. I made decisive discoveries in his films, that must be said, or written, clearly. Daniel Schmid is unthinkable without Schroeter, likewise Ulrike Ottinger, and Walter Bockmayer learned from Schroeter's films. There's a whole slew of graduates of the Munich film academy whose films are essays on Schroeter, from Eberhard Schubert to Bernd Schwamm. In France there are young colleagues to whom Schroeter's films are as important as Sternberg's. And rightly so.

And a very clever Schroeter-imitator turned up who skillfully marketed things lifted from Schroeter at a time when Schroeter was still waiting helplessly. And in Paris they actually succumbed for a long time to this trader in plagiarism, Hans Jürgen Syberberg. It was quite hard to explain in France that we were not simply epigones of the more nimble Syberberg, but that he was running a cruel clearance sale, partly with our most personal possessions. But even Syberberg, quite apart from my great desire to get this off my chest, stands for opportunities to make "great films" with Werner Schroeter's own unique inventions, opportunities that were denied their talented originator.

Then, at a time when quite a few people, even Schroeter's friends, were slowly but surely accepting the idea that he might never make a great epic film, that after all these years of shyness, hesitation, lack of opportunity, he might not get it together, in a situation in which quite a few have despaired and simply given up, and others have turned bitter and sad after a failed attempt, like Rosa von Praunheim with *Berlin Bedroll*—in this situation Werner Schroeter made the film *The Kingdom of Naples.* A great and important film. Incredible, after the terrible years of waiting, always on the verge of simply drying up. A film that without hesitation can be classed with *Ossessione* by Visconti, *La Strada* by Fellini, *Mamma Roma* by Pasolini, *Rocco and His Brothers* by Visconti, *Les bonnes femmes* by Chabrol, *Le diable probablement* by Bresson, *The Exterminating Angel* by Buñuel, and others like that. So Germany has not only three, or five, or ten film directors to show off; it has now acquired another one who was certainly needed. One with a great deal to say. A great one, to put it simply.

Finally, since this essay will certainly be read by quite a few who also read *Filmkritik,* a journal I've referred to here and there with enthusiasm, let me be permitted to mention that it published a disgusting, revolting article by Rosa von Praunheim about Werner Schroeter's most recent film. Private matters have to be mentioned; by way of explanation: a long time ago Rosa von Praunheim and Werner Schroeter were very close. While Rosa was already making films intended to reach an audience, Werner Schroeter was just beginning to make films. But Schroeter was making them for his friend then, for "love" of him. The thanks he got from Rosa von Praunheim were scorn and mockery, flaunted with the wretched superiority you find in the person who loves less. Werner Schroeter's integrity and unshakeable objectivity toward Rosa von Praunheim at times seemed almost like a form of paralysis.

Rosa von Praunheim, a man who is so progressive, whose consciousness is so liberated from all our bourgeois longings that he actually believes he alone has the right, almost a monopoly, to use the film medium to reflect his or anybody else's homosexuality. Werner Schroeter probably always obeyed his despotic orders. Now Rosa von Praunheim thinks he has traced this or that homosexual narrative thread in *Kingdom of Naples.* Reason enough, apparently, to camouflage, even from himself, his own despair, understandable enough, God knows, at not yet having made a single great film, or not having been allowed to make one. So enormous is the suffering to which filmmakers in the FRG are subjected, and I say this quite without irony, that to keep this pain, this fear, and this sadness at bay they will betray perhaps the only friend they have.

February 1979

Michael Curtiz—Anarchist in Hollywood?
Unorganized Thoughts on a Seemingly Paradoxical Idea

I launch into this consideration of the filmmaker Michael Curtiz and his work with an intentional lack of information on the readily establishable facts about this director's life and creative activity.

As I begin my consideration of Curtiz, this film author who I think has been cruelly overlooked, I want to confine myself to those films of his that have been accessible to me.

Of course I know that Michael Curtiz comes from Hungary, where he probably made as many as fifty films under his real name, Michael Kertész, before he went to America, there to make about a hundred pictures, mostly B-flicks, under the name Michael Curtiz.

But I don't know anything about his work in Hungary or about his reasons for leaving Hungary to go to America. Am not familiar with any facts, any interviews, any articles about Curtiz, or important critical evaluations of individual works, so I have no secondary sources, and as primary sources only a few films.

At my present stage, and that will change, of course, but at this moment, my thoughts are based on about thirty-five films, a wild, random, completely unplanned selection.

Almost everyone to whom the cinema, film per se, means something like love, tenderness, and lust, knows the Humphrey Bogart film *Casablanca* with Ingrid Bergman, which has become a cult film by now. I'm convinced that only a very few people know that the film is by Michael Curtiz. And those who do think Michael Curtiz created this masterpiece mainly by accident. But this widespread notion among cinephiles is wrong and unfair, and there are better things by Michael Curtiz, though the exchange by the old German couple who want to emigrate to America and are busily learning English to prepare themselves—"What's the watch?"—"Ten watch."—"Such much?"—is unforgettable in its simplicity and beauty, one of the most beautiful pieces of dialogue in the history of film. But there are more important

things by Michael Curtiz than the Humphrey Bogart film *Casablanca.*
Anarchy is not so easy to deal with. Heliogabalus, the only anarchist on the imperial throne of the "Holy Roman Empire," had to fail. Within a more or less functioning system, only a really powerful person can follow his own urgings, be an anarchist, in fact. On the other hand, the facts show that the unfettered actions of a powerful individual carry at least two risks. First, people who haven't learned anything but to conform to society are thrown off and repelled by the wishes and actions of this individual, if, indeed, they don't decide that he's mentally ill. Second, their system, within which they're useful and know how to behave, is confirmed in their eyes as right and true, and they're filled with fear of their real wishes. They'll be terrified by their true urges. Their imagination will be stifled, they'll identify dreams of the freedom of beautiful madness with power, and in this way consolidate their pathetic helplessness, till finally they'll be ashamed of their dreams.

It's quite a different story with the anarchy in the work of Michael Curtiz, which I admit I at first just postulated, hoping it was really there. Although I'm almost sure on the one hand that Curtiz would have contested with genuine conviction the idea that he was an anarchist, or would even have found it ridiculous, on the other hand I would boldly propose the following question: Didn't this Michael Curtiz leave us an oeuvre, made up of more or less good or controversial components, of course modified to suit all sorts of tastes, which adds up to a very original view of the world, no matter how disparate the works appear to a hasty eye. An oeuvre in which every single film, indeed every individual sequence, may be seen as an equally valuable building block in the specific view of the world unique to Michael Curtiz.

December 1980

The List of My Favorites

The Best Films

1. Luchino Visconti, *The Damned*
2. Raoul Walsh, *The Naked and the Dead*
3. Max Ophüls, *Lola Montez*
4. Michael Curtiz, *Flamingo Road*
5. Pier Paolo Pasolini, *Salo, or the 120 Days of Sodom*
6. Howard Hawks, *Gentlemen Prefer Blondes*
7. Josef von Sternberg, *Agent X27*
8. Charles Laughton, *The Night of the Hunter*
9. Nicholas Ray, *Johnny Guitar*
10. Vassily Shukchin, *Red Elderberry*

The Best Actresses

1. Marilyn Monroe
2. Maria Falconetti
3. Martine Carol
4. Anna Magnani
5. Jean Seberg
6. Thelma Ritter
7. Françoise Dorléac
8. Joan Crawford
9. Sybille Schmitz
10. Vivian Leigh

The Best Actors

1. Clark Gable
2. James Dean
3. Charles Laughton

4. George Sanders
5. Michel Simon
6. Hans Moser
7. Gary Cooper
8. Ferdinand Marian
9. Zeppo Marx
10. Erich von Stroheim

The Best Books

1. Antonin Artaud, *Van Gogh: Suicide through Society*
2. Arthur Schopenhauer, *The World as Will and Representation*
3. Louis-Ferdinand Céline, *Journey to the End of Night*
4. Sigmund Freud, *Moses the Man*
5. Alfred Döblin, *Berlin Alexanderplatz*
6. Joris-K. Huysmans, *Là-bas*
7. Jean Paul, *Siebenkäs*
8. Johann Wolfgang von Goethe, *The Elective Affinities*
9. Buurhus Frederic Skinner, *Walden II*
10. Djuna Barnes, *Under Milkwood*

The Best Plays

1. Heinrich von Kleist, *Käthchen of Heilbronn*
2. William Shakespeare, *Richard III*
3. Hans Henny Jahnn, *Streetcorner*
4. Frank Wedekind, *Lulu*
5. Marieluise Fleisser, *Pioneers in Ingolstadt*
6. Ernst Toller, *Hinkemann*
7. Georg Büchner, *Woyzeck*
8. Ferdinand Bruckner, *The Criminals*
9. Arthur Schnitzler, *La ronde*
10. Gerhart Hauptmann, *The Rats*

The Best Operas

1. Guiseppe Verdi, *La Traviata*
2. Gaetano Donizetti, *Roberto Devereux*
3. Richard Wagner, *Tristan and Isolde*
4. Ludwig van Beethoven, *Fidelio*
5. Vincenzo Bellini, *Norma*
6. Gioacchino Rossini

7. Franz Léhar, *Guiditta*
8. Alban Berg, *Lulu*
9. Arnold Schoenberg, *Moses and Aron*
10. Claudio Monteverdi, *Il ritorno d'Ulisse*

The Best Soccer Players

1. Helmuth Haller
2. Paul Breitner
3. Garrincha
4. Gerd Müller
5. Gento
6. Didi
7. H. Konopka
8. Peter Grosser
9. Vava
10. F. Puszkas

The Best Pop Musicians

1. Elvis Presley
2. Bob Dylan
3. Rolling Stones
4. Leonard Cohen
5. The Platters
6. Kraftwerk
7. Roxy Music
8. The Beatles
9. Velvet Underground
10. Comedian Harmonists

Hitlist of German Films

All films are listed alphabetically [by their German titles], not according to ranking!!!!!!

THE BEST: *Forty-eight Hours to Acapulco* [Klaus Lemke, 1967], *The Marriage of Maria Braun*, *The Endless Night* [Will Tremper, 1963], *Effi Briest*, *The Merchant of Four Seasons*, *Jane Is Jane Forever* [Walter Bockmayer, 1977], *Malatesta* [Peter Lilienthal, 1969], *A Degree of Murder* [Volker Schlöndorff, 1978], *Kingdom of Naples* [Werner Schroeter, 1978], *The Expulsion from Paradise* [Niklaus Schilling, 1976].

THE MOST IMPORTANT: *The Chronicle of Anna Magdalena Bach* [Jean-Marie Straub and Danielle Huillet, 1967], *Germany in Autumn*, *The Third Generation*, *Film or Power* [Vlado Kristl, 1970], *In a Year of Thirteen Moons*, *Made in Germany and USA* [Rudolf Thome, 1974], *Not Reconciled* [Straub and Huillet, 1965], *Satan's Brew*, *Beware of a Holy Whore*, and: *Artists under the Big Top: Perplexed* [Alexander Kluge, 1967] + *In Times of Danger and Greatest Peril, the Path of Compromise Leads to Death* [Kluge, 1974] + *Strong Man Ferdinand* [Kluge, 1975] + *The Patriot* [Kluge, 1979] + *Yesterday Girl* [Kluge, 1966].

THE MOST BEAUTIFUL: *Fear Eats the Soul, Ticket of No Return* [Ulrike Ottinger, 1979], *Detective* [Thome, 1968], *Eika Katappa* [Schroeter, 1969], *Gods of the Plague, A Girl and Violence* [Roger Fritz, 1970], *The Morals of Ruth Halbfass* [Schlöndorff, 1971], *Despair, Rheingold* [Schilling, 1977], *Red Sun* [Thome, 1969].

THE LEAST IMPORTANT: *Adolf and Marlene* [Ulli Lommel, 1976], *Army of Lovers* [Rosa von Praunheim, 1979], *Carlos* [Hans W. Geissendorfer, 1971], *Hitler: A Film from Germany* [Hans Jürgen Syberberg, 1977], *The Candidate* [Kluge, Schlöndorff, et al., 1980], *Ludwig: Requiem for a Virgin King* [Syberberg, 1972], *Not the Homosexual Is Perverse, but Rather the Situation in Which He Lives* [Rosa von Praunheim, 1970], *Large and Small* [Peter Stein, 1980], *The Pedestrian* [Maximilian Schell, 1961], *San Domingo* [Syberberg, 1970].

THE MOST DISGUSTING: *The Clown* [Vojtech Jasny, 1975], *Tales of the Vienna Woods* [Schell, 1978], *Grete Minde* [Heidi Genée, 1976], *Karl May* [Syberberg, 1974], *Katzelmacher, Output,* [Michael Fengler, 1974], *Scarabea* [Syberberg, 1966], *Summer Guests* [Stein, 1975], *Why Does Herr R. Run Amok?, Jail Bait.*

THE MOST DISAPPOINTING: *Arabian Nights* [Lemke, 1979], *One of the Two of Us* [Wolfgang Petersen, 1973], *Flaming Hearts* [Bockmayer and Rolf Bührmann, 1977], *Heart of Glass* [Herzog, 1976], *Cat and Mouse* [Hansjürgen Pohland, 1966], *Negresco* [Lemke, 1967], *Palermo or Wolfsburg* [Schroeter, 1980], *Pioneers in Ingolstadt, Dream City* [Johannes Schaaf, 1974], *The Scarlet Letter* [Wim Wenders 1972].

PLANS FOR '61? HOPES FOR '61?   To make many, many films, so that my life would become a film.

ACCOMPLISHED IN '61?   Saw four films every single day that God made.

ASSESSMENT OF THE PRESENT SITUATION: Blackish-brown to black, in any case mediocre and amphibian.

BEST EXPERIENCE IN THE MODERN GERMAN CINEMA: Dr. Günter Rohrbach. Horst Wendlandt. Dr. Alexander Kluge. Wolfram Schütte. H. C. Blumenberg.

WORST EXPERIENCE: Michael Fengler. Luggi Waldleitner. Hanns Eckelkamp. Christian Hohoff. Kurt Raab. Klaus Hellwig.

THE TEN BEST ACTRESSES: Hanna Schygulla. Margit Carstensen. Barbara Sukowa. Brigitte Mira. Eva Mattes. Barbara Valentin. Ruth Drexel. Karin Baal. Gisela Uhlen. Ingrid Caven.

THE TEN BEST ACTORS: Armin Müller-Stahl. Klaus Löwitsch. Dirk Bogarde. Ulli Lommel. Harry Baer. Lou Castel. Hark Bohm. Gian-Carlo Giannini. Günther Kaufmann. Volker Spengler.

The Top Ten of My Own Films

1. *Beware of a Holy Whore*
2. *In a Year of Thirteen Moons*
3. *Despair*
4. *The Third Generation*
5. *Gods of the Plague*
6. *Martha*
7. *Fontane Effi Briest*
8. *Fear Eats the Soul*

9. *The Marriage of Maria Braun*
10. *The Merchant of Four Seasons*

The Ten Most Important Directors in the New German Cinema

1. Rainer Werner Fassbinder
2. Werner Schroeter
3. Wim Wenders
4. Rudolf Thome
5. Volker Schlöndorff
6. Dr. Alexander Kluge
7. Ulrike Ottinger
8. Niklaus Schilling
9. Werner Herzog
10. Walter Bockmayer

1981

Alexander Kluge Is Supposed to Have Had a Birthday

The rumor that Alexander Kluge is supposed to have turned fifty recently is as persistent as that other absolutely ridiculous assertion that this very same Kluge got married sometime toward the end of the year! It is reported that he actually went ahead and had a private matter officially institutionalized by an official state institution. An absurd notion—several hours' worth of stirring movies by the filmmaker Kluge, as well as a whole lot of illuminating and stimulating prose by the writer Kluge, do document after all that it is one of his chief aims to call every kind of institution into question, particularly those of the state—if I interpret halfway correctly—and if his work is not indeed even more radical, that is, designed to prove that basically Alexander Kluge is interested in the destruction of every type of institution. Furthermore—an anarchist just doesn't go and turn fifty, the age at which people celebrate you. Categories like that are meaningless to him. I mean, it is precisely rumors of this sort about one of us, serving the purposes of cooptation, that make various things clear, and at the very least remind us of the necessity of continuing to struggle for our cause and of the eternal danger of growing weary in the face of gray, streamlined reality.

February 1982

Part Three

PROJECTS AND
CONTROVERSIES

Credited Debit, Debited Credit
On Gustav Freytag's Novel
Debit and Credit and the
Aborted Television Version

In the novel *Debit and Credit* there are certain nasty passages where we glimpse the author's false political consciousness and the dreadful things to come, which he of course did not produce himself, but to which he lent literary respectability, though without particular skill. These passages push us into what may be one of the most important confrontations possible, and necessary, for us to have with stories and with our history, with the nineteenth century and our social ancestors and ourselves. And film, with the help of the medium of television, is uniquely suited to bring about this confrontation. And what is special about this novel *Debit and Credit,* this fat book of, as I said, rather mediocre quality as far as the language goes, in which, furthermore, that phenomenon Fontane calls the most despicable thing that can occur in a literary work occurs: apparitions and shadows are passed off as human beings? *Debit and Credit* tells how the bourgeoisie in the middle of the last century, after a failed bourgeois revolution, developed its image of itself, established its values, values that did not extend beyond concepts of industriousness, honesty, and accountability, as well as the so-called German essence, which was actually just a way of differentiating themselves in all directions, from the proletariat and the aristocracy internally and from everything foreign externally, and especially dissociating themselves from a world view denounced as Jewish that embraced objectivity, humanity, and tolerance. These bourgeois values could obviously be incorporated into the Nazi ideology of the Third Reich without much change, but they were also values that have lived on into today's society, and that is the decisive factor that makes it imperative to confront this novel.

To put it simply, even though the Third Reich took these values and, applying terror tactics and inconceivable cruelty, declared them the essence of what is German and tried to root out anything that deviated from them or called them into question, the basic content of these values has remained engraved in all too many people's minds right up to today, without any critical reflection on them. This is what I think taking a new look at *Debit and Credit* can do: help us to recognize the historical origins of certain values and attitudes.

Precisely because of the thoughts it provokes, *Debit and Credit* is an extraordinarily exciting story to read. The characters, even though they remain shadowy, are shown in situations that are suggestive, situations that are dramatic, sentimental, and mysterious in themselves. These are elements that completely fulfill the requirements for entertainment value. Another requirement: the work must not dull the audience and confirm it in its assumptions. So it is our task to take an awful, sentimental, gripping story and put it in historical context so as to reveal Freytag's ideology of the "totality of the middle" (Hans Mayer) as potentially fascistoid. Curiously enough, that is not so difficult, if for no other reason than that Freytag the ideologue is always being outdone by Freytag the journalist, who separates experience from interpretation, consigning his own ideology to passages of commentary, which discredit themselves quite sufficiently. Without them you suddenly stumble on passages where Freytag describes a conceivable reality, descriptions for the most part of—I'm not afraid to say it—accurately observed "truth." And that is already a great, great deal.

For instance, we find a precise description of a Jewish quarter, cramped because of legal restrictions, grim, hopeless. The ideologizing passages that follow, however, carry the blithe assertion that these quarters are this way because their inhabitants wouldn't want them any other way. Freytag makes it easier for himself in the treatment of his bourgeois characters. Because he represents their identity, their actions need not be glorified by authorial commentary, and we therefore hardly have to demythologize them. They simply need to act as they act in Freytag's novel, in such a way that the audience of today can and should see them for what they are: sly, disgusting, clever, or pitiful—nowadays we do not have to feel responsible for the way our fathers set up our society, any more than we have to feel responsible for the way they ruined it—we know more about these things and can simply show it to our audience—it's their history, too.

The journalist Freytag and the Jews: if we lop off what he wants to tell us with his ranking system, even he already describes the Jews as an excluded group, who cannot behave any differently because they are not allowed to, whose conduct is determined by their curtailed civil rights. In Freytag we also see clearly that those particular rights granted exclusively to the Jews by the bourgeoisie because they did not fit the bourgeois ideology of what was honorable—primarily money-lending, making money off money—it was these "rights" that in turn made the Jews hated.

But what mattered to the bourgeoisie besides making money and seeing value appreciate? Nothing. So the bourgeoisie needed the Jews so as not to have to despise its own attitudes, so as to feel proud and grand and strong. The ultimate result of such unconscious self-hatred was the mass extermination of the Jews in the Third Reich; actually the bourgeoisie was trying to wipe out what it did not want to acknowledge in itself. As a result, come what may, the history of the Germans and the Jews is inextricably intertwined for all time, not just for the period between '33 and '45. Something like a new original sin will take root in people who are born and will be born in Germany, an original sin no less important, even if today the sons of the murderers wash their hands in innocence.

Our relationship to the bourgeois ideology, to the Jews, and to that guilt that persists in our subconscious demands that we concern ourselves with a story like *Debit and Credit,* precisely so that by making its basic elements transparent we can avert the danger of a new perversion of bourgeois ideology.

I will not discuss here the "wrong" attitude of the Germans toward the Slavs described in the novel and the early imperialism of the German bourgeoisie, which Freytag interprets as "right," along with the necessary denigration of the peoples whose lands are to be taken over. A film of *Debit and Credit* would be historically "correct" and narrate as wrong the things that Freytag, and with him his characters and his contemporary readers, considered "right."

In concluding, I would reiterate: *Debit and Credit,* with its political and literary atrocities, which can actually prove advantageous for transposing the novel into another medium, is a well-constructed, stimulating, exciting story, almost as if written for the cinema. This is exciting entertainment, that is, entertainment that entertains and is exciting and does not bore the audience, or stultify it, or confirm its assumptions, which calls into question and provokes questions, which is capable of revealing the illusory quality of things that seem safe and sure, which is also fun and enjoyable, and at the same time makes the person who is enjoying it actually want to discover the gaps and flimsy patches in his own reality, to recognize some of the contradictions that make up our reality.

March 1977

My Position on
Garbage, the City, and Death
A Statement

My play *Garbage, the City, and Death* has been accused of being "anti-Semitic." Under cover of this accusation certain parties are working something out whose purpose and implications I do not yet grasp, but that has nothing to do with me and my play.

As for the play: yes, among the many characters in the text there is a Jew. This Jew is rich, a real estate agent; he is one of those involved in changing the city in ways that harm the people who live there; but in the last analysis he is merely carrying out schemes that others thought up. These others like to leave the execution of their plans to someone apparently immune to attack because he is protected by a taboo. The place where this state of affairs can be observed in real life is Frankfurt am Main.

The phenomenon itself, though on a different level, is nothing more than a recapitulation of conditions in the eighteenth century, when only the Jews were allowed to lend money at interest, and this money-lending, which was often the Jews' only hope for survival, in the end merely gave ammunition to those who had more or less forced them to take up this activity and who were their real enemies. The situation is no different here. The city lets the supposedly essential dirty work be done by a Jew, shielded, and this makes it particularly despicable, by a taboo; for since 1945 Jews in Germany have been taboo. In the end this will backfire, for taboos have the effect of making the dark, mysterious object of the taboo frightening, and eventually opposition surfaces. Expressed differently and perhaps more accurately: Those who protest against any revelation of this state of affairs are the real anti-Semites, and one should examine their motives closely. These are the people who—when was the last time this happened?—turn on the author of a play, basing their arguments on words he invented for his characters in order to present certain ideas for critical analysis.

119

And of course there are also anti-Semites in this play. Unfortunately they exist not only in this play but also in Frankfurt, for example. Obviously these characters—actually it seems superfluous to say this—do not express the opinions of the author, whose attitude toward minorities should be clear enough from his other works. In fact, the hysterical tone of the discussion surrounding this play strengthens me in the fear of a "new anti-Semitism" that moved me to write this play in the first place.

Paris, March 28, 1976

"Philosemites are anti-Semites"
An Interview with Benjamin Henrichs about the Reactions to *Garbage, the City, and Death*

■ *Are you shocked by the furious reaction to your play? Or did you expect something of the sort?*

I was shocked, at least by the extent of it.

■ *Did you know that this play is more risky than your other works—more risky because it can offend more people?*

I don't think it's riskier than *Mother Küsters Goes to Heaven*, or *Fox and His Friends*. Those are both films that you can interpret against their theme, if you want to; in the case of *Fox and His Friends*, you can say it's a film against homosexuals, and as for *Mother Küsters*, it's a film against Communists, neither of which is true.

■ *Isn't it a mistake when an author miscalculates so badly on the impact of his play?*

Absolutely not. Plays have always been spontaneous reactions to reality—and this play's a spontaneous reaction to a reality I found in Frankfurt. I mean, the way Jews have constantly been treated as a taboo subject in Germany since 1945 can result in hostility toward Jews, particularly among young people, who haven't had any direct experience with Jews. When I was a child and I met Jews, people would whisper to me, "That's a Jew, behave yourself, be nice to him." And that continued, with variations, until I was twenty-eight and wrote the play. It never seemed to me that that was the right attitude.

■ *So you're afraid that the philosemitism that almost all of us were brought up with, which is a sort of rule of the game in the Federal Republic, could promote a new kind of anti-Semitism?*

Absolutely. Robert Neumann said, "Philosemites are anti-Semites who love Jews."

■ *Writing in the* Frankfurter Allgemeine *Joachim Fest called your play fascist. In your public statement you responded that the reactions to your play just confirmed your concern about a new wave of fascism. Do you have the feeling that in our cultural life*

121

tolerance is diminishing and hostility is on the rise? And do you really believe that five years ago the reaction to this play would have been less hostile?

I really do believe that. Five years ago the people writing about the play would have concentrated on its literary qualities and taken it for granted that a city, or the methods of changing a city, could be attacked. But that's not the reason for the present hostility: not that there's a Jew in it; not that certain supposedly obscene expressions are used; but that the recognized community is shown as something negative.

■ *You accuse the people who attack your play of subliminal anti-Semitism because they project onto one character (the "rich Jew"), which you intended to represent something else entirely, their own preconceptions and fears, their own timid goodwill toward Jews. Are you yourself completely unbiased in your thinking? Can one really be that way, should one even?*

I can't say I'm unbiased toward what happened to the Jews in the Third Reich. But I absolutely am more unbiased than the people who are attacking me. If I'd read the play myself a few years ago, maybe I'd have seen in the figure of the Jew the same lewdness, the same bogeyman quality that's been read into it—which is simply not there in the play, if you read it carefully and calmly. The Jew's the only one in this play who's capable of loving, the only one who has the ability to recognize that the language he speaks is a sort of agreement that people have entered into. No doubt about it, he's a character with some positive attributes.

■ *Have you met Jews who are sick of the official philosemitism? Jews to whom your play comes across as liberating?*

I met a Jew in Paris who saw it that way. I met a German-Jewish woman who's a critic in Amsterdam, and I talked with Erwin Leiser and his wife. Those are the four Jews I discussed the play with, and from all four I heard widely varying reactions, much more differentiated than those of you critics. Besides, it's only a play. And a person has to have a chance to approach a topic using risky, even questionable methods, not just the same old safe ones; otherwise you'll just end up with the same old dead stuff like everything else on the German theater scene. There's nothing vital going on there: everything friendly, everybody so nice, everybody wanting to please. That can't go on indefinitely.

The play shows disregard for certain safety precautions, and to me that's just how it should be. I have to be able to react to reality without regard for the consequences. If I can't do that, I can't really do anything anymore.

■ *Do you agree with Suhrkamp's decision to withdraw the play "for the time being?"*

No. How should I? I have no idea what to do next. I've never heard of a case like this. I do think they're going to release it again.

■ *Are you doing anything to see to that?*

They told me that the moment I make a statement to the press, they'll start delivering to the stores again. For now I'm going to rely on that. Five years ago they wouldn't have done this, either—given in to demands that aren't their own, that come from the outside.

■ *Isn't the whole debate coming down to this now: they're saying: he isn't an anti-Semite; after all, he said himself he isn't one, and a few people have written the same thing. But he did something awfully careless. I'm sure you can't be happy with this outcome of the debate, either. After all the turmoil you've caused, do you still believe you did nothing wrong?*

No. I believe the reaction we've seen only confirms that I did the right thing. I think it's better to discuss these things, and then they become less dangerous, less alarming, than when you can only whisper about them.

April 1976

"Madness and terrorism"
Conversations with Gian Luigi Rondi about *Despair* and *The Third Generation*

■ *What was it about Vladimir Nabokov's novel* Despair *that appealed to you?*

The crisis experienced by the hero, a Russian emigré who managed to become a chocolate manufacturer in Germany in the thirties and who suddenly has the feeling that the rug's being pulled out from under him. You could list a whole series of reasons for that: the political, economic, and social problems of those years; but the real or, at least, the most important reason is his sudden insight that everything's pointless and that nothing has meaning anymore. Why? Because old age is approaching, the age when a person just doesn't expect anything new, when a person no longer gets satisfaction from looking for things, desiring things, coming up with ideas . . . I thought about this novel by Nabokov for years, I obtained the film rights, but I hadn't found the right angle, until finally I met Tom Stoppard, and we came up with the solution almost immediately. So then we wrote the screenplay together.

■ *And what was this right angle?*

A detached perspective, not like a judge evaluating all the actions, including the admittedly negative ones, that the protagonist engages in once his crisis sweeps over him. When Hermann, the manufacturer, realizes that he can't expect anything more from life, he throws himself into the arms of madness, but he behaves not only like a madman but like a criminal. We merely recorded this madness and these crimes. This way the human face of the character can become visible, an inner logic, which to those who see only his madness and his crimes must appear as pure illogic, if not as a criminal undertaking that has to be condemned.

■ *The logicality of madness—is that approval, exoneration?*

At least not condemnation. What do people like Hermann Hermann usually do when it becomes clear to them that they're at a turning point where they have everything behind them and nothing ahead of them? They pull into their shell, they resign themselves, and rather than admit that their life's over, they'd prefer to spend the rest of it in a sea of compromises and resignation. The few who rebel, on the other hand, even if in a totally irrational way, those people achieve something, they discover something that gives them new hope. So no exoneration, but if you're comparing him to the person who gives up in the face of life, I prefer the person who's at least still capable of hope, even in madness.

■ *A film in English, even though you speak only German. How did you pull it off?*

Not so badly, I think. It's true, there was a whole bunch of words I didn't catch, especially when the actors had to speak fast, but in film it's much more important how language sounds than what its concrete content is. From my point of view, even in German the most important thing is the melody of a sentence, its tonal coloration, its modeling. And then Dirk Bogarde was in the cast. I didn't need to understand his English, any more than he needed to understand my German. During the shooting an almost extrasensory form of communication developed between us; he understood what I wanted, and I understood perfectly what he was doing.

■ *This was the first time you had the support of a large-scale production of international class. Were you happier with your "poor" films?*

I don't think there's much difference. The difference in a production with strong financial backing is simply that it isn't so strenuous. That was certainly a more comfortable feeling, but you shouldn't go thinking I had something like a Hollywood setup at my disposal. The shooting took barely forty days, and the financing just about covered the essentials.

■ *What does the title "The Third Generation" refer to?*

It refers to the three generations of terrorism, a topic that's unfortunately somewhat trendy. The first generation was that of '68. Idealists, who wanted to change the world and imagined they could do that with words and demonstrations. The second, the Baader-Meinhof Group, went from legality to armed struggle and total illegality. The third's the generation of today, which simply acts without thinking, which has neither a policy nor an ideology and which, certainly without realizing it, lets itself be manipulated by others, like a bunch of puppets.

■ *And the storyline?*

On the one hand an industrialist, on the other a policeman. To-

Dirk Bogarde and Andrea Ferréol in Despair *(courtesy Bavaria Atelier, GmbH)*

gether they decide to form a terrorist cell, the first man because it'll be useful for his business ventures, the second to justify his repressive activities.

■ *The thesis?*

Very simple: Nowadays it's capitalism that brings forth terrorism, to boost itself and strengthen its system of hegemony.

■ *How would you categorize* The Third Generation?

As a comedy, or, rather, a parlor game on the topic of terrorism. In six similar and yet fundamentally different parts. Biting and mocking, with emotions and suspense, polemics and caricature, brutality and stupidity, in an atmosphere like a dream, a fairy tale. Like the fairy tales you tell children so they're better equipped to bear their lives as people buried alive.

■ *Among other things I've heard the term "acoustic terrorism" . . .*

The film takes place in our modern housing, in our everyday setting. And what's more typical nowadays than the sounds, the noise, the shouting that constantly washes over us from television, radios, and the streets? Someone wrote about the film that you can't always make out what's being said because it's drowned out by the background noise, the loudspeakers, the radio and television announcements . . . But that's just what I wanted to point out, not really the thinking of the individual characters, who are completely secondary in comparison to the climate of noise and racket they live in. The terrorism doesn't consist in my reproducing all that; rather it's the media, which constantly hammer away at people, who in the meantime have become so hooked and helpless that by now they can't even manage to push a button to get some peace and quiet.

■ *Are you sure it's really a form of terrorism without a goal?*

Yes, because it's neither revolutionary nor constructive. If the film has any ideological program, it's to give the "fourth generation" some goals.

■ *For instance?*

Anarchy. Today only the anarchists are in a position to change society without using the methods of terrorism. The anarchists are a bit like the "first generation," which lived on ideals, but with more clearheadedness about putting them into effect.

1978/79

The Third Generation

I. The German Feature Film and Reality

In contrast to Italy, where people like Francesco Rosi, Damiano Damiani, and others are so close to the reality of their country that their
films actually intervene in this reality, so to speak, even, and indeed
precisely, under the unambiguously commercial demands of a film industry; in contrast to America, where again and again films are made
that force their way into the chronicle of current events with critical
commentary, and here too without sacrificing the commercial aspects
of an industry that in fact is commercial—how should it be otherwise;
in contrast to France, Spain, even Switzerland, where Jonas will be
twenty-five in the year 2000; in contrast to almost all the Western
democracies, there seems to be a mysterious common interest on the
part of various groups in the Federal Republic of Germany in making
sure that this kind of film does not even get made in the first place.

For years this interest in preventing any German films from being
made that might deal with German reality was guarded by nothing
more than the assertion that German audiences were not interested
in "that sort of film," an assertion that was simply believed and accepted by German producers, who in any case were confused and
timid. Reality, everyone seemed to agree, was the province of television, which in turn is fortunately a public institution and as such committed to a balanced approach to reality—or is it a balancing act, an
undiscriminatingly pluralistic approach, in which anything and everything has legal rights, especially the legal system?

Lest I be misunderstood, I should add that I do know of course that
critical films in the Federal Republic—with whatever limitations; that
varies from network to network—were possible only on television, or
at least in collaboration with television. But I also know the context
in which this criticism reaches the viewer and that it—the criti-

cism—because of the specific composition of television's evening pro-
gramming (how sad it should make us) almost at the moment it is
formulated by Peter Alexander or Anneliese Rothenberger—I know,
it can't get much worse, but isn't that nevertheless the way it is on the
whole—is eliminated on the one hand (this sentence is all right, believe me, grammatically, I mean, right?) and that on the other hand
more directors are in danger of succumbing to an aesthetic specific to
television, which really exists, or, to put it differently, people who
want to make movies for the cinema usually don't take the genre of
television, which provides their bread and butter, quite seriously.
Thus many, many people develop sloppy thinking habits, and this slop-
piness surely has an effect on feature films these same directors may
make later on, something that the audience at least senses, and that in
the end can only prove harmful to the cinema.

Certainly this issue is far more complex in its entirety than what I
have sketched here, you know what I mean? But until the very recent
past it seemed fairly clear that German reality could put in an appearance in German films at most in more or less successful translations
into the nineteenth century or the twenties, if at all. The most friendly
reception was reserved for the kind of film that very skillfully avoided
the risk that the viewer might be reminded of his own reality. (This
sentence contains more truth than you would at first suspect. Read it
again, preferably out loud, before the thought that I am being unfair
has a chance to take root in your mind.)

At this point I could easily make the transition to a concrete discussion of the theme of my film *The Third Generation,* since the refusal by the media as well, and perhaps precisely by them, to deal with
reality is to my mind one of the reasons why this very reality, this
specifically West German reality, has not succeeded in conveying to
the individual citizen what I consider the basis of democratic ideas in
such a way that a real democracy could have established itself, one
that was not merely democratic in name and in which the phenomenon of now almost incomprehensible violence in response to violence
and still more violence could not have sprung up. But I won't get to
this with my characteristic simplicity until somewhat later.

First I would like to formulate my hope, as well as I can, that these
missed opportunities or omissions or desired and rewarded manifes-
tations of cowardice will soon be more and more a thing of the past,
that a situation may come about for the German film that will be more
liberated, gratifying, and fruitful than one could imagine. I think, and
please forgive me if I am wrong, that that last sentence slipped a tiny
bit into cynicism, but just a tiny, tiny bit, right? Or is it possible that

from the succès d'estime (and from the commercial point of view the bottom line was very satisfactory, unless the rumors are even less accurate this time than usual) of the films *The Second Awakening of Christa Klages* by my colleague von Trotta and *Germany in Autumn*, a film, by the way, which for minutes at a time strikes me as more terrible than terrible, something I expressed loud and clear from the beginning, which is documented, but still a film about which I decided, with a great Parsifalesque naiveté all my own, that it wasn't the obscene moments that made this film into a film that was interesting and important to many people (and for those who may not know it, I don't find it obscene that I play with my dick in front of the camera, but rather I find it obscene when people masturbate who would like to keep the existence of their dick a secret from themselves, but also don't have enough of a grip on their brain so that they could grab it and at least jerk off with it. It's surprising, and what an accomplishment, to see how much people have masturbated with their mouths, which, just between us sisters of the revolution, actually doesn't work, with the mouth, isn't that so, with the mouth . . .?) I should have drawn a false conclusion? (This sentence is right, too, in some way, at least grammatically!) A conclusion, furthermore, which is also supported by the great commercial success of the picture *The Lost Honor of Katharina Blum*—yes, yes, self-liberation is also allowed to demand sacrifices, even intellectual ones, "God grant" that this may not be one of the unforgivable ones, one of those that are punished with black-and-blue marks on the soul.

So a commercial success for three films that confront the reality of the Federal Republic of Germany in three entirely different ways, here and now, a success, finally, that allows me to draw the conclusion that it seems to have become possible even here to pose concrete political questions using the medium of film, even and precisely cinematic film, and that the potential of the audience interested in film is large enough so that these three films may well be followed by other films, and that, in contrast to earlier, these films have a chance to reach the public. Just one thing seems very important to me, that one keep one's eye on the ball, so to speak, so that such films continue to be made on a broad basis and those who oppose making the cinema a center of communication not be allowed to use the simple absence of such films as a pretext for turning the tables and arguing that this absence automatically proves that the viewers are not interested.

This is one of the reasons for my determination to keep on making a film from time to time that is directly concerned with current political problems. I believe one can make such films more and more attractive, by means of casting and technique, and I believe that there are plenty of unambiguous moral justifications for this "speculation." If one thinks of the Italian cinema, for instance, time and again they use much-loved stars, like Franco Nero in Belocchio's films, Gian-Maria Volonté in Damiano Damiani's, or Rod Steiger in Francesco Rosi's, or, or, or . . . ; this list could be prolonged indefinitely, and in *All the President's Men* it was Robert Redford and Dustin Hoffman who gave the screen treatment of the Watergate case not only their acting ability but also their glamour. I think I needn't say more on the potential question of why I want to make *The Third Generation,* a film concerned with a problem, that of terrorism and terrorists today, more or less current at the time the film is being made, a problem with which the inhabitants of this country and those who represent this state have not yet come to terms in any way, either practically or even just intellectually = ideologically.

II. A Film—A Title

The Third Generation could mean:

1. The German bourgeoisie from 1848 to 1933;
2. Our grandfathers, and how they experienced the Third Reich and how they remember it;
3. Our fathers, who had an opportunity after the war to set up a state that could have been more humane and free than any had ever been before, and what became of that opportunity in the end.

But *The Third Generation* could also mean the present generation of terrorists, if you accept the idea that there was a first and a second generation before them. The first generation was made up of those who were motivated by idealism, which combined with excessive sensitivity and almost pathological despair at their own helplessness vis-à-vis the system and its representatives to drive them almost "insane."

The second generation was made up of those who, understanding the motives of the first, generally defended its representatives, often as "genuine" proponents of justice; but this defense was slandered for so long and so intensely as fundamentally criminal that this generation's move into actual criminality and thereby into the underground occurred more ex post facto than in fact.

Whereas each individual citizen is somehow capable of mustering

something like understanding for the actions and motives of the first
and second generation of terrorists—or not, as the case may be—it is
more than difficult to understand the motives of the third generation,
indeed, perhaps it is impossible from the point of view of the two
preceding generations; for the third generation of terrorists has, it
seems to me, less in common with its predecessors than with this
society and the violence it perpetrates, to whoever's benefit.

I am convinced they don't know what they are doing, and what
they are doing derives its meaning from nothing more than the activity
itself, from the apparently exciting danger, from petty adventures
within this system, which admittedly is administered ever more perfectly and therefore alarmingly. Action undertaken in danger, but without any sense of perspective, adventures experienced in a sort of in-
toxication for their own sake—these are the things that motivate the
"third generation." Nonetheless, the fact that this phenomenon exists
exclusively in this country does of course have to do with this country, in fact has an alarming amount to do with this country, with its
mistakes, its omissions, with the democracy it received as a gift, which
one should not look in the mouth, the same as a gift horse, a democracy whose basic values are being allowed to degenerate more and
more into taboos, a democracy that the state blindly defends against
its citizens, and which besides—this is obvious—is in turn in blind
agreement with this same citizen, who is so unenlightened (looking
over the various curricula of all the various schools can really teach
one what fear is all about) that he is incapable of noticing that this
construct around him, this state, is becoming a tiny bit more totali-
tarian from day to day. And next time, friends, it won't last just a childish thousand years; the next time has already begun, secretly, softly
and quietly, and the next time will be really long.

And, to come back to this, what a gift of God must this state see in
a kind of terrorism that springs up without motivation and poses so
little risk, even in the negative sense of being comprehensible. And in
fact, if these terrorists didn't exist, the state at its present stage of
development would have to invent them. And maybe it even did? Why
not? What, for instance, was that business with the Gleiwitz transmitter, and how did the first Molotov cocktail get into the KI, and the
Reichstag, which burned down so photogenically—that's a story, too,
and somebody in Prague indubitably requested help from Moscow,
fortunately, but why? And what luck that even without having been
summoned the Russians already had their troops well on their way to
Czechoslovakia.

By the bye, so people can more readily form a picture of what it is like, *The Third Generation* is not a so-called political film; to me, every film is ultimately political. But I wanted to mention some examples of the films I feel indebted to for *The Third Generation,* and they would be *A Touch of Evil* by Orson Welles, *Flamingo Road* by Michael Curtiz, or *Conversation Piece* by Luchino Visconti.

In this sense I also looked for actors who hadn't been overexposed by television but nevertheless had something like glamour. As far as the title goes, I'm open to persuasion, though *The Third Generation* seems attractive to me. It's accurate, besides, but be my guest; the film industry has its own laws, of course. Other suggestions for a title might be: "Grandchildren of Evil," "Hangmen of Hope," "Slaves of Order and Tranquillity," as well as "The Spreading Cancer—That's the Whole Thing." But there'll be time to chat about all this, though not to excess, face to face.

December 1978

"The walls are closing in on us birds of Paradise"
From a Conversation with Renate Klett about Political Developments and *Germany in Autumn*

You see, the problem is that we don't have censorship. If we had it, we'd know what we were allowed to do and what we weren't, and then we'd also know what we might possibly fight against. But there's nothing here you could really call censorship; I'd describe it more as a certain climate, a climate in which now and then something . . . well, it isn't exactly banned, but let's say, it's made impossible.

That's something which in my opinion will push everybody to the point where they'll take a second look at the projects they need money or space or whatever for, and ask themselves whether there isn't something in those projects that might stand in the way of their being carried through to completion. That would mean that a kind of censorship had been created, more like rumor than a codified system of censorship that tells you concretely: This and this and this is forbidden. It's a kind of censorship that in fact exists only in the minds of the people who are doing the producing.

■ *Does it affect you, too?*

No, with a few things I've taken some real risks, I've worked on things where I knew that if I did them the way I wanted to, it was possible that so-and-so and so-and-so wouldn't like them. My situation's different, because I have the option of leaving.

■ *Which you haven't done yet, even though you made a big announcement that you were going.*

It's hard to just up and leave. There are things that have been in the planning stages for a long time. It couldn't have been done so quickly. And the situation isn't really bad in that sense. In 1933 it was perfectly clear to the people who emigrated: all this is going to change, it'll have to change, it can't stay this way. That was clear to everybody. It was a fatalistic form of fascism, which only worked because of the widespread urge for self-destruction, whereas this new form—and you mustn't call it fascism; that would be a distortion—

134

what we have now is actually much worse because it's settling in
for the duration. It'll all look perfectly innocuous, people will think
they're living in a free country, etc. To me the development that's
taking place right now seems more depressing somehow, because you
really can't do anything to fight it. All you can do is keep your eyes
open, and if you do, you certainly see the craziest things, if you look
real hard.

For instance, the day Schleyer's body was found. On television they
were doing a show on soccer, with clips from several Europe Cup
games . . . the soccer fans had to have their soccer, of course, so they'd
be satisfied. After all, if their soccer was taken away, they might get
mad at Schleyer. On the other hand, from the point of view of simple
human decency, that soccer business wasn't quite right. It was fabu-
lous to be able to watch all that unfolding. So they did their soccer
and felt awkward about it the whole time . . . They were all very unsure of themselves. Yet none of it mattered to them, none; all they
care about is having people stay calm and well-behaved and friendly,
and not harbor any bad thoughts, that's the most important thing. And
you can see all that when you watch a soccer show like that. And the
directives don't have to come from way high up, not at all; they have
it right there inside them.

There really aren't any major differences anymore between your
neighbor across the street and the federal chancellor—he's a mediocre, petty person, just like my neighbor. They're all becoming more
and more alike, and that's why the walls are closing in on us, us birds
of Paradise.

■ *Now you've also had experience in the theater, where people
are becoming more and more alike, too, and the situation's gotten
perceptibly more unpleasant in recent times.*

Oh, there were signs of that earlier, too.

■ *Would you say it's the same in the cinema?*

In the cinema, I'd say, it's even worse. Because the people making
films are forced to get the money for their productions from somewhere. In the theater it's still possible to do productions that are out
of the ordinary now and then, I would think, because the people are
under contract, they get their money, and if they do their work the
way they're supposed to, now and then you can slip in a production
that'll get people stirred up. In the cinema that's out of the question.
In the cinema, unlike in the theater, you just can't approach a production with the thought that it may never open, that's just not
conceivable.

In the cinema there were those years, I don't know, between '71 and '74 or '75, when people with an interest in seeing that certain cultural things don't get done just didn't realize the tremendous diversity that the German cinema had at that point. It was too much somehow, you know? There was too much that had been stored up in the course of thirty years, and now suddenly it came bursting out, and those folks didn't quite catch on to what was going on. That's what made that period possible. And that's why we have the so-called German cinematic miracle, whatever that may be.

It's easy to say what's left: the four or five people who have the luxury of not having to be here. Someone like Wim Wenders or Werner Herzog or me is in an entirely different position in dealing with a broadcasting company, simply from the point of view of attitude. But people who produce for television and are dependent on getting future commissions, especially those people who've dared to be a little critical in their work—you should ask them some time whether they've noticed anything. They'll tell you: Oh no, nothing's changed. And they'll also explain to you that what they're doing now is exactly what they really want to be doing. Yet with so many of them it's obvious that the films they made between, let's say, 1969 and 1974 have nothing at all to do with the ones they're making today, precisely in the case of the so-called critical directors. Never mind what you think of this sort of social-criticism film—I don't like them, but that's not the issue—but just look at how scared they are, already! Even though social criticism—why, that's allowed, that can't do any harm. But even these people have become more cowardly, which wouldn't be so bad if they were conscious of it. But I think they really aren't conscious of it, and that's what's so depressing. And eventually we'll have nothing but people who aren't conscious of it, and sooner or later they'll all look alike and live in identical houses, and that'll be democracy.

■ *Did you personally have any direct experience with the harassment of sympathizers that went on last fall?*

Not directly. I mean, my phone's been tapped for years anyway, because I used to know Horst Söhnlein and Andreas Baader and Holger Meins and a few other people. So they tap my phone, but what can they do? Essentially they can't do anything to me. But of course harassment's really something that takes place more inside you, because you're constantly aware that they know you exist. So you become more cautious, more fearful. And of course this fearfulness has an effect on what you do. I made this segment for *Germany in Autumn* right away in October, because I had to make it—because I'm not a very conscious person, or whatever; it was simply clear to me: I have to do this film now, or the whole thing'll fizzle on me. Now nothing can get to me, after that film; it took care of a lot of my fear.

■ *That effect probably has to do with the fact that you're the only one who talks about himself in* Germany in Autumn.

Yes, and because I was the only one who made the film at the particular time when everyone intended to make it, I mean, right away. At that time no one could have talked about anything except himself. But the others all did their parts much later—Kluge's the only one besides me who got started right away, and he talks an awful lot about himself, too. Of course he's very different from me, and a very different kind of filmmaker, but his associative use of documentary material—that's very personal, incredibly personal and says a lot about his mind.

All the rest are things that were finished long after the fact, where people tried to do something after they'd already assimilated their fears. You can really see that in their segments, that they're made with one eye on the selection committees again, on the subsidies.

■ *That means you aren't satisfied with the film as it's being shown in the theaters now?*

No. I mean, for me it was incredibly important to be able to do that, that a situation developed where you had ten people, after all, who were also of the opinion that something absolutely had to be done. The fact that within a week they "came to their senses" in a certain way—an idiotic way, I think—that's another question. That the film exists is also okay by me. But that I'm not satisfied with the film as it turned out, that's another matter. But all that was obvious as soon as the film wasn't ready when it was supposed to have been. It was supposed to hit the theaters in mid-November. So it was clear they would have had to be done with their shooting by the end of October at the latest. So they wouldn't have had time to get their more or less powerful thinking apparatus in gear, but would really have had to re-act emotionally for a change. And it would have been an entirely different film. Maybe its formal qualities would have been much worse, but you wouldn't have had to pay any attention to the form.

■ *And in mid-November it would have hit the public much closer to home than now in the spring.*

Now it's a bit exotic for the audience, though I believe it still has some impact, even so. When we all sat down together back then, one of the reasons why we said we had to make the film was that something had to be done to combat the fear. We felt that ordinary people, who don't have any means of production and possibly have more fears than we do, shouldn't let themselves be intimidated by the feeling prevailing in Germany at that time, that criticism in any form was unwelcome and had to be crushed. To make sure that didn't happen, and because we had the means of production at our disposal, we wanted to state very clearly: People can and should and must go on talking, no matter what happens. I don't know what would have happened if the film had come out in mid-November, before they had all got a grip on themselves again . . .

They all got a grip on themselves so incredibly fast; altogether, the whole thing was incredible: the party congress in Hamburg and the dizzying speed with which the Social Democratic Party managed to get these so-called left-liberal intellectuals back into the fold. It went unbelievably quickly. If the film had come out earlier, before they'd managed to get everybody back in line—what an impact that would have had, can you imagine! Now that would have interested me! In any case I wouldn't have been here; I would have stayed in Paris.

Spring 1978

"I'd rather be a streetsweeper in Mexico than a filmmaker in Germany"

A Conversation with *Der Spiegel* about
the Politics of German Film
and Fassbinder's Announcement That
He Intended to Leave the Country

■ *Herr Fassbinder, you want to leave Germany and go to America. Why?*

I don't feel like living in Germany anymore. Maybe it's just a personal feeling on my part that it's provincial here in a certain way. But I'm not the only one who senses it. I'm fairly sure that it's less and less possible to make the films you want to.

■ *Why is that? Apart from the provinciality you mentioned.*

Maybe it has to do with the fact that until now German film has depended, and probably will continue to depend for quite some time, on this weird subsidy system, which was handled fairly liberally in the beginning. But you can see which way the trend is going by the percentage of films based on literary works.

■ *But your most successful film,* Effi Briest, *was also a film version of a literary work.*

That's just the point. If I'd continued in that vein, everything would have been great; that is, if I'd been a different person, maybe I could have convinced myself that that was what I really wanted to be doing. I've actually done things that were relatively uncompromising, to the extent possible, and now I'd more or less have to give that up; I'd at least have to think, Hm, what should I do now so the subsidy boys will fork over the money?

■ *Do you really still need money from the government?*

But of course; in order to produce a film without constraints, of course I'd need it, that's obvious. I can afford a relatively small film; something like that I can produce myself. But otherwise it's just gotten too expensive in Germany to make your own films.

■ *So you have depended on the subsidies yourself, haven't you?*

I submitted a screenplay only once, and that was *Fontane Effi Briest*. With the twenty previous films I never submitted a single one. But I don't want to pretend there was anything heroic about it. I didn't   139 say, I'm not going along with this system, though at the time maybe I was acting according to that unspoken idea.

■ *But you've just done a large-budget production of Vladimir Nabokov's* Despair.

I took on the project because it gave me more freedom than I would have had with smaller producers. When a company like Geria, the biggest tax-shelter in Germany, invests quite a lot of money in a project, of course it's interested in seeing to it that the product's good.

■ *On the other hand, earlier this year you went back to the Filmverlag der Autoren, expressing considerable optimism, after you'd already pulled out of it.*

I can't say I went back with much optimism. That was a false impression. What we had in mind back at the beginning turned out not to be do-able, of course—it was just a utopian notion, that you can get a few people together and set up an organization like the Filmverlag to support various noncommercial ventures.

■ *You're leaving the Filmverlag without anger?*

I'm leaving without anger because I tell myself that the experience I was able to get with the Filmverlag was okay for me personally. The more commercial the Filmverlag is, the better. But it's sad for the others, who I think really need something like what we originally had in mind. Sad for people who are doing their first films, which they can't place with any distributor and then can't place with the Filmverlag, either. And people who aren't just making their first film are looked over for their marketability nowadays, certainly more than before. The Filmverlag has to establish a firm financial basis now, so that it can afford to bring out difficult films again. It's the old game, I guess . . .

■ *. . . which you often played yourself . . .*

I didn't play that game. As far as the Filmverlag goes, I fought for the things I considered worthwhile.

■ *Is that another reason for your leaving, the collapse of the project for filming Gustav Freytag's novel* Debit and Credit *for WDR because people thought they caught a whiff of anti-Semitism again?*

Sometimes things come together in such a way that you sense you're working in a situation where everything that ventures into borderline territory is in danger of being boycotted. That the producer, von Sell, rejected a project without having read or discussed the available material is something I hadn't experienced before. He did that in order to set himself up as a powerful figure, so that he'd have no trouble implementing his restructuring of the broadcasting company, dissolving the cultural division. I realized that this action of his put an end to what little freedom still existed within television and didn't necessarily correspond to the wishes of certain higher-ups.

■ *And this is the freedom you hope to find in Hollywood, of all places?*

I think I'll have more freedom in Hollywood because they're unabashedly commercial. For four years Douglas Sirk has been leaning on me to come to America. He says, "The minute they want to make money off you, they give you the chance to do something so they can make money off you." Whether that's freedom or not isn't the question. All I say is, I'd rather be unfree that way than imagine I was free here. If I wanted to go on working here, I'd have to get involved with things I'd never get involved with in America under any circumstances.

■ *And what will you be getting involved with in America?*

I have a contract with a German tax-shelter company that wants to coproduce a movie filmed in Los Angeles with an American company. A classic American B-movie, nothing spectacular.

■ *You won't work in Germany at all?*

Certainly I'll continue to work for WDR, but I'll go so far as to say that even today I couldn't make a television movie like *Martha* anymore. At the time, I made the movie to show a marriage as clearly as possible as a sadomasochistic relationship, because the more crassly you show that, the more married people have a chance to identify with your characters. At the time that wasn't a problem. If I approached them with something like that today, alarms would go off. The thinking would be: This is an attack on existing social institutions. The television producer would wonder whether this wasn't one of those borderline situations where he'd have to cover himself. And since people don't like to cover themselves, it could easily happen that he'd say to me, "Don't you have something else?" . . .

■ *How about* Eight Hours Are Not a Day?

We'd never be able to make that nowadays. At most one of those depressing realistic movies about workers. Then they say, "Yes, okay, that'll depress the audience and they'll just turn it off anyway." If the situation gets any worse, I'd rather be a streetsweeper in Mexico than a filmmaker in Germany. I'd rather have censorship on paper than the imaginary freedom where you provide your own censorship.

■ *But colleagues of yours like Werner Herzog work the way they want to, don't they?*

His last two films were certainly ones he wanted to make. But in *Heart of Glass* he fell for something: he filmed the French reviews of *Kaspar Hauser*.

■ *You recently sat on the jury for the Berlin Film Festival. Did
the German films confirm you in your pessimistic fears?*

There were films there that provided an extreme confirmation of
what I mean. For instance, *Grete Minde*. Without wanting to hurt Frau
Genée's feelings—that's a film of the type I think we're going to see a
lot of from now on. I can't really understand how anyone can make
her first feature film with such an utter lack of sincerity.

■ *Heidi Genée simply said to herself, This kind of thing is what
they want, it's what you get money for...*

... it's not only a question of us right now; it's a question of the
people who are just starting out. And if they all approach filmmaking
with an example like *Grete Minde* before their eyes and say, Okay,
the best thing is to be as mediocre as possible ... It's no accident that
the only nonsubsidized film of the three German ones submitted to the
Berlin festival was *Expulsion from Paradise* by Niklaus Schilling. A
completely personal, uncompromising film. And the same's true of
Herzog's *Stroszeck,* which also didn't get a prize. In contrast to Bernhard Wicki's *Conquest of the Citadel.* I know that Wicki went to his
personal and financial limits, but even so the film isn't personal.

■ *But Wicki's film is anything but a conventional film treatment of a literary work.*

Wicki messed up on the film. That's perfectly clear. I'm very sorry
about that, because I like him. What disturbs me is that this messed-
up project can win the approval of a panel of judges. They give him
money for the impersonality of the project.

■ *So apparently the panels have neither aesthetic nor any other
criteria for evaluating things?*

I'm afraid they've found the aesthetic criteria. Finally. Unfortunately. For years they really didn't have any, which was lucky for us.

■ *They still don't have any. If you look at the Federal film
prizes:* Heinrich, Grete Minde, Group Portrait with Lady ...

No, no, I can certainly see a common denominator there: impersonality—where the artistic event becomes harmless because it
doesn't have any life anymore.

■ *What does that come from?*

It comes from the fact that the selection panels and television were
really shocked by what was going on in German films. Things were
being made that they just didn't understand. Suddenly there was a
flood of films that they couldn't get a handle on, and now they're making the medium manageable, and in the process taking all the teeth
out of it. It would contradict all my notions of the state that finances

this if it would come out and say, "We're going to finance a bulwark of freedom, and we'll let people really reflect on their reality." That's actually more possible in a purely commercial system like Hollywood.

■ *Herr Fassbinder, thank you for talking with us.*

July 1977

■ Introductory Remarks on a Projected Feature Film, *Cocaine*

1. The film *Cocaine,* based on Pitigrilli, will most certainly not be a film for or against that drug; *Cocaine* will be a film about the kind of experiences (with specifics) that someone has who constantly lives under the influence of the drug cocaine.

It is possible, even fairly certain, that relatively unrestrained or excessive use of cocaine over a fairly long period of time will shorten the user's life, in whatever fashion. On the other hand, the cocaine user will experience this shorter life span significantly more intensely, more imaginatively, and will usually be spared the cruel depressions that suddenly befall the "normal person" more or less violently, endangering him, sometimes in a life-threatening way, or at least coming over him in the form of an unconscious sadness, like a belljar popped over his head, so that he's afraid he'll suffocate.

In short, the decision in favor of a short but fulfilled life or a long but unaware and on the whole alienated existence will be left entirely up to the audience. My film won't help them at all.

2. Unlike Pitigrilli's novel, the film *Cocaine* will consist of a flashback experienced by Tito Arnaudi during his coma in Naples. Tito Arnaudi has brought on the coma on purpose, this fever-dream between life and death, by taking an overdose of cocaine. He would certainly accept death, but Tito is secretly playing with the possibility of surviving. He miscalculates, however, and dies.

Of course the decision to narrate Tito Arnaudi's experiences as a fever-dream in a coma is a simple dramaturgical trick. A trick, to be sure, that permits of any eccentricity, any willful choice of motifs, any marvelously crazy costumes, and so on; indeed, it calls for them, and not least of all it allows the actors to indulge in a necessary overplaying, a specific form of eccentricity such as the cocaine user would experience under the influence of the drug.

But not only in the staging, costumes, or acting should the film *Cocaine* capture the constantly shifting states in which the cocaine user experiences himself and life around him, states which—to put it in extreme terms—extend from great indifference toward everything to passionate pleasure in the imagination and tireless work.

Let me give one example to clarify what has just been said. Cocaine freezes the brain, freeing one's thoughts of anything inessential, and thereby liberating the essential, the imagination, concentration, and so on. This freezing of the brain, and this is the example, will be expressed in the film as follows: everything visible will appear covered with a sort of hoarfrost, glittering ice, whether in winter or summer; glasses and windows will be covered with ice flowers, and with all the interior shots in the studio, even in summertime, the actors' breath will be visible, as is usually the case only when it's bitter cold outside.

3. Since much of Pitigrilli's novel consists of interior monologue, I'll be forced to expand some of the parts, and I'll even have to invent new characters. Obviously the structure of the novel will be somewhat changed by that. But these changes will definitely improve the film, and thereby also the novel.

For various reasons, some of the scenes in the film will have to be shot in different locations. Instead of Genoa, whose character has been blasted by all the new building, I've chosen Naples. I don't know Bordeaux, but Lyon still has many of the features I need for my film. Instead of in Buenos Aires I'd like to shoot in Brazil, for various reasons, probably in Bahia, where I've situated the scenes that in the novel take place in Africa. That way we'll not only save one shooting location, but will also make the trip to South America more worthwhile.

4. Aside from the fact that there hasn't yet been a film one could really compare with my conception of *Cocaine,* there are films like *Amarcord* by Fellini, *Salo* by Pasolini, *In the Realm of the Senses* by Oshima, and my fourteenth segment of *Berlin Alexanderplatz* which can give you some idea of my conception of *Cocaine.*

1980

Part Four

LITERARY PAST /
CINEMATIC PRESENT

"Images the moviegoer can fill with his own imagination"
A Conversation with Kraft Wetzel about *Effi Briest*

■ *By now you've made a whole series of films about women:*
The Bitter Tears of Petra von Kant, Martha, Nora Helmer. *What interests you so much about this topic?*

Because when you begin to examine society concretely, you can't help bumping into the situation of women.

■ *But you could just as well bump into the situation of children and guestworkers.*

True, I could. But in spite of everything, I find women more interesting. They don't interest me just because they're oppressed—it's not that simple. The societal conflicts in women are more interesting because on the one hand women are oppressed, but in my opinion they also provoke this oppression as a result of their position in society, and in turn use it as a terror tactic. They're the really interesting figures in society; in them the conflicts are clearer.

■ *Is this factor, that in your opinion women use their oppression as a means of oppressing others, also present in your films?*

I think it is, except in *Effi Briest,* where the topic isn't a woman but a writer.

■ *What makes* Effi Briest *different from the other films, then?*

Because it isn't a film about a woman, but a film about Fontane, about this writer's attitude toward his society. It's not a film that tells a story, but a film that traces an attitude. It's the attitude of a person who sees through the failings and the weaknesses of his society and also criticizes them, but still recognizes this society as the valid one for him.

■ *What was your relationship to the literary work on which your film's based—what changes did you make, and what did you choose to emphasize?*

149

To begin with, I didn't change anything. Of course the selection that was made involves a certain tampering with the book. I tried to bring out somewhat more clearly the whole mechanism of oppression, which is hinted at much more cautiously in the book: the whole business with the Chinaman, and how Effi's husband applies his own terror tactics, all of which is embedded in a flowing narrative in the book. Of course that's already a crucial change, because it makes the criticism Fontane implies in the book come out more explicitly in the film. In the book it's more integrated into a clear, flowing narrative. It could have been left that way, but that would have seemed wrong to me.

■ *Your adaptation is very literary. You have many direct quotations from the text, off-camera commentaries, intertitles, etc. From the point of view of audience-effectiveness, this isn't an audience-friendly version.*

The task I faced wasn't to make an audience-effective film; my task was to make my attitude toward the society I live in clear by trying to make a film about Fontane.

■ *But your average moviegoer will think this is a film about Effi Briest.*

The average moviegoer you speak of probably won't go to see this film anyway. It's a film for a somewhat more aware audience. The films we make have a specific audience, which is getting somewhat bigger as the years go by. It isn't your mass television audience. If I were doing it for television, I'd make the movie differently. I'd tell myself I have a different responsibility in that situation, and I'd have to work more with the figure of Effi and show more of society and these mechanisms of oppression, and more concretely and in line with actual experience. But for the moviegoing audience, for people I can assume have a certain degree of awareness, I think it should be possible to make a movie like this, which functions in a more complicated way.

■ *Could you describe the effects you hope to achieve with the specific techniques you use, for instance the emphatically literary quality, the coolness and detached attitude toward the events in the film?*

It's important to me that people not experience the film as they do other films, which appeal to the heart or the emotions; it's an attempt to make a film that's clearly for the mind, a film in which people don't stop thinking, but rather actually begin to think, and just as when you read, it's your imagination that turns the letters and sentences into a story, the same thing should happen with this film. So everyone should have the opportunity and the freedom to make this film his own when he sees it; and in my opinion that can only happen when you have the triple alienation effect, when you have the detachment that I've built in.

■ *None of your previous films has such a forced use of the fade-in. What significance does this particular technique have for you?*

Well, fades to black usually manipulate feelings or time, whereas fades to white wake you up, because seeing just whiteness on the screen gives you a little jolt and keeps you awake, not in the sense that you might have gone to sleep, but mentally alert. But these fades to white are used the way they are in a book, when you turn the page or when a new chapter begins, and the blank space creates a break. Simply so it won't have the smooth progression that most movies have. But then again it also has a kind of cohesiveness, of course, because at a certain moment you get accustomed to the fades to white and then they don't strike the eye so much, but that's an effect we can't calculate in advance. What happens is that the film becomes brighter, even though it doesn't actually become brighter, simply because you've got used to it. Those are effects we couldn't know ahead of time, because I've never seen a film with so many fades to white.

■ *It's noticeable in the film how often mirrors are used. You have a tendency not to focus on people directly, but by way of their mirror images.*

First of all, you get a refraction that way, and second, it makes the whole thing even stranger and more distant. But that also has something to do with the actors, who get closer to their own identity in contact with mirrors. See, when they look at themselves while they're acting, they have a different attitude toward themselves, which I think is more concrete.

■ *You said in the beginning that the film was about Fontane's attitude toward his society, and that in it you also reflect your own attitude toward the society of today. How is your own position infiltrated into the film?*

Well, by leaving out my own feelings and thoughts, I accept Fontane's feelings and thoughts. I tell the viewer that his attitude is also my attitude. So it's also my attitude toward society that I see its failings and I see that it has to be changed, and yet I'm content to be a member of this society.

■ *It's characteristic of Fontane's attitude toward the society of his day that he stresses its positive elements—the sense of security and comfortableness that it provides—and also expresses these elements through the linguistic methods he uses. When I saw your film, on the other hand, I had the impression that you can't find anything positive in this society anymore. Even the decor and the*

Mirror shots from Effi Briest: *Hanna Schygulla and Liselotte Eder, Hanna Schygulla and Ursula Strätz (by permission of Fassbinder-Foundation, Munich)*

Mirror shots from Effi Briest: *Karlheinz Böhm and Wolfgang Schenck (by permission of Fassbinder-Foundation, Munich)*

language become means for portraying the web of terror in this
society.

I'd like to start with that concept of security. Of course those are the parts in Fontane that I don't agree with. I naturally left them out of my version. For me the decisive factor wasn't that he describes this bourgeois sense of security and this contentedness as something positive—that's not my attitude—but the important thing is the basic attitude toward a society. Fontane had some of the same problems in life; on the one hand he criticized his society, on the other hand he was unmistakably in favor of it. I mean, those petty-bourgeois needs Fontane fulfills for himself and his characters—those really don't interest me.

■ *But where is there room in the film for what you find positive in this society, whatever it is that keeps you from picking up a gun to fight it?*

I confirm society by accepting it, by living in it, and by taking advantage of the opportunities it offers. The opportunities are different from what they were in 1880; in those days it was a position as a district administrator, a house, the kind of security we were talking about. But that's not the topic of this film. The topic of the film is taking advantage of an opportunity this society offers and accepting it, and still knowing that it's basically wrong.

■ *Maybe you could also explain your position by outlining the differences between yourself and people like Buñuel and Chabrol, who also incorporate this dubious positive element into their movies, in a very sensuous way.*

In the case of Chabrol—I don't know Buñuel well at all—the pleasure he takes in society is certainly more perverse than mine. I think I have a cooler attitude toward society than Chabrol. That also has to do with my being German, while Chabrol is French. In France the whole thing looks a bit different; in France you have all that great food, which has an entirely different cultural meaning and also simply gives people a lot of fun. We don't have all that. In Germany the things that are fun are all a little more meager than in France. It may be that the difference between Chabrol and me lies somewhere in that area. There's a whole bunch of films by Chabrol, let's say from *Les biches* to *Le boucher,* which I completely accept and find absolutely terrific. But now he's going in a direction that I can't accept, where the fun he gets out of society doesn't interest me anymore, in *Docteur Popaul* and *Nada.* He's starting to become inhuman, isn't interested in human beings anymore. But those are films that would be bearable only if they had something to say about human beings.

■ *Taken as a whole, your work in film can be divided into two parts. The first would be more literary, the second more concerned with social criticism. How do you feel about the two?*

My personal interest of course isn't in making movies like *Eight Hours Are Not a Day*; my personal interest is more in literary topics, or topics that work with cinematic experience. The fact that I made things like *Eight Hours Are Not a Day* has to do with my having grasped certain societal mechanisms and recognizing perfectly calmly that you have to do something for the audience. And with other films like *Effi Briest* and the earlier ones, there I was doing something for myself.

■ *How do you explain the fact that the critics and part of the public have an ambivalent attitude toward you? On the one hand you're acknowledged to be brilliant, a boy wonder, and incredibly productive, and on the other hand you always run up against criticism, rejection, and anger.*

When you put the question that way, I think it simply has to do with envy, or rather with people's real fear that there's someone out there whom they consider so potent, and when they compare him with themselves, they're almost afraid. I also don't think the way people react really has much to do with the films or other things I do. I notice that every time. It's also a problem of timing. I keep working steadily, but sometimes it just happens that in one week or one month three different things of mine appear, even though they were made over the course of a year. People always react normally to the first one, with the second one they're already a bit nervous, and with the third one they just fly off the handle, because it's simply too much.

■ *How do you manage to work so steadily and so intensely?*

I don't do anything special. I just work, one thing after the other. I have the great advantage that I almost always work in a group, with a couple of friends and other people, and of course that's a whole lot easier and gives you a whole lot more support than when you just muddle along by yourself, as many other people do. That's probably it. But it probably also has to do with the fact that I don't just make one film a year, and spend three-quarters of the year preparing for it; instead, while I'm preparing, I'm already doing something else, too. When you have the technical aspects under control, you can pay a lot more attention to questions of content. When you don't have to think so hard about camera placements, but just know that in a certain series of shots the camera has to be placed here, then you can pay much more attention to content, at least during the actual shooting.

■ *But when you do several things a year, with everything over-*

*lapping, from conception to execution, doesn't that create problems
for you each time you have to get into the material?*

All my things are incredibly interconnected. There are time pe-
riods when three or four things are being done at once, all of which
relate to each other. It's not that I would work on entirely different
projects that way. See, I have one theme that I'm doing three or four
things with. There was a time when *Eight Hours Are Not a Day, Jail
Bait,* and *The Merchant of Four Seasons* were all being made, and they
all have a lot to do with each other. And then the time when *Effi Briest*
was being made along with *Nora Helmer* and the script for *Martha.* I
couldn't work any other way.

■ *Could you also briefly describe the way you work? To what
extent is the team you always work with involved in the actual
execution, and to what extent do you impose your own concept?*

That varies from film to film. In the case of *Effi Briest* I imposed
what I wanted. There was one view that was fundamentally different
from mine, and that was Frau Schygulla's. She wanted it to be a film
about Effi Briest, about a woman toward the end of the nineteenth
century and her problems. Then it would have turned into a film like
the one by Gustaf Gründgens; it would have been a film that tells a
story. I just wanted it to be different, and in that case I imposed my
will. The cameramen do exactly what I want. I look at every take, and
for every take I say exactly what kind of lighting I want, and I try out
every traveling shot myself. That's how it was possible to have half the
film shot by one cameraman and the other half shot by another without your noticing it in the film.

■ *What did the film cost? I know the shooting dragged on fairly
long, with several interruptions.*

If we include the salaries that didn't get paid but for which we gave
shares, the film cost more than a million marks. In actual money it cost
between 750,000 and 800,000 marks. Of that I was given 250,000 as
a prize for the screenplay, and the rest came out of my pocket, my
earnings from the last four years.

■ *Why did the shooting take so long?*

It began with my wanting to shoot in all four seasons. That didn't
work out, because the leading actor got sick in the middle, and then
the whole project was up in the air because we didn't know whether
he'd ever be able to work again, and that made everything really
complicated.

■ *Let's turn to the international renown that has now come to
you quite unexpectedly . . .*

It wasn't unexpected in the least. It was perfectly clear to me that this would have to happen some day. *The Merchant of Four Seasons* was actually the beginning, with people abroad starting to pay attention, and observing more attentively, realizing that there was someone out there doing interesting things. First they got all excited about German productions like Werner Schroeter's, because they thought it was somehow special that such things could be coming out of Germany. But in the end it was clear that some day they'd come around.

■ *To what do you attribute the fact that critics abroad don't really know what to do with* Effi Briest*?*

Well, it's a film that really only works in the German language. So it's incredibly difficult for them to get into it, because they don't pick up on the specifically German quality of Fontane's language, which is the whole point and the basis of the film.

■ *Can you describe what it is about Fontane's language that interests you so much that you give it such a large part in your film?*

It's because I find it so precise, because it describes things and situations so precisely and for that reason is never unambiguous . . .

■ *. . . isn't that a contradiction?*

That's what's so precise about it, that it always describes a thing from two sides; even when he says a thing is this way, he says in the next sentence, Yes, but you can also see it another way. Fontane never pins himself down. He says—let me put it very crudely—Effi is very happy, though you could also think that maybe she isn't. That goes all the way through the book, and to me it's absolutely fascinating that he isn't unambiguous and doesn't say, This is how it is—and that's that, but he always leaves himself room to maneuver by doing it this way.

■ *Isn't there a danger, when you're so caught up in a particular kind of language and the pleasure you get from displaying it in the film, that the cinematic images may become tautological, that the images may just be in the way, because the film actually lives in and through the words? If the film were just blank film, people could think up their own images.*

I think the images are constructed in such a way that they almost function like blank film, so that even though there are images there, you can fill them again with your own imagination and your own emotions. What makes that possible is the triple alienation effect: the mirrors, the fade-ins and fade-outs, and the emotionless acting style. The detachment that's created this way almost forces the moviegoer, I think—though I find that wrong; let me put it differently: he has freedom like with reading, where the sentence you've read doesn't take shape till your imagination goes to work; what I mean is, he has the freedom with this film to make the film for himself, even though the images are there. It isn't a film like most other films, which overwhelm the moviegoer. This is one which in my opinion gives the moviegoer room to maneuver, and that's what makes this film special.

■ *In the part of your work that's socially critical you place considerable importance on the moviegoer's identifying with characters in the film, in contrast to your "literary" films. For example, in* Fear Eats the Soul *people are supposed to identify with Mira, or in* Eight Hours Are Not a Day *with the main characters. Wouldn't that make them films that overwhelm the moviegoer? Why do you do one thing in one set of movies and then contradict it in the technique you use in other films?*

Because on the one hand you can recognize that something's important and right, and in spite of that have different personal interests, just like Fontane.

■ *So you think it's important to make some films that aim for audience identification?*

Yes. I came to that realization through people like Yaak Karsunke, Peter Märthesheimer, I don't know, many people. They didn't tell me, "Do identification," but they told me, "It's important to change the world."

■ *But why with those kinds of form?*

Because it doesn't work any other way. Because it's pointless to make films for the public that the public can't feel involved in. That would be idiotic. As for *Effi Briest,* that's a film which will only appeal to a special audience, to people who view movies more consciously. While *Eight Hours Are Not a Day* wasn't understood at all by the people I thought would certainly understand what was right and good about it. It was really only understood by the people for whom it was actually made. We had an incredible number of discussions with workers and union members; it went incredibly well. They were able to take the so-called fairy tales in *Eight Hours Are Not a Day* and rethink them in terms of their own situation, and that's what they did. That was certainly another reason why we couldn't go on with it.

■ *What are you working on at the moment?*

I'm shooting a film called *Fox and His Friends,* which is about a young entrepreneur whose company's on the verge of bankruptcy, and who manages to trick money out of someone to save the firm. It has to do with a private struggle between an entrepreneur and a nonentrepreneur who'd like to become an entrepreneur. It's a movie production in color. I play one of the main roles in it, the nonentrepreneur, and Peter Chatel plays the entrepreneur, and then there are many older stars in it. At the moment I don't have any other projects, just ideas. The series of films about women is finished. What interests me now are models. Models for many things. I'd like to make a film about the origins of the Jewish religion.

■ *To what extent would that be a model?*

The Jewish religion was an experiment by good old Mister Moses. There's a beautiful book by Freud which would be the basis for the film; it's called *Moses the Man*. The basic idea is that Moses was an Egyptian, and a pharaoh had invented this one-god religion and then died, and the Egyptians were very discontented because it was a very inhuman religion, a very abstract one, and they fought to bring back their polytheistic religion, which for them was much more practical and human. And now Moses was suddenly out of work, because he'd been an Egyptian priest, and he went looking for a people he could try out this religion on, so he could experiment with how it worked, and he took the Jews, who were living there in a slavery that they totally accepted—they were already integrated into Egyptian life— and he took them and said, "You are the Chosen Ones, you are a better race." And they believed it, because a thing like that is thrilling, after all. And that's how it got started. Then I have another idea: I'd like to film B. F. Skinner's book *Walden II*. It's about a model for society.

July 1974

The Cities of Humanity and the Human Soul
Some Unorganized Thoughts on Alfred Döblin's Novel, *Berlin Alexanderplatz*

About twenty years ago—I was just fourteen or maybe fifteen already, and in the throes of an almost murderous puberty—I had embarked on my completely unscholarly, extremely personal grand tour through world literature, guided only by my very own associations, when I encountered Alfred Döblin's novel *Berlin Alexanderplatz.*

At first, to be quite honest, the book didn't turn me on at all; it didn't knock me over or hit me over the head as some books had, though not many, I admit. On the contrary, the first pages—maybe two hundred—bored me so completely and utterly that I might easily have put the book aside, in which case I would not have finished it, and then almost certainly would never have read it again. Strange! I would not only have missed one of the most stimulating and exciting encounters with a work of art; no—and I think I know what I'm saying—my life would have turned out differently, certainly not as a whole, but in some respects, in many, perhaps more crucial respects than I can even say at this point, differently from the way it turned out with Döblin's *Berlin Alexanderplatz* embedded in my mind, my flesh, my body as a whole, and my soul—go ahead and smile.

In fact the author skirts around his theme, or rather the actual theme of the novel *Berlin Alexanderplatz* for many chapters, for many, many pages, possibly out of cowardice, possibly out of an inexplicable timidity toward the prevailing morality of his time and his class, possibly out of the subconscious fear of a man who was somehow personally implicated. The "hero" Franz Biberkopf meets the other "hero" of the novel, Reinhold, a meeting that determines the future course of the lives of these two men, on page 155 of the 410-page paperback edition, more than a third of the way into the novel, and at least 150 pages too late, or so it seemed to me on first reading, an impression, by the way, that has basically not changed for me, though it has necessarily undergone some refinement.

For whatever reason, but fortunately for me at any rate, I got through that first third of *Berlin Alexanderplatz,* which, as I said, bored me more than it might have confused, disturbed, or even aroused me; I read on, suddenly found myself reading in a way that you would hardly call reading—more like devouring, gobbling, gulping down. And these expressions still don't do justice to that way of reading, which dangerously often wasn't reading at all, but more life, suffering, despair, and fear.

But luckily Döblin's novel is too good to permit a person to go under or lose himself in it. Again and again, I was forced, as any reader is, to return to my own reality, to analyze everybody's reality. A criterion, by the way, by which I would measure any work of art. It may be that *Berlin Alexanderplatz* helped me to recognize this requirement for art, to formulate it, and not least to apply it to my own work. So I encountered a work of art that was not only in a position to provide life support, and I'll talk about this, too; this work of art, *Berlin Alexanderplatz,* also helps you get a theoretical handle on things without itself being theoretical, forces you to behave morally without itself being moralistic, helps you accept the ordinary as the real thing, as sacred, without itself being ordinary or sacred, or making much of itself as an account of the real thing, and all this without being cruel, something literary works as significant as this one often are.

But *Berlin Alexanderplatz* didn't only help me in something like a process of ethical maturation; no, it also provided genuine, naked, concrete life support when I was really at risk during puberty, because I was able to apply the story to my own problems and dilemmas, oversimplifying, of course; I read it as the story of two men whose little bit of life on this earth is ruined because they don't have the opportunity to get up the courage even to recognize, let alone admit, that they like each other in an unusual way, love each other somehow, that something mysterious ties them to each other more closely than is generally considered suitable for men.

Yet it's by no means a question of something sexual between two people of the same gender; Franz Biberkopf and Reinhold are in no way homosexual—they don't have problems in this area even in the broadest sense; nothing points to that. Not even Reinhold's unambiguously sexual relationship with a boy in prison, no matter how happy Döblin makes it out to be. I would argue that this has nothing to do with the bond between Franz and Reinhold. No, what exists between Franz and Reinhold is nothing more nor less than a pure love that society can't touch. That means that's all it really is. But of course both of them, Reinhold even more than Franz, are creatures of society, and as such naturally not in a position even to understand this love, to accept it, simply to take it as it is, to become richer and happier from a love that in any case occurs far too seldom among human beings.

And indeed, what would a person raised just like us, or similarly, see in a love that doesn't lead to any visible results, to anything that can be displayed, exploited, and thus made useful? Such a love must— that's the sad situation with love, and how terrible—such a love must strike those who have learned that love is usable, or at least useful, in the positive as well as the negative sense (we've also learned to enjoy suffering)—such a love is bound to create fear, quite simply, in them, and that means of course in us. Every one of us.

That's the way I must have read *Berlin Alexanderplatz* that first time, or in some such way. And, to be quite specific, this reading helped me to admit to my tormenting fears, which were almost paralyzing me, my fear of my homosexual longings, to give in to my suppressed needs; this reading helped me avoid becoming completely and utterly sick, dishonest, desperate; it helped me avoid going under.

About five years later I read *Berlin Alexanderplatz* again. This time something entirely different shook me up or awakened me to an experience that again helped me to understand to a much greater extent what *I* really means—an experience that helped me not to do unconsciously something that I would like to describe roughly as "living life secondhand." At this second reading, from page to page it became clearer to me, amazed at first, then more and more alarmed, finally so struck that I almost felt obliged to close my eyes and ears, that is, to repress; it became clearer and clearer to me that a huge part of myself, of my behavior, my reactions, many things I had considered part of me, were nothing more than things described by Döblin in *Berlin Alexanderplatz*.

Very simply, I had unconsciously turned Döblin's imaginings into my life. Yet once again it was the novel that helped me to overcome the alarming crisis that resulted and to work at establishing something that could eventually become, I hope, more or less that thing one calls an identity, to the extent that's even possible with all this screwed-up mess.

Next I saw the *Alexanderplatz* film by Piel Jutzi, which I found quite a good film, by no means bad, taken by itself. Though in making the film they had completely forgotten Döblin's novel. The book and the film have nothing to do with each other. Each of them, and that certainly includes the film by Jutzi, is art, independent of the other. And since film is the medium with which I identify most, I decided at the time that some day—and why only some day, I don't know; maybe when I would have sufficient skill—I would make an attempt to venture on an experiment using my cinematic resources, an experiment in documenting, by way of Döblin's *Berlin Alexanderplatz,* my involvement with this very special literature.

It took ten years before I got that far. And if the situation hadn't been as it was, namely that I had to do it or someone else would, I probably would have given myself more time. But chronologically speaking, in many of my works of the last few years I slipped in many of what you could call quotations from Döblin's novel. And then at some point, because a book was being done on me, I reviewed all my old films over a period of three days. And again—this time it really took me aback—I realized that there were substantially more quotations than I had dreamt, and most of them unconscious.

So then I read the book again; I wanted to understand more clearly what was going on between me and Alfred Döblin's novel. Many things became clear, fundamental things, but probably most important was the recognition, and the resulting admission, that this novel, a work of art, had helped determine the course of my life.

Certainly anyone who hadn't read *Berlin Alexanderplatz* would ask at this point what kind of a story Alfred Döblin would have to have told for it to take on such a vast, almost existential significance for even one reader, which is, after all, a highly unusual impact for a single work of art. Well, a person asking about the story of *Berlin Alexanderplatz* would have to be told honestly that the story itself is actually no big deal. On the contrary, really. The story of the former teamster Franz Biberkopf, who gets out of prison and swears to stay clean, and what becomes of this resolution, is more like a series of dreary little stories, some of them incredibly brutal, each of which could supply the most obscene tabloids with the most obscene attention-grabbing features. So the crucial part of *Berlin Alexanderplatz* isn't the story; this is something the novel has in common with some other great novels in world literature; its structure is, if possible, even more ludicrous than that of Goethe's *Elective Affinities*—the essential part is simply the way in which this incredibly banal and unbelievable plot is narrated. And the attitude toward the characters, whom the author exposes in all their dreariness to the reader, while on the other hand he teaches the reader to see these characters, reduced to mediocrity, with the greatest tenderness, and to love them in the end.

At this point I do want to try to give a simple plot summary. As I said, the former teamster Franz Biberkopf is released from prison, where he had spent four years for killing his former girlfriend Ida with an eggbeater; during the hard times of the twenties she had walked

Cover of the program for Piel Jutzi's adaptation of Berlin Alexanderplatz *(1931), starring Heinrich George as Franz Biberkopf (Deutsches
Literaturarchiv, Marbach am Neckar, Germany)*

the streets for him. The released prisoner first experiences the usual
impotence, which he overcomes by almost raping his victim's sister,
so that after that he's in a position to begin an affair with the Polish
girl Lina, and in such a way that she can mistake it for love and get

Franz to swear that he'll stay clean from now on, so help him ... ah, well.

Economic conditions are catastrophic; all attempts to get on a firm footing fail, whether selling tie pins, pornographic literature, or the Nazi *People's Observer,* which gets him into trouble with former friends, communists, with whom he once made common cause simply because he liked them. What's left are shoelaces, something people always need, and he peddles them with his uncle, until the uncle exploits the trust Franz places in him and blackmails and threatens a widow to whom Franz had given a bit of happiness, for which he'd gotten money. Franz, who has an unshakeable faith in human goodness, is so hurt that he withdraws from the world and other people, does nothing but drink for weeks on end, but then finally returns to life and other people.

Then he meets someone called Reinhold, who's a small-time crook, but remarkably fascinating somehow, so fascinating that Franz enters into a strange deal with him; he takes over his women when Reinhold's through with them, because this Reinhold gets tired of them too quickly. It's almost pathological with him: first he has to have one, come hell or high water, and then he has to be rid of her, suddenly, violently, but it's hard for him, even so; he has trouble with it. But Franz, who is clearly somehow fascinated by him, and whom Reinhold considers rather dumb, this Franz takes them off his hands, the women, first one, then a second, but when it comes to the third, he refuses. Reinhold should learn to stay with a woman longer, because it's healthy, and the other way is sick, and because Franz wants to help Reinhold, for real. And that the other one can't understand this and is offended, this Franz Biberkopf can understand and accept.

Shortly after this, it happens that Franz helps out with an undertaking that he thinks consists of handling a regular shipment of fruit, but suddenly realizes is stealing. He's standing guard, and wants to run away, but doesn't make it. After the robbery Franz is riding in the car with Reinhold when Reinhold suddenly gets the feeling they're being followed. Now fear of being followed mingles in Reinhold with his rage at Franz. And then—there's something somnambulistic about it—Reinhold suddenly pushes Franz out of the car. Franz is run over by the car behind them, and it must look as though he's dead. But Franz Biberkopf isn't dead; he only loses his right arm. His former girlfriend Eva and her pimp nurse him back to health, and without a right arm he goes back to the city, meets a petty gangster for whom he fences some stolen goods, which brings him a degree of prosperity. Then this Eva brings him a girl he calls Mieze, who, as it turns out, walks the streets for him. Franz accepts this, and for a while the two of them are happy. But Reinhold interferes in this relationship, too, has several rendezvous with Mieze, until at last he kills her. Franz is arrested for this murder, is committed to an insane asylum, where, over a rather long period, he undergoes a "reverse process of catharsis" to become an ordinary, useful member of society. Nothing else special happens with him. He will probably become a nationalist, that's how much the encounter with Reinhold has ruined him. That's all there is to the story.

Basically nothing more than a threepenny novel, nothing more than just a series of several tabloid features. So what makes this plot into something so great? It's the how, of course. In *Berlin Alexanderplatz* the same degree of grandeur is accorded to the smallest, objectively speaking, and most mediocre emotions, feelings, moments of happiness, longings, gratifications, pains, fears, deficiencies of consciousness, of seemingly inconsequential, unimportant, insignificant individuals, the so-called little people, as is normally accorded in art only to the "great" ones. The people whose stories Döblin tells in *Berlin Alexanderplatz,* especially the protagonist, the former teamster Franz Biberkopf, later pimp, homicide, thief, and pimp again, are credited with such a differentiated subconscious, combined with an almost unbelievable imagination and capacity for suffering, that one would have to look long and hard for their equal in world literature, at least to the extent I'm familiar with it, even among the highly cultivated, clever intellectuals or great lovers, to name just a few types of characters.

Döblin's attitude toward his characters, who are, objectively speaking, certainly poor, insignificant creatures, is, I would contend, in all likelihood influenced by Sigmund Freud's discoveries, even if Döblin disputed that on several occasions. That would make *Berlin Alexanderplatz* probably the first attempt to transform Freudian insights into art. Let that be said first.

Second, Döblin narrates every scrap of plot, no matter how banal, as a process that is significant and grand in its own right, usually as part of an only seemingly mysterious mythology, and then again as a translation into religious motifs, whether Jewish or Christian.

As someone who had converted from Judaism to Catholicism, Döblin had more problems with religion than most. Perhaps that was the reason he tried to master these problems, to discover in the ordinary that which is peculiar to religion, and to describe it as such.

In simple terms, that probably means that no motif of the plot stands merely for itself, even though that would be more than sufficient, but is a motif in a second, different, more impenetrable and mysterious story, part, that is, of a novel within the novel, or perhaps also part of a private mythology of the author's, but I don't want to have to decide that at the moment.

Third, then, is the narrative technique Döblin invented for *Berlin Alexanderplatz*, or perhaps merely chose. By the way, I don't consider this question of whether it was invented or not at all important, for what's decisive is whether an author chooses the right means for expressing his intentions, not whether he's also their inventor; that may interest literary historians, but to the reader it doesn't really matter; he's lucky enough to be reading a novel whose author found the proper form, and Alfred Döblin did just that, with somnambulistic certainty, in *Berlin Alexanderplatz*. And whether Döblin knew James Joyce's *Ulysses* before he wrote *Berlin Alexanderplatz*, or whether he didn't know it, doesn't make his novel any better or worse. Besides, I could imagine that two writers might well hit on practically the same narrative technique simultaneously; why not, after all? As in history itself, in literary history not everything can be explained from within. A mystery, even if it be only hope, will always remain.

To me the question whether Döblin knew *Ulysses* is less exciting than the idea that the language in *Berlin Alexanderplatz* was influenced by the rhythm of the elevated trains that ran past the window of Döblin's Berlin study. The language is certainly shaped by such things—mostly the noises of the big city, the specific rhythms, the constant madness of an unceasing back-and-forth. And consciousness of life in a big city, a very specific alertness to everything that living in the city means, certainly provides the source of the montage technique Döblin uses in this novel, one of the few big-city novels that exist. Life in a big city: that means constant shifts in one's attention to sounds, images, movement. And so the means used for narrating the chosen elements shift, as the interest of an alert big-city resident may shift without his losing himself as focal point, as is also the case with the story.

I leave it to others to say more, and more specific, things about Döblin's particular narrative style; I can only point out that Döblin also wrote other works, works of art, which will possibly mean more to later generations, which will perhaps some day be more important than *Berlin Alexanderplatz* is today. And I can wish that Döblin might be read more, far, far more than he is read today. For the sake of the readers. And of life.

March 1980

■ Preliminary Remarks on *Querelle*

1.

Contrary to popular opinion, the making of an authentic film from a piece of literature is in no sense simply a matter of accomplishing the most "congenial" possible translation from one medium, literature, into the other, film. Cinematic transformation of a literary work should never assume that its purpose is simply the maximal realization of the images that literature evokes in the minds of its readers.

Such an assumption would, in any case, be preposterous, since any given reader reads any given book with his own sense of reality, and therefore any book evokes as many different fantasies and images as it has readers.

There is no such thing as the ultimate objective reality for any work of literature. Consequently, the intention of a film that tries to come to grips with literature cannot be the realization of the author's world of images in some fixed and final consensus of separate and contrary fantasies. Any attempt to turn a film into a *substitute* for literature must inevitably result in a compound fantasy based on the lowest common denominator and will therefore, by definition, be a mediocre and lifeless product.

A film that comes to grips with literature and language has to make of this confrontation something absolutely intelligible, clear, and transparent. Not for a single moment may it turn its own fantasy into a composite one. Always, at every stage, it must make it clear that this is but one possible way of dealing with a work of art in another medium. This is the only way:

— through an unequivocal and single-minded questioning of the piece of literature and its language;
— by scrutinizing the substance and the posture of the author's work;

—by developing an imagination instantly recognizable as unique;
—and by abandoning any futile attempt at "consummating" the
work of literature.

This is the only way to turn literature into film.

2.

As far as discrepancy between objective plot and subjective fantasy is
concerned, Jean Genet's *Querelle de Brest* may be the most radical
novel in world literature. On the surface, its story, when divorced
from Genet's world of images, is a fairly uninteresting (in fact, third-
class) tale about a criminal, and as such it is hardly worth our while.

What is worthwhile is to confront Jean Genet's narrative method,
his extraordinary imagination, which conjures up a world that seems
alien at first, a world in which singular laws seem to be in force, in the
service of an astonishing mythology.

It is tremendously exciting to discover, at first slowly and then
more and more compellingly, how this strange world with its own
peculiar laws relates to our own subjective sense of reality, how it
brings surprising truths to the surface of this subjective reality of ours
by forcing us (and I am fully aware of the pretentiousness of this notion) toward certain recognitions and decisions that, no matter how
painful they may seem to be, bring us closer to our own lives.

This also means that we get closer to our own identities.

Only those who are truly identified with their own selves no
longer need to fear fear. And only those who are rid of their fear are
capable of loving nonjudgmentally. The ultimate goal of all human
endeavor: to live one's own life.

3.

I cannot form a picture of the world of Jean Genet, and consequently
of my own treatment of it, in its original settings. That is because every
action that takes place within this world, every gesture, means something else; in each case it is something essentially more, something
greater, generally something sacred.

For this reason Rolf Zehetbauer and I have decided that the film of
Jean Genet's *Querelle* will take place in a kind of surreal landscape. It
will be a composite of the specific segments and signals of all the
settings referred to by Genet. Within this landscape there will be

several walls for projection. They will enable us to project particles of the real world into this artificial world, and thereby to expand it infinitely.

Another essential reason for using such a landscape is that for each separate scene there will then be the possibility of bringing any one of the other motifs into that central image and having it function as a sort of counterpoint to the action. Whether it will then act merely as a contrapuntal motif, or take over as the setting for the action, is something to be determined from situation to situation.

1982 (Translated by A. S. Wensinger and Richard Wood)

Part Five

MONOLOGUES AND
CONFESSIONS

"Of despair, and the courage to recognize a utopia and to open yourself up to it"
Two Monologues and a Text on *Despair*

You can't talk about the meaning of life without using phony words. Imprecise ones. But there aren't any others. If there's anything, it's movement. At some point a solar system got established, which doesn't move anymore because it moves according to laws. To get it moving, something has to come along and smash things. That's why human beings were invented. But that wasn't part of a plan. We're no longer allowed to say: We're here to . . . The plan of the powerful takes place in our causal thinking, which is always intent on setting up value systems, creating meaning. All history, all mythologies grow out of this notion of planned chains of causality. Now, if we destroy the various cogs in this system, all the neatly ordered gravitational forces don't work anymore, and everything collapses. And suddenly there's movement, and that's something. But we, we just stand around, the creators of values. That's what we're here for. We're not capable of accepting the opposite of things as they are. So we're nowhere near freedom. We won't become free unless we accept destruction the same way we accept the ordered solar system, which makes for our paralysis. This has developed because the individual doesn't know that it can be stopped. I'm not talking about intellectual knowledge, but about the physical certainty in everything the individual does. The possibility of understanding this is withheld from him for a long time, and he experiences it physically only much later. If the certainty that he had to die became physically palpable for the individual very early on, he would lose the existential pains—hatred, envy, jealousy. No more fears. Our relationships are cruel games we play with each other because we don't recognize our end as something positive. It's positive because it's real. The end is life in concrete form. The body must understand death. In Bremen I had a terrible night when I was directing a play there. A dream of death. I was completely unprepared for it. After that I had neurotic heart symptoms and went running from one

173

doctor to another. Of course there was nothing wrong with me. It was already much too late when it got to me at twenty-six, this experience of mortality that came in my sleep. I couldn't make use of it in my relationship anymore. That's the subject of my new play. It's called *End Endless*. Destruction isn't the opposite of what exists. Destruction is when this concept no longer exists, when it doesn't have any meaning anymore, when it has a reality that makes it disappear. What people invent then—that would be exciting.

June 1977

In the life of every human being there comes the terrible, wonderful moment that forces its way into the consciousness of some like a lightning bolt and into the subconscious of others like a sacred pain, the moment when you recognize the finitude of your own existence. But with all sorts of false notions in our heads we've learned to see as right, compelling, definitive, and unchangeable much that is false and disgusting, particularly this strange, unnecessary, but apparently useful paralysis that comes over us simultaneously with the longing for a utopia of our own. We've been taught to embrace so many false, sticky thoughts as our own that even the struggle for various utopias only admits of certain means, which are false, too—not more false, not that, but just as false as everything else. And so the terrible recognition that we will come to an end, instead of liberating us, which it actually could and should, rather shores up our tormented pursuit of pleasure, our happiness in our mediocre unfreedom. The enjoyment made possible by this recognition of the ultimate meaninglessness and actual fortuitousness of every existence—indeed of every existence from that sacred moment of recognition on, which should confer meaning on it again in free decision and great strength in the fight for something wonderful, possible, meaningfully conferring meaning in the midst of meaninglessness—is not taught as enjoyment to be experienced, not as pleasurably liberated pleasure, but as fear, which in pleasureless pleasure makes absence of freedom palatable. This admirable jungle seems to have no way out, except through the decision in favor of death, except perhaps for the path described in *Despair,* the path into madness, which one can choose for oneself. But the "land of madness" is like that of death: only possibly can they be adequate sources of hope. And we've received only incomplete tidings of the lovely anarchy that's supposed to make sensational happenings in freedom possible in the "land of madness." One day, when I demand a decision of myself, I hope I'll have the courage to choose one of those paths, and not to settle for the easy way out.

March 1, 1978

Despair—A Summary of the Contents of a Film That Doesn't Permit a Summary of Its Contents

Before the fashionable concept of the "mid-life crisis" was invented, making an odd condition into something minor by naming it, opening it up to cheap self-pity, and thereby depriving this condition of its possibly really menacing aspects, this strange, apparently inexplicable period did exist in the lives of many people, a period when they became dissatisfied with what they'd accomplished, their possessions, their acquired ability to "be happy," with everything called satisfaction, and wanted to break out, or at least wanted something, but didn't know what.

Men suddenly feel the urgent need to exchange the woman they call their own for another, to despise the work they do and know, to dream of islands, of adventures, of some kind of trip through some kind of world. Inexplicable? Not in the least! They simply can't get around the fact anymore that their life is over, that everything that will happen from now on will be repetition, and so their satisfaction, of whatever sort, is hollowed out like a stone on which the same water drips day in, day out.

Hermann Hermann, chocolate manufacturer, emigrant from a Russia which, after twelve years in Berlin, seems to him more like a stale mocha torte than something that would be worth his yearning, has a particularly hard time with the crisis, when he recognizes that he isn't good for anything but to go on competently repeating what he's already competent at. For his wife is so much his wife, has become so much a part of him, that any change in this area would be an amputation, out of the question. He's never seen his profession as satisfying, so even despising it wouldn't be any sort of change. Lonely islands, traveling somewhere to flee from nothing real, nothing definable, isn't Hermann Hermann's sort of thing, the earth as a ball that leaves dirt on your shoes, and where mountains remain mountains, and the sun does what it's always done, not acceding to the wishes of this person or that, and the moon also remains the moon and forces this person as well as that to let what is happening happen.

All around him things may swing into motion that are frightening, but even this fright doesn't help him get out of his skin; on the contrary, his skin opens its pores to fright, so that finally one step after another becomes softer, more cautious, but step continues to be called step, and steps, which are now and forever called steps are not even—steps.

Somewhere Hermann Hermann's despair sets in, making him do things that turn whatever happens into his happening, which allow his strange, hapless possibilities to become a great transformation, a refusal to be dead in life.

Of this despair and the painful search for something in motion, and the courage to recognize a utopia and to open yourself up to it, however poor it may be—of these things I tell in this film.

1977

In a Year of Thirteen Moons

1. 1978, A Year

The film *In a Year of Thirteen Moons* will show the encounters a man experiences during the last five days of his life and will try, using these encounters, to determine whether this man's decision not to have any more days after the last of these five days is reprehensible, understandable at least, or perhaps even acceptable.

The film takes place in Frankfurt, a city whose specific structure practically demands biographies like the one that follows, or at any rate doesn't make them appear particularly unusual. Frankfurt is not the place for pleasant mediocrity, for equalizing contrasts, not peaceable, not fashionable, or nice; Frankfurt is a city where you encounter the general social contradictions on every street corner, everywhere and constantly, even if you don't stumble over them right away, those contradictions that are quite successfully covered over everywhere else.

2. A Biography

Sometime during the Second World War Anita Weishaupt bears a son. Frau Weishaupt is married and already has two children by her husband, but when the third child comes into the world, Anita Weishaupt's husband hasn't been with her for two years; nothing is known of him, whether he's dead or a prisoner-of-war, nothing. Whatever may have happened to her husband, Anita Weishaupt is sure of one thing: this third child, though brought into the world by a married woman, is still born out of wedlock, and in case of her husband's return would cause her marriage to break up. But Anita Weishaupt doesn't even have to think that far ahead, for quite apart from the fate of her husband, this child would have a negative effect on her existence, since financially she is extremely dependent on her husband's parents, whom this child would give a long-sought pretext for cutting Anita off with a clear conscience. Anita Weishaupt, a person burdened with excessively great existential anxiety, for these reasons gave birth to her child in secret and turned it over to an orphanage shortly after its birth. Since at this time people's minds were full of war and fear and destruction, Anita Weishaupt actually succeeded in carrying out her plan without any complications. She left the Catholic orphanage where she had deposited her son with no feeling other than great relief. No worry about the child, no troubled conscience, no sorrow, no anger at having to give up something which, after all, was like a part of her. That shows how much fear a human being can feel among other human beings. Anita Weishaupt forgot this child; she probably had no other choice. Years later, when she was reminded that there was something else there, something that was a human being and might perhaps have a right to her, a right at least to a tiny little chance, even if she herself didn't have the necessary strength—she betrayed the child, so as not to have to betray herself.

Anita Weishaupt had no chance to assert herself in her world, so how could she have given another living being a chance? Her son was supposed to be called Erwin; she had already told the nuns, and she signed a statement giving the child up for adoption. So the child was baptized Erwin, and the nuns liked him, for he was a very quiet child, which was pleasant; they called him a good boy and in those really bad days at the end of the war and the three years that followed they always slipped him enough so that he wouldn't be hungry, preferably too much rather than too little. They had to do it secretly, because there was seldom enough for all the children to eat their fill. It particularly impressed the nuns to see how quietly and, they thought, in submission to God's will, Erwin went through the usual childhood diseases; so it's not surprising that soon all the nuns in the orphanage developed something like motherly feelings for Erwin. Such feelings can easily become a burden to the one on the receiving end, especially because each of these "surrogate mothers" of Erwin's wanted to be his favorite. So Erwin learned to lie, for he had soon discovered that things went better for him when he told the nuns what they wanted to hear. Erwin also constructed a system of different behaviors, for he had also soon learned that each of these mothers had a different image of her child, which had to be confirmed. Since Erwin was extremely intelligent and very skillful, no one noticed, except Sister Gudrun, who was really fond of him, that the quiet, good child was turning into an uncommunicative, sad child, a child, furthermore, who felt under constant pressure to continue getting what he took for love.

When Erwin was old enough, he was sent to school. Without being particularly ambitious, he was a good student, during the first year and a half. Then something happened that was to change Erwin's life decisively. More and more often older couples came to the orphanage, usually on Sunday afternoons, walked around, looked Erwin and his fellow students over so carefully that Erwin sometimes couldn't stand their gaze and ran away. And yet there must have been something good about these people, for one or another of Erwin's friends would suddenly disappear, and Sister Gudrun would explain to him that those who were gone had found parents. And parents, Sister Gudrun explained to him, were something wonderful, it was so wonderful for a child to have parents, because parents try to be there for their child, to help him, to love him, and to make everything possible come true for him. From then on Erwin didn't run away anymore on Sunday afternoons when he was looked over; on the contrary, he returned the looks attentively, for the parents shouldn't only be there for him, he wanted to be there for his parents, wanted to love them. Erwin didn't want only to receive, he also wanted to give, and maybe that was even more important to him. Now everything moved very quickly. Erwin found his parents and they found him. Their name was Weber, and they owned a little house on the edge of the city, not very large, but for Erwin all this meant almost more than freedom; in fact this is how he had pictured heaven. He didn't have to lie anymore, play a part, make himself liked. The Webers knew something important; they knew and were willing to accept that everyone has defects, everyone. And their son was also allowed to have defects and shouldn't have to pretend. The Webers agreed with each other and reached an agreement with Erwin; there was something one might call trust among the three of them. Trust and patience. So the Webers decided to adopt the child, after they had thought about it more than seems to be usual in such cases. Now it was just a question of the formalities. Frau Anita Weishaupt had officially given her son up for adoption, to be sure, but that was during the war, and many things had been different then. Perhaps Anita Weishaupt had even changed her mind in the meantime.

Sister Gudrun took on the task of looking up Erwin's mother to discuss her child's future with her.

She found Frau Weishaupt in a fairly large and handsome apartment. In the apartment there were by now four children, and Anita Weishaupt was very pregnant again. As soon as Anita Weishaupt opened the door and caught sight of Sister Gudrun, something like horror spread over her face, and she tried to get rid of Sister Gudrun at the door, claiming she knew nothing about a child called Erwin. But Sister Gudrun didn't give up, although she sensed that this woman had actually managed to forget her own child, but precisely because the nun found that so terrible and inhuman, she felt sorry for this woman. Yet she couldn't spare her this conversation. So Anita Weishaupt let the nun into the apartment, nervously closed the doors to the rooms where the other children were, and drew Sister Gudrun into the living room, where she quickly closed the door and leaned up against it, as if she wanted to brace herself against someone who might come in. Then she spoke quickly, in broken sentences, almost as if she were out of breath; she explained to the nun that her husband had come back from a prisoner-of-war camp and mustn't hear anything about the child—that would result in a catastrophe, it would ruin her life and that of the other children and of the one about to be born. Sister Gudrun nodded and explained why she had come: it had to do with the adoption of her child Erwin. At that Anita Weishaupt shook her head violently and said that she had signed the papers long ago to give Erwin up for adoption. Sister Gudrun replied that they had felt it was their duty to give the mother another chance maybe to decide to keep her child. At that Anita Weishaupt began to cry violently and sobbed, and said over and over, no, no, no. Then Sister Gudrun began to have a bad premonition, so she asked whether Anita Weishaupt had already been married when Erwin was born. At that Anita Weishaupt nodded, and Sister Gudrun suddenly sat down helplessly on a chair and said very softly but quite clearly that in that case the father, Anita's husband, had to sign the form that gave Erwin up for adoption. At that Anita Weishaupt almost stopped breathing; she looked at Sister Gudrun for a long time, than shook her head very slowly, and said that under those circumstances an adoption would never be possible for the child Erwin. Sister Gudrun sadly shrugged her shoulders, stood up, thought for a moment whether she should try again to change Anita Weishaupt's mind, but quickly decided that it would be pointless. Then she left, full of dull pain, and when she was out on the street she wept bitterly.

Now the Webers didn't visit Erwin anymore, and Erwin was also not allowed to go to their house as in the previous weeks. At first he didn't think anything and waited; then he realized all by himself that he was waiting in vain, but although he tried, he didn't succeed in forgetting the Webers. He had felt something with them that didn't want to leave his body. Then he began to think, but no matter how hard he tried to reconstruct every second he had spent with the Webers, hoping to figure out what mistake he might have made, he couldn't manage to achieve clarity in his mind. Then he became feverish. The doctor came and couldn't explain this kind of fever. So the fever mounted, went up so high that for days the boy was in danger. But the doctors still couldn't explain this phenomenon, and one day they gave the boy up for lost. Then Sister Gudrun came and sat by the feverish child's bedside, and although she didn't know whether Erwin could hear her or not, she told him the whole story of his mother and why the Webers wouldn't come anymore, and Sister Gudrun tried, although it was very hard for her, to be fair to Erwin's mother. The boy didn't show any reaction to the story, but from then on the fever went down as if miraculously, and Erwin became completely well again.

No one who met him could tell that somewhere inside his skull the fever hadn't stopped burning. Nevertheless, the boy had changed visibly. He became a bad pupil, sometimes intentionally mixed up the system he had constructed with the nuns so badly that none of the people who dealt with him had the feeling they had earlier had that he was a good child. Erwin seemed unpredictable, and the nuns didn't like unpredictable children. They were actually afraid of unpredictable children. In addition, Erwin began to steal one day; but he always stole things he could have had easily, so that no one in his world wanted to have anything more to do with him, except Sister Gudrun, who was the only person with whom Erwin developed something like a trusting relationship. A trusting relationship that among many other things enabled the nun to find out something very important, namely that Erwin had no memory, at least consciously, of what she had told him about his mother and the things connected with her. Yet Erwin never mentioned the Webers again and also didn't ask any questions.

In school Erwin never recovered the interest and attentiveness that had made him a good pupil earlier. On the contrary, Erwin seemed to resist almost obstinately every new experience, so that here, too, situations arose where Sister Gudrun just barely managed, with great persistence and against the wishes of all the other nuns, to prevent Erwin's being sent to a special school. For her sake, it seemed, Erwin put out just enough effort in school so that he finished primary school by the skin of his teeth.

But then, when he and the others his age were asked what they wanted to be when they grew up, for each one was to be found an apprenticeship, Sister Gudrun was ill. So the only person to whom young Erwin was important enough for her to intervene on his behalf and beyond the call of duty wasn't there. But her special intervention would have been necessary in order to fulfill Erwin's desire to become a goldsmith, for in contrast to the bakers', masons', or gardeners' apprenticeships that were offered, you had to search for an apprenticeship with a goldsmith, indeed sometimes had to persuade a goldsmith to take on an apprentice when he had no intention of doing so. Of course nothing of the sort happened; on the contrary, the nuns packed Erwin off to a butcher—it almost looked as though they had reasons for something like revenge against the boy—and told him this apprenticeship was the only one they had been able to find for him, given the grades with which he'd finished school.

Since Erwin on the one hand didn't know enough about life and on the other hand hadn't learned how to fight, he accepted the decision without protest and soon afterward began his apprenticeship with a master butcher named Wünsch. Butcher Wünsch had been getting his apprentices from the orphanage for years, and they had lived for years in a little room above the store. Master Wünsch had had good experiences with the apprentices from the orphanage. In contrast to boys who came from a family, the boys from the orphanage were so grateful for a little kindness that they were willing to work much longer hours far more often than they would have had to, were much easier to handle, since they hadn't learned much about defending themselves, and in addition were usually loyal and often stayed on at the butcher shop as excellent workers for a long time after they completed the apprenticeship.

Master Wünsch was not an especially kind employer, but he wasn't especially harsh or mean, either. Besides, he wasn't especially interested in teaching his apprentices a lot; he was more interested in them as manpower. But that was an attitude that suited Erwin's needs and made his apprenticeship easier, because he hadn't wanted to learn this trade in the first place.

The room over the shop where he lived was small and usually cold, too, but it was the first time Erwin had lived alone in a room of his own. So for a long time this room seemed like paradise to him. The period of his apprenticeship passed uneventfully on the whole. The days came and went for Erwin. The only thing that occasionally made him suffer was the moodiness of his boss's wife, who was usually extremely friendly, almost too friendly, and then suddenly, without reason, would turn nasty and insulting. But in the long run Erwin learned to deal with that, too.

The Wünschs had a daughter who was Erwin's age. Her name was Irene, and she went to the university-preparatory school. When Erwin began his apprenticeship, Irene was quite pert toward him and tried to play tricks on him, while Erwin had a dream one time in which he loved this girl very much, and when he woke up after this night and this dream, he still believed in this love. Over the years he kept trying to show this girl signs of his affection, tried to give her little presents, presents in which Erwin often invested almost all he had. Nevertheless it took a good three years before Irene managed to overcome the particular behavior she had adopted toward Erwin, a mixture of silliness and arrogance, and to see in her father's apprentice not only the apprentice but also, if not a human being, at least a man. Now Irene sometimes went out with Erwin, sometimes to a restaurant, now and then to a dance. They realized that they had a hard time talking to each other, finding a common language, and perhaps it was that very thing that made the relationship between the two larger and more important than is actually possible.

In 1960, and that must have been a coincidence, both of them took their major exams at the same time. Irene took the university-entrance examination, and Erwin the journeyman's test. They both passed, and celebrated accordingly.

For her excellent performance on the exam Irene wanted just one present from her parents: she wanted an apartment of her own. But this wish was not fulfilled. Primarily it was her father who wanted to keep his daughter at home. Maybe he loved her, maybe he trusted only his own methods of upbringing. Irene was hurt by her father's attitude.

At first she viewed the matter in a dangerous, fatalistic way. Then Erwin borrowed a motorcycle and took Irene for a ride through godforsaken parts of Frankfurt. This ride on the motorcycle must have made a great impression on Irene. During the ride she must have felt something that might be a mixture of an actual sense of freedom and the idea that it's possible to feel free, even to be free to a certain extent, and nevertheless to have a partner who, without really owning anything, could give one a feeling of security, a sort of security completely free of obligations.

On one of the following days, when Irene had just had another huge and apparently definitive blowup with her father, the two young people slept with each other. From that very first time Irene became pregnant, and when a doctor confirmed her condition, she didn't for a moment think of getting an abortion, but she also didn't think of telling her parents while she was in such an early stage of her pregnancy.

Erwin, who in the three years during which he had loved Irene from afar, had developed a relationship with his own body, realized that this body was capable of filling him with lust and of satisfying this lust pleasurably. During this period he masturbated a lot, without any sense of shame. Only the strange thoughts he had while doing it worried him sometimes. They were thoughts over which he had no control, thoughts and images that came and went without his being able to influence them. So the notion formed in his mind at some point that as long as he still saw odd images while he satisfied his lust and had thoughts that seemed to think themselves, this lust and its satisfaction could never be the ultimate. Then the idea of experiencing this pleasure with Irene became more and more urgent, and finally overwhelming.

Irene for her part knew there was something like lust and satisfaction, but it was all theory for her, mixed with fear that her imaginings might become reality some day. But then, when she was through with school and the freedom she so longed for was forbidden by her parents, she forced herself to put an end to her fear of real lust and its satisfaction. That's how she came to sleep with Erwin, became pregnant by him, and never wanted to get rid of the child.

Then, when enough time had passed and a termination was no longer possible, she boasted to her parents of the child she was carrying and decided, without having thought about it before, that she would marry Erwin now. Her parents reacted with anger and shock, but the more they tried to sabotage the relationship, the more firmly Irene clung to her decision. So it happened that the two of them really got married one day; they were eighteen and wanted to run their own lives from now on.

Now, when there was nothing more to be done, her parents came to terms with it all and helped them get a little apartment and furnish it so that they could feel comfortable there, since these little details were so crucial and important to Irene in helping her bear what she had made up her mind to do, for she knew one thing very clearly: she liked this boy called Erwin, but she didn't love him. One day, much later, when it was too late already—she had simply not had the courage earlier.

Irene gave birth to her daughter, who was to be called Marie-Ann. The two of them had decided on that beforehand, and during the days while Irene was still in the hospital after the delivery, something absolutely decisive happened to Erwin. It all began quite harmlessly. Erwin ran into a former classmate, who invited him to come for a beer at his regular bar. Erwin wasn't much in the mood, but finally he went along anyway.

As they entered the bar, the world suddenly seemed to come to a stop for Erwin, for fractions of a second or for eternities; something happened to him, came over him so suddenly and terribly, that he almost forgot to breathe. Objectively, of course, nothing really happened. Two young men came into a bar that was half-full; the people were rather remarkable, true, but then again not so remarkable that they could have noticed something in Erwin for which he wouldn't have found any words, if he'd been asked. It was nothing, except that among the patrons in the bar was one whose name was Anton Seitz. He was sitting there and looking at the door when Erwin came in with his friend. Their eyes met, and Erwin was sure of one thing: this person into whose eyes he was looking would assume a crucial place in his life. This Anton Seitz waved the two of them over to his table and said hello to Erwin's friend, who in turn introduced the two of them. So they sat there at a table, and nothing happened. Then at some point the conversation came around, as it usually does, to what each of them did, and when Erwin said he was a butcher and worked in a butcher shop, this Anton Seitz seemed to take a more intense interest in Erwin for a few seconds, but that could have been no more than a mistaken assumption on Erwin's part.

Quite suddenly Anton got up, said he was in a hurry, shook Erwin's hand, and said quickly that they could meet the next day in some other bar, maybe around six in the evening if Erwin had the time and felt like talking with him some more.

After Anton left, the whole place suddenly seemed so dreary and empty to Erwin, and soon he went home. But Erwin quickly realized that, no matter how hard he tried, he couldn't get this Anton Seitz out of his mind. Finally he even admitted to himself that as far as he could remember he had never in his life longed for anything as much as the next day and six o'clock on that day.

In the morning Erwin went to the store as usual, did the necessary grocery shopping, and then worked in the slaughterhouse. Long ago Erwin had developed a great ability to separate himself from that person working with the meat and to be happy somewhere else, he wasn't exactly sure where, occupied with other things entirely. On this day, too, the part of him that he felt was his real self drifted far away, while his body was busy cutting steaks off a carcass of beef. But today something happened that had never happened before: apparently he had gone too far away, so far that he didn't have his body under control, and consequently he cut deeply into his finger with the very sharp knife he was working with. The sudden pain brought him back to himself, and he saw that the finger was just dangling by a flap of skin on one side and bleeding as he had never seen anyone bleed before. Erwin just barely managed to concentrate enough so he didn't keel over. Then he silently showed his wound to the butcher's wife, who first turned away in disgust, but then went to the telephone right away and called an ambulance. At the hospital they said it was touch and go whether the finger could be saved or would have to be amputated. But Erwin was lucky; his finger was sewn back on and could be saved.

On the stroke of six, his hand heavily bandaged, Erwin was sitting in the bar that Anton had mentioned, waiting. Something, and this something seemed to be happiness, made his throat tighten up. Every second he looked at the clock. He kept his eyes on the door, got more and more nervous as 6:15 came, then 6:30. Suddenly something over-whelmed him, a great inner void. This void tormented him, and it tormented him all the more because he simply didn't understand what was happening to him, no matter how he tried to figure it out. Then suddenly the door opened, and Anton came in. When Erwin saw him, a strange trembling passed through his entire body, something he had never felt before. Gone was the void, replaced by a feeling that Erwin didn't know was happiness. Anton came over to Erwin's table, Erwin stood up and shook his hand, turning beet-red like a young girl, but he didn't notice. Nor did he notice that he was stammering now; he didn't notice anything, any details; he knew only that he was there and that he wasn't only glad to be there, that for the first time in his life, at least consciously, the question as to why he was there at all and had to live on this earth no longer presented itself. It was enough for him to be there, and this being there suddenly didn't seem to need any meaning above and beyond his existence. Anton sat down and talked about meat. Anton talked a lot, probably developed some theories or other, but Erwin wasn't really listening to him. He just realized that suddenly he was making promises to do things that were at the very least illegal, and could perhaps also be dangerous. But first of all, he couldn't have refused this person anything, and second, the possible consequences were clear to him, but all that was strangely uninterest-ing to him.

So for almost two years Erwin was involved in illegal deals with Anton, knowing how dangerous they were but not feeling at all afraid.

During this time he carried on his marriage with Irene, with their daughter Marie-Ann, as well as he could, but he hardly had time for his family; most of the time he was off with Anton for some reason, and most of the time he didn't even know why. And one day when Anton asked him why he was always looking at him like that, Erwin replied without a moment's hesitation that he did that because he loved him. Anton nodded in a friendly way, shrugged his shoulders, and said only that if Erwin were a girl he would probably love him, too. And these very sentences, matter-of-fact as they were, passed be-tween the two several more times, but that was all. Anton often felt like talking about himself, about his previous life. Erwin often had the impression that it wasn't Anton talking but that something was talking through Anton. They were always the same stories. Anton had spent almost all of his childhood in a concentration camp, and it was pure chance that he had survived, at least it was chance in one of Anton's versions. There was another version in which Anton owed his survival to his own skill, and in other versions there were other reasons, and somehow, in spite of the large discrepancies, everything seemed to be at least a little true. At any rate Anton had survived, and had come out into freedom with only one wish in his head, to go to America, and on the way to America he got hung up in Frankfurt and there succeeded in a relatively short time in acquiring a respectable name in the so-called underworld. Besides, he realized one day that there was probably no difference between the city of Frankfurt and America, and Anton had learned another important thing in the years of freedom, and he kept coming back to it: he had learned that there was no great difference between life outside and what he had lived and seen in the concentration camp. Of course people outside were not so obviously imprisoned, but ultimately they were all imprisoned, and all of them outside were afraid, and this fear was no smaller than the fear he had come to know in the camp, just somewhat different. Sometimes it happened that Anton got into arguments when he presented such theories. But miraculously he never really got into a fight. He probably had something like a seventh sense.

One day Erwin was arrested. By some stupid chance someone had become aware that Erwin was involved in racketeering with meat. Erwin never betrayed his partner Anton. He took the rap for the whole thing, with the police, the examining magistrate, and in court. Since Erwin had no police record, and besides had a wife and child, he got away with twelve months in jail and no probation. Erwin experienced these twelve months that he spent behind bars as nothing more than a gift to Anton, and strangely enough, Irene didn't abandon him when the whole thing came out in the open; on the contrary, she visited him in prison as often as it was permitted, and now it was as though Irene were beginning really to love him. Erwin for his part liked Irene as much as before; whatever might happen, Irene had a part in his life, and because Erwin almost never saw people with whom he could have talked, he told Irene one day about his relationship with Anton. He didn't make a secret of the fact that he thought he loved Anton. Just at first Irene was as if paralyzed, but soon afterward she gave Erwin to understand that he could talk to her about it and that this story basically didn't change anything for her.

Anton never came to visit him, and Erwin could understand that. But one thing made him sad, and that was that he never got a letter from Anton, a letter he waited for with new hope each day for twelve months. And yet immediately after his release Erwin combed through all the bars he had been to with Anton. He looked for him, but he couldn't find him; someone told him Anton had opened a brothel and was really a big man in the business. Erwin found Anton very quickly in this brothel, and Anton was really glad to see him again, even thanked him for leaving him out of the other business, reached into his pocket, and handed Erwin a bunch of banknotes. Erwin, who for twelve months had been waiting for this moment when they would see each other again, just stood there stiffly and looked at Anton, looked and looked, until Anton felt uncomfortable, as he had several times in the past, and he asked him the reason again, and Erwin said again that he loved him, and Anton said again that if Erwin were a girl, then ... and quickly changed the subject, explaining to Erwin that in his brothel he had introduced approximately the same organizational principles, the same structure of command and obedience, duty and fear that he had once experienced in the concentration camp, and how well the whole thing worked. At that Anton clapped his hands, happy as a little child, and was apparently very contented.

Erwin left the brothel as if numbed, and then he did something very strange, something he had never given any thought to before. He hailed a taxi, had himself driven to the airport, booked the next flight to Casablanca, and there, without a trace of hesitation, had himself transformed into a woman in a comprehensive operation. He had to stay in Casablanca for about three weeks, until all the follow-up operations were done, and then he went into town from the hospital, bought himself women's clothes and a wig and flew back to Frankfurt.

At his departure from Morocco, as upon his arrival in Frankfurt, there were the usual difficulties, but finally the one country let him leave and the other let him enter.

Erwin again hailed a taxi, because he wanted to be with Anton as quickly as possible. Again he met him at his brothel, where Anton didn't recognize him right away, and probably thought he was dealing with an applicant for one of his rooms. But Erwin shook his head and said that wasn't the case at all, that he was Erwin and had now taken the name Elvira, and when Anton was puzzled and couldn't figure out what was going on, Erwin-Elvira reminded him that whenever Erwin had said he loved him, Anton had said if only he were a girl, and now he was a girl. Anton quickly got a grip on himself, looked Erwin-Elvira over from all sides, at last nodded like an connoisseur, as if he'd been evaluating a particularly fine piece of work, a chest or a table, if you will.

At that Elvira became insistent. The time for fooling around was over for her; all this was a big, serious matter in which she placed great hope. But Anton just shook his head and then laughed, laughed until he cried, but Elvira didn't like this laughter, so there was nothing for him to do but to explain very clearly that of course he hadn't meant it that way, and now from one minute to the next Elvira knew what was what. It became absolutely clear to her that this love could never be consummated, and at the same time she became aware of the terrible implications of what this operation now meant for her. She just nodded very quietly at Anton, shrugged her shoulders as though it were nothing, and went away. In a drugstore she bought sleeping pills, and then she took a room in a hotel. There she swallowed the sleeping pills, but the hotel owner had thought from the first that this guest was very strange, and he knocked on the door, but couldn't hear anything, and the door was locked. Then he ran down to the desk, looked at the registration form, and there Elvira had written in the address she shared with Irene. The hotel owner called Irene. Irene couldn't think what woman might be staying in a hotel under her address, but she came into town anyway, as fast as she could. Now that Irene was there, the hotel owner broke open the door with his shoulder, and they found Elvira in bed, already in a coma. The hotel owner called for an ambulance immediately, while Irene began to see more and more clearly what had happened here, and strange to say, it made her love Erwin, or the woman lying there, more than she had ever been able to before. The hotel owner dashed back into the room, pushed Irene aside, picked up Elvira and slapped her hard, again and again, in the face. But that didn't help either; Elvira remained unconscious. Fortunately it didn't take long for the ambulance to arrive and take Elvira to the hospital. Going by her passport, they took her to a men's ward, and they succeeded in saving her life.

When Elvira woke up on the men's ward, some of the other patients were amazed by her, while others were very nasty to her. Then Elvira lay back in the pillows, and at last very small, delicate tears ran over her face, and when the doctor came with Irene, and Irene stroked Elvira's hair, Elvira just asked why they hadn't let her die. Then Irene sat down on her bed, put her arms around her, kissed her, cried with her, and said stupid things like life was beautiful, and you could never know what might come next. But even as she spoke she realized that those were just general sentiments that were occurring to her, and she told herself she should make an effort to have a sensible talk with

Elvira some time about life, to the extent it's even possible to talk sensibly about life.

After Elvira was released from the hospital, she rented a studio apartment in the inner city and worked as a barmaid at a bar on Kaiserstrasse. Elvira took a long time before she accepted being a woman, and even longer before she came to terms with it, for she hadn't become a woman because she particularly wanted to be a woman. A long time passed during which Elvira had the uncomfortable feeling that she was doing something homosexual whenever she had any contact with a man, and it didn't have to be sexual; Elvira wasn't homosexual in the usual sense. Even her love for Anton had never reached a stage where Elvira really pictured physical union with Anton.

During the first three years after the operation Elvira worked as a barmaid or a hostess. In this period she had no sexual contact whatsoever. On the contrary, she tried to forget that she had any such thing as sexuality. But Elvira did do one thing, though hardly anyone who knew her would have guessed it: within the various bars where she worked she pursued a clearly traceable downward path, which ran absolutely parallel to the unmistakable ascent of Anton Seitz, who in the meantime had earned so much money with his brothel that he began to buy up houses, and speculate on houses. The real estate market was hot in Frankfurt. You could get rich and richer by buying up old houses cheap, driving out the tenants with the strangest tricks if they didn't move out on their own, and when they were all out tearing the buildings down and then either making big money on the land or building yourself. Anton Seitz was soon a big man in this business, and he got bigger and bigger, and when he had reached something like the pinnacle of his career as a real estate agent, Elvira decided that she wouldn't work in a bar anymore but would go out on the streets. After just a short time Elvira was one of the best known and best liked prostitutes in Frankfurt, the city of fairs and conventions. By this time Elvira had also come to terms with her role as a woman. She even managed to enjoy men as a woman and find pleasure with them.

During all these years Elvira hadn't broken off her relationship with Irene, which was terribly important to her. Irene had in the meantime become a tenured schoolteacher, and she never stopped trying to give Elvira pleasure in many ways. Even if most of Irene's attempts failed, she did succeed in interesting Elvira in one thing or another, for Irene knew that only living and having new experiences offered Elvira a chance not to be destroyed by herself.

One day, when Elvira had just reached something like the pinnacle of her career as a prostitute, she met Christoph Hacker, out of work and full of self-doubt, with whom she fell in love, at least in a certain respect. Christoph Hacker was an actor, had had engagements for quite a few years at theaters in the provinces, and had been forced one day to recognize that the path he was on was a downward path, for in contrast to the usual one, where an actor moves with each engagement to a larger, more important city, the cities from which Christoph Hacker received offers were getting smaller and smaller, so that one day he couldn't help admitting to himself that he was probably not the great talent he had once taken himself for. This recognition is of course terribly painful, besides which one loses all the hopes for the future that previously kept one alive. So when Christoph Hacker met Elvira, he was in a borderline situation in his existence, in a situation that hardly let him come up with reasons for staying in this world. But when Christoph Hacker met Elvira, he met a person who from the first moment on fascinated him so much that even the simple existence of this person was enough of a reason for Christoph Hacker to see some meaning in life. Since the very fact of entering into such a relationship meant a risk to Elvira, she wanted to begin her life with Christoph Hacker with a clean slate.

So she told him everything that she thought constituted her life, left nothing out; perhaps she wanted her narrative to give Christoph Hacker a chance not to get involved with her. But nothing could get Christoph Hacker to give up Elvira. And so they looked for an apartment, fixed it up completely to their liking and according to their needs. Elvira kept her old studio apartment, which she would still be needing for her work.

In the first part of their time together, Christoph Hacker occupied himself mainly with fixing up the new apartment, and when this work was finished, he hung around for a few months, until one day he made the decision to try working once more. Christoph felt out the market in all directions, and then decided to work as a salesman, but not as a salesman for vacuum cleaners or magazine subscriptions, but rather as one who sold some kind of stocks. These were stocks whose value usually didn't last much longer than a year, but new ideas can be developed all the time for selling these stock-like papers. There are still enough people who go all dumb and empty-headed at the thought of a 240 percent return on their investment, for instance.

Elvira helped Christoph in every respect as he was building up this business. She did it by giving him strength, and she did it by giving him what is most important in this business, the means for making a good showing. Elvira and Christoph Hacker lived together for about three years, until Christoph Hacker was so well established that he was earning enough for both of them, and Elvira had plenty in the bank. That made it possible for her to leave the streets from one day to the next. In the first period she found enough to keep her busy, and she thought the fact that Christoph wasn't there from Monday to Friday was more good for their relationship than otherwise; and yet sometimes during those years it happened that Elvira stood there in her spotless apartment, didn't want to go to any of the bars where she had been earlier, but also found that cultural things such as listening to music, reading books, watching movies, or whatever didn't give her life enough of what's called "content." She had tried out many things; she bought herself a camera, with which she took pictures, but she soon gave that up. At some point she bought herself a video camera and wanted to make her own films, but that, too, was too lonely for her. A couple of times she accompanied Christoph on his trips, but then she just sat around in hotel rooms, so she gave that up, too. So it was fairly logical that Elvira took up drinking, became more and more immoderate, sometimes took pills along with the alcohol that intensi-fied its effect, and in between had spells of a kind of ravenous hunger that was more greed than hunger, and now that she was completely out of control most of the time, Elvira got fatter and fatter, so that one can almost say she was coming apart at the seams. As might have been expected, the more Elvira deviated from the image Christoph Hacker had of her, the less desire he had to come home, so that he sometimes stayed away for as much as three to six weeks. In her clearer moments Elvira realized that her chances as a woman were zero if she didn't fit the image people had of her.

As a result, the thought automatically began to form in the back of her mind that she would rather be a man again. This notion grew and grew in her head, until finally it dominated all her thinking. Occasion-ally, when Christoph Hacker wasn't home, she tried to find men to spend at least a night with her, but she had less and less luck, and since she somehow found it humiliating as a woman to pay a man, it often happened that she went out in man's clothes and found male prosti-tutes, so she could enjoy the illusion of tenderness for at least a few minutes.

3. A Film

Dressed as a man, Elvira Weishaupt has bought herself a male prosti-tute. By chance the boy notices that Elvira isn't a man. He's so ashamed in front of the woman that he can't think of anything to do but beat her up. Elvira's clothes get ripped, her long hair comes out from under her cap, and there she is, after being beaten, torn apart and destroyed from head to toe, a terrible mirage, a mixture of man and woman, stumbling along Kaiserstrasse on her way home. When two drunks make fun of her, she manages to muster so much pride and disdain that they fall silent and slink away.

It's early in the morning, and the sun is coming up. Elvira Weishaupt enters her apartment, where surprisingly Christoph Hacker, the man with whom Elvira Weishaupt lives, has come home, apparently only half an hour before. Elvira hadn't expected to see Christoph this night, and now she suddenly stands before him in her dreadful getup and her ruined appearance. An ugly quarrel ensues, in which both of them give vent to their apparently long bottled-up pain. Then Christoph Hacker suddenly grabs his suitcases and wants to leave. Elvira throws herself onto the suitcases, doesn't want to let him go, begs and pleads, but he doesn't give in. She follows him to the stairs, but he's too fast for her. When she reaches the bottom of the stairs and runs outside the building, he's already in his car. Elvira tries to get in front of the car so he can't drive away. She's still weeping and pleading, but Christoph simply drives off. Elvira throws herself to one side, into the gutter, just in time.

Then Red Zora, a prostitute with whom Elvira is friends, comes running over from the other side of the street. She picks Elvira up, cries with her, and drags her along to a snackbar at the corner. There they have a beer, and while Elvira weeps, tells what happened, and becomes very angry, she demolishes an incredible number of grilled sausages. Then she leaves in a hurry, because she thinks Christoph Hacker will be home again; apparently there have been such scenes before, and every time Christoph Hacker has come back. Full of hope and longing, Elvira comes into her apartment, quite sure of finding Christoph there, but the apartment is empty. Then Elvira goes through the apartment, which suddenly seems completely unfamiliar to her, and where she suddenly doesn't seem to know her way around. Then she sits down, takes a book, and reads. The book is a sci-fi novel called *World on Wires*. Elvira falls asleep reading, tears running down her cheeks. The next morning Elvira is awakened by someone ringing the doorbell over and over again. She quickly pulls on a bathrobe and opens the door. Outside stands Irene Weishaupt, who is still married to Elvira, who was once called Erwin. Irene has a magazine in her hand and is scolding Elvira. Apparently Elvira gave an interview to someone, in which she talked about her relationship with a person who has become one of the richest and most powerful men in Frankfurt. Irene is clearly frightened for Elvira; the man will want to crush her, destroy her, eliminate her, Irene says, and Elvira counters with the idea she has gotten out of *World on Wires,* which seems very reasonable and convincing to her, that the world in which she finds herself is only a rough model for a higher world, a model where apparently genuine living beings are used to try out various reactions. Under the circumstances no conversation is possible between the two, and Irene stomps out of the apartment.

Later Elvira meets Red Zora in a bar. Elvira has spruced herself up a bit, but it's still unmistakable that she's in deep despair. Elvira tries to explain the idea from *World on Wires* to Red Zora, too. All of this seems so confused to Red Zora that she says she'll take Elvira along to her psychotherapist; maybe he can get Elvira out of this state. Elvira agrees; it doesn't matter to her who she talks to. At the moment she just has to talk to someone. At the psychoanalyst's it turns out that Elvira wouldn't have a chance to be psychoanalyzed anyway, because as an orphan she wouldn't be taken on by any psychoanalyst.

Elvira and Red Zora leave the psychoanalyst's not knowing what to do. But then Elvira suddenly has a desire to go to the orphanage where she was raised, and maybe to talk with the nun to whom she was close. At the orphanage she asks for Sister Gudrun. Sister Gudrun comes and at first has trouble recognizing in Elvira little Erwin, with whom she once dealt. But then the two of them go into the garden, and Sister Gudrun tells Elvira about her childhood, and after Sister Gudrun has revealed the whole, awful truth, Elvira breaks down. It's almost as if she were having an epileptic seizure. Sister Gudrun and Red Zora try to calm Elvira, and call a taxi for her. Red Zora goes along, after promising the nun that she'll watch Elvira until she goes to sleep. Back at the apartment Elvira takes sleeping pills and tranquilizers, too many, actually, but Red Zora makes sure she doesn't take so many that it could be dangerous. Then she sits down by Elvira's bed and waits until she's asleep.

The next day Elvira has done herself up very nicely and is standing with a bag of French bread, cheese, and red wine in front of the office building belonging to her former friend, Anton Seitz. Then she goes into the building, almost timidly, goes up the stairs, hears voices above her, and quickly ducks into an empty office, still hears voices and footsteps, peeps around the corner, and sees Anton going down the stairs with his male secretary. Elvira doesn't have the courage to speak to him. Then she goes into the empty office, sits down in the dirt without thinking of her clothes, breaks off a hunk of bread, eats the bread with cheese, and drinks red wine along with it. During this time darkness falls. When dawn comes the next day, Elvira is still sitting there, just as on the previous evening, in the empty office. Suddenly she hears footsteps; they're coming closer, and a bum comes into the office; he has a rope with him, which he fastens to a hook. He climbs up on a box and breaks his neck as he kicks the box away. Elvira is watching him the whole time.

Somewhat later in the day she walks past the dangling corpse out into the stairwell, goes up the stairs, rings the bell at the door to Anton Seitz's office, goes inside, tries to apologize to Anton for the interview, but he just laughs. Altogether, a character like Elvira doesn't fit into these surroundings, and as a result they have nothing more to say to each other. Even so, Anton wants to go with her, and they're driven to Elvira's apartment by Anton's chauffeur. At the door to the apartment Red Zora is sitting, crying, with a black eye that someone gave her. Elvira tries to comfort her, and goes to get a gauze pad with boric acid to put on the eye, but when she comes back into the room, she sees Anton and Red Zora lying on the floor in a tight embrace, making love. Then Elvira dashes into her bathroom, strips off her clothes, goes to the closet, pulls out a man's suit and puts it on, grabs a scissors and chops off her hair, hastily washes off her make-up, and runs out of the house. In this suit and with her unevenly cropped hair she arrives at Irene's house in a small suburban development outside Frankfurt. Irene is sitting there in the garden with Marie-Ann, their daughter. Both of them laugh at Elvira at first, but then they quickly notice that there isn't much to laugh about. But when Elvira says that she wants to live with Irene, Irene can only say no. She loves Elvira, she loves her very much, but she can't live with her anymore. Elvira does understand that, but at the moment she can't bear it. Suddenly she runs off and doesn't let the two women hold her back.

Then Elvira wanders aimlessly through the night, and then suddenly goes into a building. There she rings the bell of the poet Burkhard Hauer, who opens the door and laughs at her. Elvira says she wants to talk to him; she had such a good talk with him when he did the interview with her, but the poet refuses and closes the door. Elvira no longer understands the world.

The next day the poet finds Elvira in his cellar. She's already dead.

1978

■ Answers to Questions from Schoolchildren

Editor's note: In 1979/80 a German school class sent out the following questionnaire. The first twenty-six questions were asked of all the respondents; the last six questions, the so-called Personal Questionnaire, were formulated individually for each participant in the survey.

■ *Do you find it difficult not to feel like an outsider in a group of people you don't know?*

Depends on the group. In most of them, yes.

■ *Do you consider it likely that there could be an evolutionary regression that would take us back to a very primitive stage of existence?*

No.

■ *Do you believe in the existence of extraterrestrial beings?*

Yes.

■ *How do you picture your old age?*

I don't expect to experience it.

■ *What do you think of Christmas without a Christmas tree?*

People who have been brought up so hypocritically that they need such symbols should just be left alone until we have a society where such things aren't necessary anymore.

■ *How do you react to negative criticism?*

Positively.

■ *What party game do you like best?*

The Truth Game.

■ *What do you think about the hostility toward children in the Federal Republic?*

There is a larger problem, that of people who have been showered with too much fake love, and thereby help to preserve society in its present form.

■ *Do you see the mentally ill as a burden to our society?*

In our society there's no one who isn't mentally ill.

■ *Do you think that suicide can be justified on principle?*
Yes.
■ *Do you find it difficult to show your feelings uninhibitedly to someone close to you?*
No.
■ *Under what conditions would you be prepared to make a great sacrifice?*
For love.
■ *In time of personal crisis would you consult a psychiatrist or a psychologist?*
Certainly.
■ *What degree have you earned?*
None.
■ *Would you be willing to adopt a handicapped child?*
No.
■ *Do you think other people like you?*
I make it so hard for other people to like me that only a few are left.
■ *Do you look forward to the future, or do you approach it with pessimism?*
That's not an issue for me.
■ *Who is your hero, and why?*
Heinrich von Kleist, because he succeeded in finding someone who wanted to die with him.
■ *Were you brought up in an authoritarian way? If so, do you regret it?*
No.
■ *When and why were you last embarrassed?*
I'm always embarrassed when a person in uniform looks at me.
■ *What does your self-confidence rest on?*
On my skill.
■ *What do you consider most important in a relationship between partners?*
Constantly reexamining the values on which the partnership is based.
■ *Do you see nuclear energy plants as a threat?*
No.
■ *Do you allow yourself to be influenced by other people's moods?*
Depends on the moods.
■ *What do you think is needed for a perfect Sunday morning?*
Caviar, champagne, the Eighth Symphony of Mahler, "radio activity" by Kraftwerk, the Sunday *Bild* paper, a book so exciting you

don't want it to end, a friend, a good friend, and the possibility of unplugging the phone.

■ *In your experience, what trait or what kind of behavior has turned out to be particularly helpful in establishing contact with others?*

I can't answer that like a normal person; for me it's my so-called prominence.

■ *Are your television plays based on true happenings?*

There aren't any true happenings. The true is the artificial.

■ *Do you allow yourself to be influenced by others in your choice of a topic, or do you pick everything for yourself?*

From the moment you make up your mind not to live on a desert island you no longer pick everything for yourself.

■ *What party do you vote for in the Bundestag elections?*

I don't vote anymore.

■ *Do you believe in the things you show in your films?*

Yes.

■ *Do you like to play sports, and if yes, which ones?*

Table tennis, swimming, faire l'amour.

■ *How do you visualize your professional and private future?*

There isn't any past, there isn't any present, so there isn't any future, either.

Hanna Schygulla—Not a Star, Just a Vulnerable Human Being Like the Rest of Us
Disorderly Thoughts about an Interesting Woman

What I really want to talk about is the very beginning—about getting to know Hanna Schygulla, about myself, about the first work we did together and the way things were then.

Most of what I'll have to say, with obvious minor differences, is essentially applicable to our present relationship and collaboration—provided we keep in mind the more or less successful attempts of an officious world to turn us into easily manipulated ciphers or marketable goods.

We first met at one of those drama schools of which Munich has too many, most of them existing only to cater to the superhuman ambitions of countless stagestruck boys and girls—and in the process exploit them for their money.

My reasons for attending this school, and Hanna Schygulla's as well, differed considerably from those of our fellow students.

The stage, the theater, the desire to become actors at any cost were not our reasons. Nor were we there for the acting classes (expensive, by the way, clearly beyond the means of most young people), which consisted of instruction in diction and proper breathing, role study, and a weekly "étude" evening on Wednesdays, when all the students would get together to attempt something best described as improvisation on an assigned theme. These Wednesday evenings were demonstrations of the greatest desperation on the one hand and the most brutal sadism on the other.

Rarely since have I seen human beings behave so ruthlessly, so scornfully and contemptuously toward other human beings. The mere fact that the teachers failed to teach their students anything so elementary as respect for the dignity of others (assuming that sheer indifference had not long since stifled any genuine feeling for them)—that fact alone would have made it easy to recognize that they were not qualified to serve as the role models these young people needed. 199

Anyone should have been able to see that, to draw the obvious conclusion and react accordingly. But that, clearly, everyone was afraid to do.

Well, my reason for staying at this school in spite of all this is easily explained. Ever since I'd begun to think about my own future, I'd wanted to make films.

There were no proper film schools in those days, and a brief trial made it clear that I was completely unfit to work as a director's assistant, since almost every camera position, camera movement, or directorial decision struck me as both ridiculous and wrong. I soon abandoned any attempt at interfering, at contesting this or that decision, after my first timid sallies were shouted down as irritating interruptions of the work in progress. So I did some sound, learned to work at the cutting table, and helped out with props and sets—but as far as I was concerned, my real training in filmmaking consisted in viewing three or four movies every day without fail.

One day I heard a rumor that in two or three years a film school would be opening in Berlin. But it was said that to be considered for admission you would need a real degree of one kind or another.

Lacking any better inspiration, I applied to a drama school and was accepted, probably because I could come up with the tuition, which, as I mentioned, was not inexpensive.

Hanna Schygulla, on the other hand, was at the university studying German literature and, if I remember this correctly, English and French as well. She was probably planning on becoming a teacher. Somewhere along the line, however, she began to get bored. Her life seemed to her lacking in mystery, too predictable, too confined, too plodding.

Secretly—her parents were violently opposed—Hanna Schygulla began to take acting lessons on the side, to find out more about herself and her real needs. So she enrolled in the drama school, much the same way a person would go to a psychoanalyst. Naturally it didn't take long for Schygulla to see through the swindle and, sadly disappointed, turn her back on the school. The entire experience lasted no more than a year.

Hanna Schygulla and I were soon recognized as rather unruly interlopers, that is to say, outspokenly critical. But oddly enough, we were also considered the two most interesting and gifted people at the school—difficult people, to be sure, but endowed with the most promising, though perhaps abnormal, indeed rather alarming, talent.

That may seem strange, but in retrospect it's a matter of simple logic. It was only natural that the very students whose aims had abso-

lutely nothing to do with stage-acting should be secretly more interested—and consequently more interesting—students. This was because they, Hanna Schygulla and I, were free to focus their full and
uninhibited attention on the behavior patterns of both classmates and
teachers. We felt no obligation to submit to the supervision accepted
by the other students, who had evidently lost all willpower and, in
their basically pathological yearning for the stage, had become both
blind and deaf.

After the Wednesday evening études, the students usually went out
to a cheap bar for two or three glasses of wine. The chief topics of
conversation tended to be their hopes for a contract, their ideas about
and desperate longing for a career in the theater, but also their various
anxieties and the attendant fantasies and paralyzing fears—which not
infrequently gave rise to thoughts of suicide.

Hanna Schygulla and I hardly spoke at these gatherings; mostly we
observed those doing the talking and, I think, were probably both
trying to analyze what was said. Only rarely did we say anything on
those evenings. She would talk about literature and life, I about movies
and life. But hardly anyone was interested in Schygulla's thoughts
or mine.

On one of those evenings it suddenly became crystal clear to me,
literally from one minute to the next, as if I'd been struck by lightning,
that Hanna Schygulla would one day be the star of my films (there was
never a moment when I doubted that I would be a filmmaker)—she
would be an essential cornerstone possibly, maybe even something
like their driving force.

Schygulla certainly had no inkling of what I was thinking, not a
clue, while I was dead sure that this was how things would turn out.
Of course, I never breathed a word of this to Schygulla, not even a
hint, perhaps out of cowardice, or perhaps out of my unshakeable
conviction (crazy or arrogant as it may sound today) that sooner or
later my wishes and my needs would be fulfilled. Besides, Schygulla
and I had a kind of basic unanimity that didn't require words.

From the very beginning we hardly spoke to each other; a little
more at the start of our work in theater, but later on less and less—
actually almost not at all.

Incidentally, I'm certain that in all those years Schygulla and I
never exchanged a single sentence about personal things, and I mean
not one. So what?

A short time later Hanna Schygulla left the drama school to continue her studies at the university, but that didn't jeopardize the plans
I had for her in the slightest. By the way, in spite of my diploma from

Fassbinder and Hanna Schygulla in Love Is Colder than Death *(by permission of Fassbinder-Foundation, Munich)*

the drama school, I managed to flunk the qualifying exam for the new film academy in Berlin. Thank God a friend of mine (a former actor) financed two short films for me soon after my sad and shameful defeat in Berlin.

There was no role for Hanna Schygulla in the first of these films, but there was in the second. Over the years, however, I had somehow managed to forget her name. The drama school, where help would almost certainly have been forthcoming, had meanwhile become an absolute taboo as far as I was concerned (an accumulation of personal affronts had driven me to this extreme), and even on several visits to the university I couldn't track her down. So I made the second of my short films without Hanna Schygulla.

Shortly after that, the first wave of the "Young German Cinema" sloshed over the arts-and-leisure pages of the Federal Republic's newspapers. One film after another was released; but following a period of euphoria (the duration of which varied, depending on which paper you read), a general hangover set in. I was not the only one to be robbed of the hope that a flourishing new German film industry would spring up, an industry that had seemed to promise that I, too, might become a regular film director—that is to say, someone who makes films.

My fall was all the harder, the collapse of my illusions all the more radical. My hopes were wiped out, now that the first wave of the "Young German Cinema"—for a few years a source of support for some, of hope for others—had been exposed with almost embarrassing clarity as rigid and restrictive rather than liberating, a kind of paralysis rather than something vital, idle promises rather than actual fulfillment. It made my dream of the birth of a new German film industry plummet, it paralyzed my thinking, and it produced in me a dark mood of bleak depression that I couldn't control. This was how things stood when I had a visit from Marite Greiselis, the most pleasant and, in a positive sense, the craziest of my fellow students at the drama school, the one who had taken the role in my second short film that Schygulla was supposed to play. She invited me to come and see her as Antigone in an exciting production at a small theater in the heart of Munich, blessedly not in Schwabing, which probably motivated my promise to show up and, in fact, was the reason that I did go to see the production—because the theater was *not* in Schwabing.

Much to my astonishment, the performance I saw fascinated me extraordinarily.

Normally nothing bores me more than the usual solid, well-produced play, even if it's presented on a high artistic plane, even the highest. In this case, however, I was really excited by what was happening on the stage, by the way it was happening, and by how it was affecting the audience—I was excited quite against my will and in such a concrete way that it almost knocked the wind out of me. Something like a reciprocal trance was being generated between the actors and the audience, something like a collective longing for a revolutionary utopia.

Even before the performance was over, my mind was absolutely made up: to work here, in this theater and as a member of this group. It never crossed my mind that the group might not want me; it was a decision made in almost guileless naiveté.

When the play was over, a healthy mix of actors and members of the audience assembled at the little bar in the theater. Probably the majority of the group took a great dislike to me, but Marite Greiselis (who didn't really count because she was a friend) along with Peer Raben, the director of *Antigone,* and Ursula Strätz, the manager, concluded that beyond the shadow of a doubt I must have great artistic potential; and I was offered a lead part in their next production, *Astutuli,* by Carl Orff.

Now the animosity of one member of the group or another boiled over, but their opposition only served to make the situation more of a challenge to me, and gave me the strength to confront all possible difficulties with relative aplomb—indeed, even with good humor. Very soon, actually just two or three days later, one of the members of the *Antigone* cast broke several fingers, and Peer Raben asked me if I could get ready to take over the role the very next evening; any interruption in the run of an Action Theater production was a palpable threat to the existence of the enterprise. I accepted at once.

As it turned out, my theatrical debut the next day was so gruesome that it was really almost funny. And so things went—for better or worse.

A few days later, when the last spectators had left after the evening performance, a drama of jealousy was acted out in the theater, with consequences that were both incomprehensibly harsh and final.

In a fit of blind rage, one of the actors attacked his lover, Marite Greiselis, with a hunting knife, and his rage was so terrible, so monstrous, that it didn't even faze him when someone else brought a chair down on his head with all his might. The actor received the maximum sentence for his crime, ten years in prison. Marite Greiselis has been in a wheelchair ever since, paralyzed from the waist down.

But the show must go on. And because no one else could come up with a good replacement in the role of Antigone, I thought of Hanna Schygulla. This time I was lucky; I located her in one of the endless corridors of the university, and after what seemed like an eternity I managed, by applying all my powers of persuasion, to make her agree at least to read for Peer Raben and to decide only after that whether the role was one she could do something with, that is to say—as she emphasized over and over again—whether it would promote her own "personal development." Hanna Schygulla came to read, and since every member of the group was painfully aware that the continued existence of the theater depended on the successful casting of the central character, people tiptoed around her as if everyone's life were in her hands.

Those are the simple, unadorned facts; that's how it began, the special status of Hanna Schygulla within the group, which subsequently often caused problems.

She liked Peer Raben's reinterpretation of the classical Greek material, thank God, and three days later we were ready to reopen the theater with Hanna Schygulla as Antigone. Her performance, as everyone realized without a tinge of envy, was magnificent, of extraordinary pathos and intensity. She was so good that her presence in the cast made the entire production even more intense, more consistent, and thus more unified. On the other hand, she began very soon and with excessive vehemence (so much so that one had to think she was afraid of losing her identity) to point out repeatedly to each person in the group that she didn't consider herself a member, and that, furthermore, she hadn't the slightest intention of ever becoming a member. It was to be clearly understood, she maintained, that she was consequently not subject to the fundamental group ethos, according to which each member owed complete allegiance to the demands of the collective effort and was expected to come forward automatically to help out with any aspect of any production, unless some major obstacle, obvious to all, stood in the way. She made it clear that nothing in the world would draw her into any automatic participation.

On the contrary, she claimed a right to work with the group again only if a particular role and production concept were of sufficient interest to her.

And, needless to say, no matter how essential certain other theater activities might be—publicity, etc.—she wouldn't dream of concerning herself with such things.

Hanna Schygulla's position in all this was justified by the importance of her university studies and her decision to become a teacher, a profession she considered intrinsically more significant and potentially more revolutionary than doing plays. Accordingly, virtually all the other members of the group—no matter how impressed each of them was by her extraordinary, truly indescribable stage presence—regarded her guest performances at the Action Theater as a one-time thing, since continuing to work with someone with that kind of attitude seriously threatened any utopian ideal of a collective.

Only Peer Raben and I, without being particularly obtrusive or eager to join in the discussion (both of us were basically sympathetic to the idea of collective efforts), felt that a unified, vigorously functioning group could never be threatened by the participation of individual colleagues who took the kind of position that Hanna Schygulla maintained with such winning candor; on the contrary, we were convinced this was the only way such a group could come to recognize its true strengths and its superiority to troupes organized according to the usual hierarchical system. Only through conflict could the happiness of the individual assert and sustain itself in the liberation that resulted from collaboration with a group in which all were equals.

Years later, when all the others had long since forgotten or at least repressed the beautiful ideal of cooperative group work (and for the most diverse reasons, ranging from simple lethargy to genuine sorrow and existential disillusionment at the collapse of each new attempt at collaborative effort), it was Peer Raben and I who kept on trying, in the face of countless vicissitudes, to foster the birth of new groups, and I further venture to assert that of all the many people who once stepped forward to produce evidence that this utopia could be realized, the only ones left are Peer Raben and I, and perhaps Ingrid Caven. Nor did Hanna Schygulla, who at times seemed to have discovered a bit of latitude for such hope, have in mind the liberation of the imagination of the many, but rather the gratification of her own vanity. But please understand me correctly: that remark is not meant to be disparaging; rather, it should be understood as it's intended. In many respects Hanna Schygulla has the good fortune, I believe, to be fundamentally no crazier, no more far-out, no more splendid than most human beings, no matter who or where.

And never mind whether clinging to your old ideals, sometimes even when you know better, even when they threaten to become an obsession, is really more positive than accepting, perhaps very painfully, a world without illusion, that is, opting to be practical and adapt to a reality stripped of the dreams you once had. So what?

But back to our true adventures. As was bound to happen eventually, Peer Raben's *Antigone* reached the end of its run. He had long since canceled the rehearsals of *Astutuli,* using some threadbare excuse, and instead of that had put himself enthusiastically at the disposal of my apparently stronger, more unfettered energies.

This he did for two reasons: first, because my compulsion to create something was irrepressible, and second, because by this time the group had sunk into a kind of blissful Boy Scout camaraderie; for example, they had taken to sitting around in a circle in the evenings and singing, accompanied by a guitar—a fairly mindless feeling of sloppy togetherness spreading unchecked.

So there they were, a group of people who originally had come together to set something in motion; and since one of the things that had brought them together was that they had a space, a theater, they had decided that they would do plays and that furthermore they would become a group that could work together under brand-new, liberated, nonhierarchical conditions.

But besides that, for a good number of these people—for the majority of them, in fact—this theater space had become (and not just in fun, indeed, quite the opposite) a living room, a bar, a bedroom, and here it was that they tended to hang out, around the clock. At the same time, this segment of the group soon completely lost sight of the fact that in any such space costs inevitably arise—recurring, persistent expenses like rent, electricity, and telephone, and additional expenses for things like food, beverages, and cigarettes, and now and then someone would need something like a new pair of socks or underwear or whatever.

Probably not one of these people gave thought to this particular aspect of the group arrangement—that is, how all of it was to be paid for if they weren't producing anything. These were the responsibilities Ursula Strätz had assumed when she became the theater manager. Groceries were taken care of by the two or three members who had relatively well-paying jobs outside the theater. It was mainly the members of the group who were using the theater as a kind of cozy, convenient, centrally located home who had the weakest grasp on this most elementary fact: that no theater has even a halfway chance of making it unless some serious acting is going on.

Ursula Strätz was drinking heavily at that time, the result of which was that she kept coming up with far too many ideas—and among them far too many crackpot ideas; and that, in the final analysis, amounted to having no ideas at all. The two or three other colleagues who knew the financial situation and who also had a genuine drive to do theater (somewhat too undirected a drive for my taste, I might add) seemed to me to be essentially either too lazy or too complacent to develop any original ideas—or, if they had any, to be willing to fight for them.

I had a feeling that, consciously or unconsciously, they were relying on my possibly pathological need to be active, even though I strove mightily (but evidently to no avail) to conceal this compulsiveness of mine, this pressing desire to do something, to make something, to get something going—in short to get things *done*—ceaselessly, constantly, without a moment's pause, if I could have my way. A pathological compulsion, no doubt, as I said.

And then, when nothing had happened for too long a time, so long that I couldn't stand it anymore, I proposed that our next production should be Büchner's *Leonce and Lena*. In the first place, I love the play. In the second place, it spoke to the political situation of the day without our needing to wrench it out of context and bring it up to date; we could obviously just let it be what it is—for all its seriousness, merry and lighthearted, happy in the midst of sadness.

And to top it off, the play contained the role of Valerio, one of the very few parts absolutely perfect for me. For a long time, my fervor matched only by the futility of the undertaking, I tried to convince Hanna Schygulla of how wonderfully important the role of Lena could be, especially for her own "personal development." In the end, however, I was left without any counterarguments.

The role of Lena, she said, was tiny—basically nothing more than a dramaturgical necessity—and if I were honest, I would have to admit that *Leonce and Lena* is a man's play, that the women in it are nothing more than window-dressing, almost stage props. She, Hanna Schygulla, was after self-development, and in a forward direction; she wanted to discover and experience something about herself, something new—that's what was important to her, and I ought to realize that; she had no desire just to stand there onstage as a pretty face.

Leonce and Lena was put on without Hanna Schygulla, which at least spared me a certain amount of stupid, petty, unprofessional wrangling with the rest of the cast.

On the other hand, in order to provide the members with an opportunity to function as a real group, I suggested that at least three or four of us should collaborate on directing the play, a practice that could then be extended and improved upon in subsequent productions.

At the beginning of such a project, I emphasized, everyone must be sensitive enough to understand that collective directing must be learned and practiced gradually, very cautiously, in the hope of releasing the latent subtleties and fragile interpretations that have to be permitted to emerge before there can be any sort of dramatic continuity or, indeed, any intelligent development of communal ideas.

The composition of the directorial team worked in my favor. To all outward appearances the team seemed to be functioning, but as far as real work was concerned, no one interfered with me.

The team consisted of Peer Raben, who of course kept his mouth shut; then Ursula Strätz, whose suggestions were as badly thought out as they were impractical; but at least she had enough of a sense of humor that instead of arguing we could all enjoy a good laugh at her lunacies.

After me, the fourth team member was the actress Christin Peterson, who also played Lena. From the beginning Christin held back with an elegant sense of reserve. Furthermore, I soon had the happy idea that all the actors should be on stage at all times, so that they could take on any task that might crop up. Christin was playing Lena, Strätz the governess, and Peer Raben the role of Leonce; and since it's nearly impossible to direct from the stage, and someone has to sit in the house to see whether the desired effect is being achieved, I sacrificed myself for this job. In any case, when I'm acting there's nothing I hate more than rehearsing.

The first time I played my role all the way through was on opening night. The response was wildly enthusiastic, and my performance in particular was singled out for praise in most of the reviews. There were perhaps two reasons for this. First of all, everything I did on stage was of course fresh and relaxed, as if I were doing it for the first time.

No one could have guessed that such an impression was absolutely correct. Second, I played Valerio with an outspoken, nearly outrageous aggressiveness toward the audience, probably the result of my anxiety that the audience might not like me, which meant that from the outset I had to show them that I disliked them ten times more than they could ever dislike me, so that it would be quite understandable, the logical consequence of my own provocation, if they didn't like me.

I suppose this was my way of keeping from being hurt.

The outcome was completely unexpected. The audience, which is generally passive and probably equally masochistic, found my aggressiveness exhilaratingly frank, and enjoyed it thoroughly.

Ever since then I have preserved this posture toward the audience whenever I act (which is seldom enough), though my reasons for it have changed. I simply refuse to bid for the audience's favor; I reject the craving to be loved, even though being loved might just be the most important thing in the world for me.

As I said, most of our reviews for *Leonce and Lena* were hymns of praise. The only real exception was the opinion of the critic for the *Süddeutsche Zeitung,* and his review differed from those of his colleagues in an unforgettably witty way (at least I'll never forget it). He wrote, "All the children on earth ought to read *Leonce and Lena*; they simply shouldn't always do it in public." That's all there was. Over and out. Unless you want to make an issue of the little logical slip in that sentence: what children are "always" reading *Leonce and Lena* where in public?

Be that as it may, we were amused by this critique, perhaps because it was the one exception to all the other paeans.

Whether these splendid reviews had something to do with the first telephone call I ever received from Hanna Schygulla is a question about which I neither want to nor can speculate. No matter. What had happened was that Ursula Strätz, in one of her rare lucid moments, had managed to get me interested in Ferdinand Bruckner's play *The Criminals.*

I was so enthusiastic after reading the play that I resolved to make it the first production for which I would be totally and officially responsible.

Over the telephone, I offered Hanna Schygulla a role in the play. It wasn't even the lead, but she immediately accepted. I then began casting the other parts with actors from the Action Theater; only one of the "bums" who were living in the theater got a role.

I managed to make a joke of the rebellion that naturally arose among the six others, and at the same time embarrassed them so much with my adroitly formulated arguments that without further discussion they packed up their stuff and disappeared for good.

I cast the remaining parts with actors who had given up the actor's life for so-called respectable professions, also with a high school student I had met at the theater bar after a performance, and with Irm Herrmann (with whom I was living at the time). Her resistance to being in the cast of *The Criminals* was stubborn and long. She's the only actress-in-spite-of-herself I've ever known. It wasn't until later that she, too, tasted blood.

Working on this production (I would describe it today as something like choreography with a text) made me very happy. I was truly overjoyed with the results. Thinking of it now still makes me happy.

Everything about it was taken very seriously. If I remember correctly, I succeeded in establishing a sense of mutual trust between the actors and myself, so that again, even though for a short time, we could call ourselves a real group. In my work with Hanna Schygulla, however, there appeared for the first time something symptomatic of our relationship to come, something that decisively shaped our future collaboration. And that is that every time Schygulla was unsure of herself, she panicked—her body tensed up, refused to obey—and then she began to discuss things.

At first these discussions were halfway connected with the situation that was giving her trouble, or at least with the play we happened to be rehearsing. Later, the topics had less and less to do with the matter at hand. It frequently ended up with her wanting to talk about the Meaning of Life.

Needless to say, these usually fruitless discussions interrupted and delayed the rehearsals which, as it was, had to be scheduled into a few evening hours because of the daytime jobs some of the cast had.

And so I had no recourse (assuming I wanted to go on working with Schygulla) but to look for possible ways—cheap tricks, in part—to convey by nonverbal means the effects I wanted to have her produce on stage. I had to learn how to direct Actress Schygulla so casually that she wouldn't even know she was being directed.

The result was that Hanna Schygulla was firmly convinced that of course she was not bringing someone else's fantasies to life, that she wasn't submitting to the imagination and will of another. Her performance was carried along by her conviction, evidently so important to her, that she was fulfilling herself 100 percent, that the conception of her role was exclusively her own.

Naturally the other actors weren't in a position to see through this stratagem of mine—they saw nothing more than preferential treatment, my seeming deference to Hanna Schygulla. As you can imagine, this perception brought the idea of a collective effort to the brink of the precipice.

Hoping that the essential needs of the group would be met somehow, I decided to risk it. And then outside help arrived. Ursula Strätz's husband had been in the hospital, and while there he had been fed all kinds of rumors and gossip concerning his wife and me. When he was released, he could apparently think of nothing better to do than to come in a state of lunatic fury and totally wreck the Action Theater.

When he was finished, there wasn't a chair left intact; the stage was completely destroyed, likewise the ticket booth and the bar.

Curiously enough, this wanton destruction of their theater, to the point where it could hardly be used for anything, least of all a performance, served to reinforce the cohesion of the cast of *The Criminals.*

We abandoned the Action Theater in the Müllerstrasse, left what remained of our permanent house, and founded the "anti-theater," a group theater that was conceived as a kind of touring company or, at best, a theater without a permanent home.

For the first production of this new group—a decision arrived at after serious discussion and a vote—we settled on the Peter Weiss play *Herr Mockinpott.*

The group chose—this too was voted on—Egon Schmidt and me as codirectors.

As an indication of the group's new solidarity, every member was to be involved in its first production, in no matter how tiny a role.

Except for Hanna Schygulla, everyone lived up to that commitment. Schygulla claimed urgent obligations to her studies, which were just then, she said, entering a critical phase.

It eventually came out that Schygulla had long since given up her studies at the university.

The real reason she had no time for our new production was something quite different.

Peter Fleischmann had invited Schygulla to do a screen test for the female lead in his first film, *Hunting Scenes from Lower Bavaria,* a screen test that for some peculiar reason went on for weeks.

It turned out in the end that she didn't even get the part she'd tested for.

Back from the screen test. Just then we were working on plans for the production of Marieluise Fleisser's play *Pioneers in Ingolstadt.* I persuaded Schygulla to take the leading role, this time with little effort.

One day I realized, in a great burst of insight, that whenever it was a question of leading roles I really didn't have to muster all my powers of persuasion to talk Hanna Schygulla into accepting them.

Fassbinder and Hanna Schygulla in Katzelmacher *(by permission of Fassbinder-Foundation, Munich)*

Within the group, however, it seemed that my casting of Schygulla met with an icy reception—in fact, with what at first seemed to be impenetrable resistance.

It took several days of pleading, all sorts of threats, and Peer Raben's unselfish support to break down the general resistance. And then Schygulla's performance turned out, as it nearly always did, to be of the highest quality—no one contested that. But quality or not, one thing was abundantly clear: Hanna Schygulla would represent a permanent threat to any theater company, no matter how constituted.

Our next production had to be done without Schygulla in any case, even though all she was getting in Peter Fleischmann's film was a small supporting role.

For years there had been contact between the old Action Theater and Jean-Marie Straub, the film director. Straub had decided to work up a new version of Ferdinand Bruckner's *Sickness of Youth* and then stage it.

When he finally finished reworking the material, what was left was an approximately ten-minute-long extract.

Straub planned to produce this work, as he had long before promised he would, at the Action Theater. His cast, however, consisted exclusively of members of the new anti-theater. It was only because of our special interest in Jean-Marie Straub that we decided, for this one

production and for this one time only, to return to the hastily reno-
vated Action Theater.

Since Straub's piece was going to be scarcely ten minutes long,
however, and since small theater groups generally get the biggest run-
arounds from publishers when it comes to the production rights for
the sort of plays that interest people like us, I decided to fill out the
evening by writing a play of my own, my first.

It was *Katzelmacher* [British translation: "The Cock-Artist."]

Both directors, Straub and I, had decided to use Hanna Schygulla,
and so this time there were practically no complications as far as she
was concerned.

Soon after this double-bill production there arrived that moment
of general alarm when the government promulgated its emergency
decrees against terrorism, the *Notstandsgesetze.*

The company decided spontaneously to present a series of tableaux in reaction to these decrees. Each person chose one specific
theme that he or she could work on alone until it took on some sort
of dramatic shape; these separate pieces would then be put together
one evening in the theater. In that way the play as a whole would not
emerge until the moment it was on stage—no rehearsals, no safe-
guards, like jumping into cold water.

Hanna Schygulla, normally ready at the drop of a hat to voice her
views on politics, unfortunately chose to withdraw from this project,
intended as it was to demonstrate political commitment rather than
one's personal brilliance in a role.

Shortly after this evening's presentation, which we called "Axel
Cäsar Haarmann," the Action Theater was permanently closed by the
city authorities, under the flimsy pretext that the theater had a license
for dramatic productions but not for political cabaret. And so the anti-
theater withdrew to the now almost legendary back room of Widow
Bolte's, a bistro in Schwabing. As for the group and Hanna Schygulla,
things now went along with fewer problems, much the way an injus-
tice if repeatedly perpetrated will gradually cause confrontation to
give way to lethargy.

If a play had a major role for Schygulla, it was understood that she
would be in the cast. If not, then no Schygulla, and that's just the way
it was.

Basically the same arrangement, with no further discussion, continued in the films we did together.

In any event, the major roles were there for her to play. From year
to year I was able to refine my method of directing so that she hardly
noticed she was being directed. If, for whatever reason, it was more
important for me to cast her in a smaller role, I literally had to come

Fassbinder and Hanna Schygulla in The Marriage of Maria Braun *(by permission of Fassbinder-Foundation, Munich)*

begging. Most of the time my supplications were graciously acceded to, and she would play a smaller role for a change; but she also never let me forget that she was doing it only because of my fervent appeals.

She continued, however, to have bigger problems with so-called supporting roles, especially if Margit Carstensen played the lead.

But who would be so petty as to fault someone for having such normal human reactions?

And Hanna Schygulla is furthermore very clever, for she has learned how to be conspicuously terrible in minor roles that don't interest her.

Accordingly, I plan not to ask her anymore to play a part that doesn't further her "personal development" as a human being. Although much of this may not have sounded so very happy—Hanna Schygulla's relationship with me and especially with various theater groups—it must nevertheless be said that the very existence of Hanna Schygulla was important to my work, as I knew at the beginning, when it first popped into my head.

And even if what made her important to me was nothing more than her absolute desire and need to prove her importance to me—so what?

Honni soit qui mal y pense!

1981 (Translated by A. S. Wensinger and Richard Wood)

The Sad Eyes of Cannes

This year there was absolutely no rational reason to subject myself to the Cannes Film Festival, with its mostly absurd, often gruesome distortions of what film is all about, or at least as I see it, besides which in previous years I regularly came to the conclusion sooner or later that I would absolutely never go to Cannes again, no matter what. But as it happened, I've had a film at Cannes every year, and I love every film, of course, as if it were a child or something, and feel it should have the best possible care at the very least. So I adopted the clever saying, "What do I care about the stupid things I said yesterday?" and that helped me not to be plagued by a guilty conscience every year. Besides which I basically support anything that is good for film, even festivals, if only they were a little more the way I imagine them, the New York Film Festival, for instance, or the Film Days at Hof, let's say.

But Cannes . . . so I went to Cannes, or at least I think I think I went to Cannes this year, precisely for the reason that I didn't have a film being shown, no stress, no interviews, with the same old questions over and over again, which always call for the same old answers, until eventually you're almost in danger of coming to hate your beloved film, and would rather not have made it. Especially since a surprisingly large proportion of incredibly stupid, uninformed reporters are sent to Cannes, probably because it really isn't a question of film there. So I would be spared all that and various other things—no appointments, sleeping as late as I liked, meeting friends some time in the evening, friends one otherwise seldom sees, going out to eat with them, and talking, talking, without having the conversation twisted by some stupid purpose.

But suddenly I had another idea—call it crazy if you like, maybe it is. I had the idea of not watching any movies in Cannes. For one thing, they begin at a specific time, and for another thing, I found the notion of getting an impression of films only through people who had seen them incredibly exciting. In this way I hoped to learn more, or at least something different, about film in itself and its effect on people than if I'd seen them myself.

May 1982

Notes

The texts have, with one exception, been taken from the two volumes edited by Michael Töteberg and published by Fischer in Frankfurt am Main: *Filme befreien den Kopf. Essays und Arbeitsnotizen (Films Liberate the Mind. Essays and Working Notes,* 1984) and *Die Anarchie der Phantasie. Gespräche und Interviews (The Anarchy of the Imagination. Conversations and Interviews,* 1986). These books are abbreviated throughout the notes and in the following bibliography as *FbK* and *AP.* Most references to secondary literature have also been abbreviated; full citations may be found in the bibliography. Notes on persons, events, institutions, and cultural phenomena are usually keyed to their first appearance in the text. The few exceptions may be found by using the index.

"The kind of rage I feel"

First published in *film* [Velber bei Hannover], August 1969, 19–22; text based on *AP,* 30–37.

3. your plays: Much of Fassbinder's work in the theater had been devoted to irreverent adaptations of classical dramas, for example, Sophocles' *Ajax* and Goethe's *Iphigenie auf Tauris.* One of his early plays, however, *The American Soldier* (first performed on 9 December 1968), did in fact draw its inspiration from a gangster film, Irving Lerner's *Murder by Contract.*

5. Chabrol: Claude Chabrol, to whom, among others, *Love Is Colder than Death* is dedicated, eventually became the object of one of Fassbinder's most scathing critiques (see "Shadows, to be Sure, and no Pity" in this volume). In an interview given around the time of Fassbinder's interview with Mengershausen, however, Fassbinder stressed their affinity: "Like me, Chabrol is working toward social change by starting at the bottom, that is, by analyzing feelings" (*Abendzeitung* [Munich], 18 June 1969).

a Godard film: For example, *Breathless,* which Godard himself said was supposed to be like *Scarface* and ended up like *Alice in Wonderland.* See *Godard on Godard,* ed. Jean Narboni and Tom Milne (New York: Viking, 1972), 175.

5. Delon in *Le samourai:* Although Fassbinder was apparently not yet familiar with the films of Jean-Pierre Melville, Ulli Lommel intentionally chose a hat almost identical to the one worn by Alain Delon in *Le samourai* (1967). Fassbinder uses the German title of the film, which translates into English literally as *The Ice-Cold Angel.*

6. *White Heat:* In Fassbinder's first film, the short *The City Tramp,* the character he himself played has a poster for this Raoul Walsh film on his wall.

Hawks: Fassbinder commented in a 1974 interview that "most" of the films of Howard Hawks are "gay stories." See Iden et al., 62–63.

Hanna: Hanna Schygulla, who plays Joanna, Franz's girlfriend.

7. Godard films: In 1974 Fassbinder called Godard's *My Life to Live* "the most important film I've seen in my life" (Iden et al., 61). Later, he also articulated their differences in a paradigmatic reversal of a famous statement by the French director: "Film, Godard says, is telling the truth twenty-four times per second. Film, I say, is lying twenty-five times per second" (*FbK,* 130).

8. Straub: Jean-Marie Straub and Danièle Huillet, his wife, left their native France for West Germany in 1958, where they began to make difficult, challenging films, including two shorts loosely based on texts by Heinrich Böll. In 1969 they moved to Rome. They now live alternately there, in Paris, and in Hamburg. Their films, which also include adaptations of Brecht and Kafka, have often provoked critical consternation as well as political censorship.

Action Theater: For an eyewitness account of Fassbinder's involvement in this underground theater and its successor, the "anti-theater," see Yaak Karsunke, "History of Anti-Teater: The Beginnings," in Iden et al., 1–10. Fassbinder's essay "Hanna Schygulla" (in this volume) also deals in detail with this period.

Sickness of Youth: Ferdinand Bruckner's drama (1926), which is set in the Vienna of 1923, deals with sexual confusion caused by the loss of bourgeois values. Straub's production reduced the three-act play to a ten-minute version. Fassbinder was fascinated by the "comic solemnity" with which Straub directed the play. He also admired Straub's Brechtian approach, which resulted in "a distance between the role and the actor, instead of total identity" (Iden et al., 63–64).

patron: Hanna Axmann von Rezzori of Munich, an amateur painter, backed Fassbinder's early film production and actually played the role of a financial backer in *Rio das mortes.*

9. cost shares: The Fassbinder estate contains a contract for *Cold Steel* (a provisional title for *Love Is Colder than Death*) that clarifies this unfamiliar term, *Grundsummen* in German. The usage in the contract suggests that Fassbinder meant "basic investment amounts." Investments, for which cash amounts were agreed upon in advance, could be made in the form of capital funds or services.

10. Lohmann: Dietrich Lohmann went on to work as Fassbinder's cameraman for several other films, including two of the best, *The Merchant of Four Seasons* and *Effi Briest.*

"At some point films have to stop being films"

First published in *Film-Korrespondenz* [Cologne], February 1974, 3–6; text based on *AP,* 47–52. The title used here is taken from the republication of the interview in *Zoom-Filmberater* 2 (1976).

12. Vohrer: A reference to the prolific but mediocre German director Alfred Vohrer (1914–86).

13. Brigitte Mira: Born in 1915 in Hamburg, Mira began her long and varied career on provincial stages from Kiel to Graz. After the war she worked in cabarets and took small roles in film comedies. In the 1960s she was known especially for her performances in operettas and musicals. The part of Emmi in *Fear Eats the Soul* was her first leading role in a film.

14. Böhm . . . Mira: Like Brigitte Mira, Karlheinz Böhm had a rather different screen image prior to his Fassbinder roles. He was best known as the romantic leading man opposite Romy Schneider in the so-called Sissi Films, based on the life of the Austrian empress Elisabeth.

family series: *Eight Hours Are Not a Day*

Finck . . . Luise Ulrich: Both Werner Finck and Luise Ulrich brought conventional, well-known movie personas to Fassbinder's subversive miniseries. In fact, Ulrich (1911–86) had a career that included pre–World War II productions of UFA (Universum Film A.G.), the dominant German studio until 1945, and sentimental comedies of the fifties.

head of a theater: Fassbinder served as general director of Frankfurt's Theater am Turm for one controversial season, 1974–75.

"I've changed along with the characters in my films"

First published in the German edition of *Playboy,* April 1978, 53–68; text based on *AP,* 108–28.

17. Barbara Valentin: Valentin played a notable part in Fassbinder's films of the early 1970s, especially in *Fear Eats the Soul* and *Effi Briest.* She also made an important cameo appearance in *Berlin Alexanderplatz.*

20. Ingrid Caven: Fassbinder and Caven were married in 1970 and divorced in 1971. She had important roles in his early films, and in the late 1970s achieved considerable success as a singer in a style reminiscent of Marlene Dietrich. In a 1978 interview, Fassbinder characterized his relationship to her: "Of all the actresses and actors I've been involved with, Ingrid is the least willing to let herself be reduced to being an actress, and the one who, more than anyone else, remains something other than an actress, in other words, the one who, more than the others, carries on a dialogue on an equal footing" (Hayman, 96).

Armin Meier: Meier was working as a butcher when he and Fassbinder met around 1973. Fassbinder dedicated the film *Fox and His Friends,* which centers on an exploited, uneducated homosexual, to "Armin and all the others."

Meier appeared in small roles in several of Fassbinder's films. In the director's segment of *Germany in Autumn,* Fassbinder and Meier act out their tortured relationship against the background of the political hysteria caused by the terrorism scare. In 1978 Armin Meier committed suicide.

21. Michael Ballhaus: Between 1970 and 1978 Ballhaus served as the cameraman for fourteen Fassbinder films, including *The Marriage of Maria Braun.* He is one of the leading cinematographers of the New German Cinema, and since 1982 he has become an important presence in American films as well. His recent credits include John Sayles's *Baby, It's You* and two films by Martin Scorsese, *After Hours* and *The Color of Money.*

22. thirteen and a half hours: The television series eventually ran for fifteen and a half hours; the feature-film version was never made.

quotes: In several films, including *Love Is Colder than Death, Gods of the Plague,* and *The Third Generation,* Fassbinder himself, Harry Baer, and Günther Kaufmann play characters named Franz, who resemble the central figure in Döblin's novel, Franz Biberkopf. In *Fox and His Friends* this character's name actually is Franz Biberkopf. There are many other, less obvious borrowings from *Berlin Alexanderplatz* in Fassbinder's work.

23. television version: The actual cast included Günter Lamprecht as Franz, Barbara Sukowa as Mieze, Gottfried John as Reinhold, and Hanna Schygulla as Eva. Franz Buchrieser did indeed play Meck.

25. *Le bonheur:* Varda's film was released in 1965.

29. Douglas Sirk: Sirk's directorial career began in Germany in 1934, but his most famous films—the ones Fassbinder admired—were, of course, made in Hollywood.

30. Herbert Achternbusch: Achternbusch is another Bavarian writer-director whose filmmaking is if anything more insistently auteurist and autobiographical than Fassbinder's was. His films openly use parody and comedy and consciously assume an avant-garde position. Like Fassbinder, Achternbusch has proved particularly adept at violating taboos. His film *Das Gespenst* (*The Ghost,* 1982), for example, which involves a travestied retelling of Christ's Passion, resulted in charges of blasphemy and the loss of state subsidies. See Achternbusch's unconventional eulogy, "A Rose for Rainer Werner Fassbinder" (1982) in Rentschler 1988, 199–201.

"This is the only way we can do films here"

First published in *Frankfurter Rundschau,* 20 February 1979; text based on *AP,* 129–40.

31. Rosi, Damiani, or Cayatte: Francesco Rosi and Damiano Damiani, both born in 1922, and André Cayatte, born in 1909, have all had directing careers marked by a continuing interest in politics and social problems. Fassbinder dedicated *Love Is Colder than Death* not only to his favorite directors but also to a pair of characters in Damiani's *El Chuncho* (1967), a "spaghetti Western" with a social message.

31. *Knife in the Head:* Reinhard Hauff's psychological thriller (1978), based on a screenplay by Peter Schneider, is a film that dealt obliquely with certain social and political repercussions of the West German government's reaction to the terrorist activities of the 1970s.

treatment: Fassbinder uses the English word.

"Foreword": See the essay *"The Third Generation"* in this volume.

32. *Germany in Autumn:* This openly political film (1978) included stylistically quite heterogeneous segments by Fassbinder, Schlöndorff, Edgar Reitz, Alexander Kluge, and others, each director reacting in more or less direct fashion to the dramatic events that began in September 1977. After the kidnapping of the industrialist Hanns Martin Schleyer by the terrorist group RAF and the hijacking of a Lufthansa airliner in Mogadishu had failed to win the release of terrorist leaders imprisoned at Stuttgart's Stammheim prison, Schleyer was murdered and the terrorists, Gudrun Ensslin, Fritz Raspe, and Andreas Baader, were found dead in their cells, apparent suicides.

33. Filmverlag: The Filmverlag der Autoren was a publishing and distribution company set up on a cooperative basis in 1971. By 1974 it had incorporated, and in 1977 Rudolf Augstein, publisher of *Der Spiegel,* saved the company from bankruptcy by assuming a majority interest. Fassbinder, who had been one of the founders, severed his connection with the Filmverlag in 1977. In a recent attack on the Filmverlag's current business practices under Augstein's ownership, Wim Wenders recalled that it had once supported the "idea that cinema is not only a business, but also a form of expression, and therefore not only a question of cash, but also one of art" ("The Filmverlag against the Authors" [1985], in Rentschler 1988, 37).

34. *Katharina Blum: The Lost Honor of Katharina Blum* (1975), Volker Schlöndorff and Margarethe von Trotta's prize-winning film based on the novel by Heinrich Böll, attempts to analyze the press's exploitation of terrorist activities.

The Second Awakening of Christa Klages: A film (1977) by Margarethe von Trotta about a woman who commits a bank robbery in order to save a daycare center from closing. The treatment of her flight from the police is clearly constructed as a liberal reaction to the repressive political climate of the period.

The Earth Is Uninhabitable Like the Moon: Fassbinder wrote a screenplay based on Gerhard Zwerenz's novel (1973) about corruption in Frankfurt's construction industry. In 1986 Zwerenz published the screenplay as an appendix to a new edition of the novel (see "Die Erde ist unbewohnbar wie der Mond").

Berlin crowd: A reference to a group of directors associated with the German Film and Television Academy who made films about workers and their problems. One of the best known is Christian Ziewer's *Dear Mother, I'm OK* (1972).

filmmakers' syndicate: A forerunner of the Filmverlag der Autoren.

35. Caterina Valente movies: German musical comedies and revue films from the 1950s featuring the Paris-born actress.

36. WDR: Westdeutscher Rundfunk (West German Broadcasting), abbreviated as WDR, is one of the major regional television and radio networks. Its headquarters are in Cologne.

37. Mogadishu business: See note to p. 32.

"German Model": A reference to the postwar governmental policy based on an ideology of nonplanning that understeered the economy and strictly controlled conflicts between interest groups.

38. Brandt . . . Wehner: Willy Brandt, who spent the war years in exile in Norway, was chancellor of West Germany from 1969 until 1974, when he resigned because of a spy scandal within his own staff. Herbert Wehner (1907–90) was one of the most influential leaders of Brandt's Social Democratic Party and served for several years as its chairman.

Holocaust: First aired in the United States in April 1978 by NBC, the American miniseries was broadcast by WDR in January 1979. A useful analysis of the West German response to the series may be found in Andrei Markovits and Rebecca Hayden's article, "'Holocaust' before and after the Event: Reactions in West Germany and Austria" in *New German Critique* 19 (1980): 53–80.

Debit and Credit: Gustav Freytag's significant but anti-Semitic novel (1855) that parallels the lives of a good German and an evil Jew. See "Credited Debit, Debited Credit" in this volume.

Peter Zadek: Zadek, who is still active in the theater, was one of West Germany's most innovative and provocative directors in the late 1970s.

39. *The Journey:* Vesper's fragmentary novel, written in 1969–71 and published posthumously in 1977, is considered one of the most important literary treatments of the student movement in West Germany.

40. *The Man in Jasmine:* Unica Zürn (1916–70), who has begun to attract the attention of the feminist movement, figured in Fassbinder's work in several ways. He tried unsuccessfully to obtain the rights to the autobiographical work mentioned here. Fassbinder probably read the Ullstein edition published in 1977 with the subtitle, "Impressions from a Mental Illness." He had in mind a film that would feature a female counterpart to the character played by Dirk Bogarde in *Despair,* which is dedicated to Van Gogh, Antonin Artaud, and Zürn. Excerpts from Zürn's works are read in *The Third Generation.* Hanna Schygulla reported in an interview that she and Fassbinder had planned to rent a house together and produce an "extemporaneous study of the poet and painter Unica Zürn." See Gabriele Presber, *Die Kunst ist weiblich* (Munich: Knaur, 1988), 26.

"Reacting to what you experience"

First published in *Süddeutsche Zeitung,* 8 March 1979; text based on *AP,* 141–45.

41. Jean Paul: Jean Paul Friedrich Richter (1763–1825) was a literary outsider of his time who opposed the political conservatism of Weimar Clas-

sicism embodied by Goethe and developed an idiosyncratic humorous style in his novels. In the "List of My Favorites" published in this volume, Fassbinder includes Jean Paul's *Siebenkäs* (1796–97) in his selection of "Best Books."

42. Beckmann ... Nolde: Both Max Beckmann (1884–1950) and Emil Nolde (1867–1950) belonged to the generation of modern German painters who began their careers before the onset of Expressionism. While Nolde remains best known for his Expressionist work, Beckmann maintained an objective, figurally oriented style well suited to his allegorical purposes. Both artists were classified as "degenerate" by the Nazis; Nolde stayed in Germany but was forbidden to paint, and Beckmann spent the war years in Amsterdam.

43. Arnolt Bronnen and Brecht: Like Brecht, his friend and collaborator, Arnolt Bronnen (1895–1959) began his literary career as an Expressionist playwright; unlike Brecht, he became an ardent supporter of the Nazi regime.

Bourbon Street Blues: Sirk supervised this production at the College of Television and Film in Munich.

44. Tennessee Williams play: *The Lady of Larkspur Lotion,* a one-act play.

Thomas Mann: The quotation actually paraphrases a famous sentence in *Tonio Kröger,* which Fassbinder used as part of the motto for *Beware of a Holy Whore:* "I tell you I am sick to death of depicting humanity without having any part or lot in it" (Thomas Mann, *Stories of Three Decades,* trans. H. T. Lowe-Porter [New York: Knopf, 1930], 103).

"I make films out of personal involvement, and for no other reason"

First published in *Kino* [Hamburg] 3 (1980): 29–40; text based on *AP,* 146–66.

45. *The Good-for-Nothing:* Alf Brustellin and Bernhard Sinkel's film *Taugenichts* (1977) is based on the once popular Romantic tale (1826) by Joseph von Eichendorff.

Döblin: Alfred Döblin (1878–1957), the author of *Berlin Alexanderplatz,* the great city novel of 1929 on which Fassbinder's television series was based.

47. Alexanderplatz ... Kurfürstendamm: Locations in the divided city that symbolized East and West Berlin.

48. ten chapters: Actually *nine.*

49. Durbridge dramaturgy: Film versions of Francis Durbridge's detective novels kept people in West Germany off the streets and in front of their televisions in the 1960s. Episodic structures that emphasized suspense rather than convincing plot development characterized these popular adaptations.

other two projects: *Eight Hours Are Not a Day,* which was canceled after five episodes; and the television series based on Freytag's *Debit and Credit.*

50. Kracauer: Siegfried Kracauer (1889–1966), who began writing film

reviews for the *Frankfurter Zeitung* in the 1920s, is best known for his influential film history, *From Caligari to Hitler: A Psychological History of the German Film* (1947).

52. Günter Lamprecht, Gottfried John, and Barbara Sukowa: Lamprecht plays Franz Biberkopf, the main character; John is Reinhold, the gangster; and Sukowa plays Mieze, Franz's girlfriend.

54. the only new one: Baumann, played by Gerhard Zwerenz.

57. Luggi Waldleitner: Working with Waldleitner, an old-guard producer, marked a departure for Fassbinder, and critics, especially on the left, were quick to accuse him of collusion with the conservative establishment. In 1985 Waldleitner commented on his cooperation with Fassbinder: "We had to work with these so-called leftist directors because there wasn't a single good director in the conservative camp who would sell beyond the borders of the Federal Republic."

Günther Rohrbach: As head of production at WDR and as executive producer for Bavaria Studios, Rohrbach worked with Fassbinder on *Berlin Alexanderplatz* and other projects.

58. life story of Lale Andersen: The script is based on her autobiography, *Der Himmel hat viele Farben* (*The Sky Has Many Colors*, 1972).

Haganah: The Zionist self-defense organization founded in Palestine in 1920 by Vladimir Jabotinsky.

59. Niklaus Gessner: An example of Gessner's work is *Peking Blond* (1966), a film featuring a jewel thief who exploits her connections with the American secret service until she is betrayed.

60. Michael Fengler . . . Bernadette Lafont: Fengler, one of Fassbinder's earliest associates, later produced *The Marriage of Maria Braun*. Lafont is a French actress who appeared in many French New Wave films, including those of Claude Chabrol and François Truffaut.

"Why these problems with Franz Biberkopf?"

First published in *Frankfurter Allgemeine Zeitung,* 29 December 1980, 15. The text is based on the newspaper publication and, unlike the version in *AP,* 181–85, is unabridged.

62. Springer press: The media corporation owned by Axel Springer, which publishes the widely read tabloid *Bild* and other conservatively oriented papers.

63. *Tagesschau:* The evening news program on ARD, the First German Television Network.

65. Piwitt in *Konkret:* See the article "Herrenballett," November 1980, 9. Piwitt accused Fassbinder of treating the proletariat of the 1920s from a false, "gay" perspective.

66. Syberberg: Hans Jürgen Syberberg is best known in the United States for his monumental film, *Our Hitler: A Film from Germany* (1977). This film uses a complex mixture of Brechtian and Wagnerian aesthetics to analyze the phenomenon of Hitler as an image of commercialized culture.

"I'm a romantic anarchist"

First published in *tip* [West Berlin] 6 (1982): 36–40; the text follows the abridged version in *AP,* 186–94.

67. Frank Ripploh: Ripploh had just become well known as a director in his own right, for the critical gay film *Taxi to the Loo* (1981).

68. "longing": The German title translates literally as *The Longing of Veronika Voss.*

gossipy report by Rosa von Praunheim: See André Müller, "'Meine Seele ist weiblich': Ein Gespräch mit dem Filmemacher Rosa von Praunheim'" ("'My Soul is Feminine': A Conversation with the Filmmaker Rosa von Praunheim"), *Die Zeit* [Hamburg], 11 December 1981.

69. Walter Bockmayer: See the essay, "The German Cinema Is Being Enriched" on Bockmayer's *Jane Is Jane Forever,* in this volume.

Oberhausen people: A reference to the signatories of the Oberhausen Manifesto of 1962, which has been seen as an seminal document for the rise of the New German Cinema.

71. butcher: Perhaps a reference to Fassbinder's companion, Armin Meier, who had been a butcher.

Imitation of Life

First published in *Fernsehen und Film* [Hannover], February 1971, 8–13; text based on *FbK,* 11–24.

77. Samuel Fuller . . . a screenplay for Douglas Sirk: See Sirk's recollection of the difficulties with Fuller's script for *Shockproof* (1948) in *Sirk on Sirk,* ed. Jon Halliday (New York: Viking Press, 1972), 77–78.

a film by Jean-Luc Godard: *Pierre le Fou* (1965), in which Fuller, playing himself, explains to Ferdinand, played by Belmondo, that "film is like a battleground: love, hate, action, violence, death . . . In one word, *emotion.*" See Charles Barr et al., *The Films of Jean-Luc Godard* (London: Studio Vista, 1967), 101.

a hymn: "Des Larmes et de la Vitesse," *Cahiers du Cinéma* 94 (April 1959). Rpt. in *Godard on Godard,* 134–39.

A Time to Love and a Time to Die (1958): The film was based on Erich Maria Remarque's novel *Zeit zu leben und Zeit zu sterben,* which appeared in 1954, first in English and then in German.

Asta Nielsen: The great Danish silent film star (1881–1972) began making movies in Copenhagen in 1910.

77. Max Brod . . . Kafka: Brod, Kafka's friend and editor, is mentioned in Sirk's recollections of a visit to Vienna. See *Sirk on Sirk,* 78.

78. UFA: Universum Film A.G., during the 1920s Germany's largest and most powerful film company, was founded during World War I by the German army and continued production throughout the Second World War.

81. the last films of Fritz Lang: For example, *The Tiger of Eschnapur.*

83. Hedleys: Should be Hadleys.

84. *Music:* A play (1907) by Frank Wedekind (1864–1918), whose provocative treatment of sexuality and unconventional theatrical style decisively influenced Brecht and other major German playwrights of the 1920s.

story by Faulkner: The novel *Pylon,* which Sirk had tried to film in Germany before he emigrated to Hollywood.

85. Jiggs: The name of the character played by Jack Carson.

88. Sandra Dee: She plays the role of Susie Meredith, Lana Turner's daughter.

Sarah Jane . . . Annie: In these two instances, Fassbinder uses the names of the characters, played by Susan Kohner and Juanita Moore, respectively.

Lana Turner: Fassbinder later unsuccessfully tried to engage her for one of his films. See Iden et al., 67.

89. Josef von Sternberg: The cinematographer Xaver Schwarzenberger, referring to his and Fassbinder's conception of the lighting design for *Berlin Alexanderplatz,* remarks, "We used the idea of an *hommage à* Sternberg as the starting point—the result of course is quite personal." See Fassbinder with Baer, 503.

. . . Shadows, to be Sure, and no Pity

First published in Peter W. Jansen and Wolfram Schütte, eds. *Claude Chabrol* (Munich: Hanser, 1975), 7–16; text based on *FbK,* 28–35.

90. Gerhard Zwerenz: Zwerenz is a prolific leftist writer who came to West Germany from the German Democratic Republic in 1957. Many of his works, including the autobiographical novel *Kopf und Bauch (Head and Stomach),* deal with the predicament of the underprivileged in society. Fassbinder's play *Garbage, the City and Death* borrowed characters from Zwerenz's novel *The Earth Is Uninhabitable Like the Moon.* In Daniel Schmidt's film based on the play, *Shadows of the Angels* (1976), Fassbinder played one of the leading roles. The director created the role of Baumann in *Berlin Alexanderplatz* specifically for Zwerenz. Zwerenz in turn wrote a novelization (1979) of *The Marriage of Maria Braun,* as well as a memoir of the filmmaker, *Der langsame Tod des Rainer Werner Fassbinder (The Slow Death of Rainer Werner Fassbinder),* 1982.

Theodor Fontane: This quotation is taken from Fontane's review of the first three volumes of Gustav Freytag's novel *Die Ahnen (The Ancestors);* it appeared in the *Vossische Zeitung* (Berlin) in 1875. In the original text the phrase "all guilt is avenged on earth," from a poem in Goethe's *Wilhelm Meister's Apprenticeship,* is set off by quotation marks and "that" is italicized. See T. Fontane, *Werke in Fünf Bänden* (Munich: Nymphenburger Verlagshandlung, 1974), 5:480.

91. *Nada:* This film (1973) tells the story of a gang of mostly young anarchists who give their organization the nihilistic designation "Nada." Their terrorist kidnapping of the American ambassador goes awry, and all but one of them are shot down by the police.

"Gestapo!": In one of the film's most striking scenes, Paul, wearing a

German officer's cap, frightens a Jewish student out of his sleep by yelling "Gestapo!"

91. Marcoins: The name is actually Marcoux.

Cahiers du Cinéma: The quotation is taken from Louis Marcorelles's review in No. 102 (January 1960).

92. Michel Bouquet: Bouquet (b. 1926) had roles in *Le tigre se parfume à la dynamite* (1965), *La route de Corinthe* (1967), *Le femme infidèle* (1968), *La rupture* (1970), and *Juste avant la nuit* (1970–71).

93. hostile images: Fassbinder uses the word *Feindbilder,* a pun that suggests both cinematic images that convey hostility and the (often prejudiced) images that one has of one's enemies, in this case the audience, as the following sentence makes clear.

Eighteen-minute sketch: *L'homme qui vendit la tour Eiffel* was an episode in the film *Les plus belles escroqueries du monde* that also included contributions by Roman Polanski and Godard.

"Tiger" films: *Le tigre aime la chair fraiche* (1964) and *Le tigre se parfume à la dynamite* (1965)

Terence Young: Fassbinder is comparing Chabrol to the successful director of the early James Bond movies, including *Doctor No* (1962), *From Russia with Love* (1963) and *Thunderball* (1965).

94. Colonel Rémy: Chabrol himself later took a more skeptical view of *La ligne de démarcation* and of Rémy, whom he called "great, but an old reactionary" (Jansen and Schütte, eds., *Claude Chabrol,* 96).

two other films: *Marie-Chantal contre Dr. Kha* and *La route de Corinthe,* respectively.

96. four television movies: *Monsieur Bébé, Nul n'est parfait, Une invitation à la chasse* and *Les gens de l'été,* which were made in 1973 and 1974.

The German Cinema Is Being Enriched

First published in *Die Zeit,* 24 April 1977; text based on *FbK,* 40–42.

97. *Jane Is Jane Forever* (1976): In a 1977 interview Fassbinder summarized the film's importance: "*Jane Is Jane Forever* is a very painful but funny film, with a couple of scenes which will certainly go into film history. It's about an old woman who is terrified of old age and starts to imagine she's married to Tarzan and lives that fantasy to the bitter end. And in describing what fear of old age does to an old woman like that the film really questions the sickness in our society which creates that kind of fear in people" (C. B. Thomsen in Rayns, ed., 96). Bockmayer (b. 1948), who often works together with Rolf Bührmann, began his career with Super-8 films such as *Whispering Pretzels* (1975) and *Screaming Pretzels* (1976), both of which Fassbinder also admired. Bockmayer and Bührmann's films often parody the *Heimatfilm* and Bavarian folklore, but their more recent efforts have been criticized for making too many concessions to popular taste. Fassbinder himself was already disappointed by *Flaming Hearts,* which is set in both Bavaria and New York

and is perhaps the best known of their films to have been distributed in the United States.

Chin-up, Handstand, Salto Mortale—Firm Footing

First published in *Frankfurter Rundschau*, 24 February 1979; text based on *FbK*, 76–80.

100. *Kingdom of Naples:* Schroeter's first commercially successful film (1978). The German title translates literally as "Neapolitan Siblings"; the subtitle *Regno di Napoli* provides the Italian basis for the American title.

101. Novalis, Lautréamont . . . Céline: Novalis (1772–1801), the most famous of the early German Romantics, celebrated the mystical longing for death in his works. Lautréamont (1847–1870), a late Romantic poet of Satanism and Byronic rebellion, was discovered and hailed by the French Surrealists as an important precursor of their movement. *Voyage to the End of the Night*, the best-known novel of Céline (1894–1961), derives its powerful effect from destructive nihilism conveyed with satiric energy.

102. Daniel Schmid: The Swiss director (b. 1941), whose films include the adaptation of Fassbinder's play *Garbage, the City and Death*.

Ulrike Ottinger: Ottinger, born in Konstanz in 1942, worked as a painter and photographer in Paris from 1962 to 1968 and began making films in West Berlin in 1973. Her most distinctive film, *Ticket of No Return* (1979), also known as *Portrait of a Woman Drinker*, provides "an intellectual feast for the eyes" and creates "an exceptionally intensive Berlin film, closely linking hyper-fashion and sub-culture." See Pflaum and Prinzler, 79.

Hans Jürgen Syberberg: The most obvious similarity between Syberberg and Schroeter is their mutual interest in an operatic aesthetic for the cinema.

Rosa von Praunheim: Praunheim's films about gay life have frequently aroused protest and provoked censorship.

103. *Filmkritik:* See Rosa von Praunheim's article, "Mit herzlichem Gruss an Champagner-Schroeter von Rosa von Praunheim" ("With best wishes from Rosa von Praunheim to Champagne Schroeter"), in *Filmkritik* (January 1979): 2–5. This polemic includes a swipe at Fassbinder: "I find the bawling of Fassbinder's transvestite in *A Year of Thirteen Moons* just as disgusting and self-pitying as Schroeter's sentimental masochism."

Michael Curtiz—Anarchist in Hollywood?

Written in 1980. First published in *FbK*, 94–96.

105. Heliogabalus: Fassbinder's point of reference here is Antonin Artaud's novel, *Heliogabalus, or: the Crowned Anarchist*. Fassbinder's beginnings as a playwright go back to his exposure to the Living Theater in Munich in the 1960s, which combined Brechtian theatrical devices with the spontaneity and physicality of Artaud's "Theater of Cruelty." In his only documentary film,

Theater in Trance, Fassbinder himself speaks texts taken from Artaud's *The Theater and Its Double.*

The List of My Favorites

Written in 1980. First published in *text + kritik* 103 (July 1989): 86–87. A publisher's request prompted Fassbinder to make these lists of his favorites. Rowohlt Verlag, which was gathering material for a German edition of the American publication *The Book of Lists,* asked Fassbinder to submit compilations of the ten best films and the ten best actors. He apparently enjoyed the exercise and did more than was asked, but never sent off the results.

Hitlist of German Films

First published in Joe Hembus, *Der deutsche Film kann gar nicht besser sein* (Munich: Goldmann, 1981), 39; text based on *FbK,* 127–29. The directors and dates of the movies named, except for those by Fassbinder himself, have been added in brackets.

Alexander Kluge Is Supposed to Have Had a Birthday

First published in *Berlinaletip* (a special issue of the West Berlin magazine *tip* published during the Berlin Film Festival), 17 February 1982, 2; text based on *FbK,* 115. See *October* 46 (Fall 1988) for an issue devoted exclusively to Kluge.

112. filmmaker Kluge . . . writer Kluge: Alexander Kluge, one of the few signatories of the "Oberhausen Manifesto" to have become a major filmmaker, has achieved recognition for both his films and his literary work. His education as a lawyer has also enabled him to remain an important force in the sphere of cultural politics.

Credited Debit, Debited Credit

First published in *Die Zeit,* 11 March 1977; text based on *FbK,* 36–39. The subtitle is an editorial addition by Michael Töteberg. The planned television series based on Gustav Freytag's *Debit and Credit* was canceled by F. W. von Sell, the general manager of WDR (West German Broadcasting). Sell insisted that the "historical treatment of anti-Semitism and anti-Slavism on the basis of the novel would be subject to too many risks and misunderstandings." For detailed accounts of the controversy, see Hans C. Blumenberg, "Chronologie einer Affäre," *Die Zeit,* 11 March 1977; and Wolfram Schütte, "Da stimmt doch was nicht," *Frankfurter Rundschau,* 12 March 1977.

115. ancestors: Perhaps an allusion to Freytag's *The Ancestors.*

115. Fontane: Here Fassbinder paraphrases a comment from Fontane's review (1875) of Freytag's later novel *The Ancestors.* Fontane had also published an anonymous review of *Debit and Credit* in 1855.

German essence: A famous phrase from Emanuel Geibel's poem "Germany's Calling" (1861), which contains the lines "Some day the German essence / Will surely cure the world." Nationalistic rhetoricians made this line a "familiar quotation," stressing the image of a sound Germany confronting a sick world.

116. "totality of the middle": This phrase is quoted from Mayer's essay "Ist Gustav Freytag neu zu entdecken?" ("Should Gustav Freytag be rediscovered?"), which appeared in the *Frankfurter Allgemeine Zeitung* on 26 February 1977 and later as the foreword to a paperback edition of *Debit and Credit.*

My Position on *Garbage, the City and Death*

First published in the *Frankfurter Rundschau,* 31 March 1976, in response to charges of anti-Semitism brought against the play when it was published by the Suhrkamp Verlag. This version of the statement had been edited without Fassbinder's consent. The text used here corresponds to the manuscript in the Fassbinder estate; it appears in R. W. Fassbinder, *Die bitteren Tränen der Petra von Kant / Der Müll, die Stadt und der Tod. 2 Stücke,* 2d rev. ed. (Frankfurt/M.: Verlag der Autoren, 1986), 108ff. It varies slightly from the version published in *FbK.* For an analysis of the scandal caused by the disrupted premiere of the play in Frankfurt in 1985, see Markovits et al.

"Philosemites are anti-Semites"

First published in *Die Zeit,* 9 April 1976; text based on *AP,* 82–85.

121. Robert Neumann: An Austrian-Jewish novelist and critic (1897–1975) who made his reputation as a parodist.

Joachim Fest: Fest, the author of a controversial biography of Hitler, accused Fassbinder in an article in the *Frankfurter Allgemeine Zeitung,* 19 March 1976, of being a left-wing fascist. In a 1977 interview Fassbinder contrasted his planned television series *Debit and Credit* with Fest's "Hitler film, which is terribly reactionary and actually the attempt of a bourgeois citizen to relieve himself of his guilt" (*AP,* 87).

122. Erwin Leiser: Born in 1923 in Berlin, Leiser spent the war years in exile in Sweden. He is a filmmaker and film historian best known for *Mein Kampf* (1960), a critical documentary about the Third Reich that makes skillful use of period footage.

123. Suhrkamp's decision: Despite the publication of Fassbinder's statement, Siegfried Unseld, the owner of Suhrkamp Verlag, had the book withdrawn from bookstores and shredded.

"Madness and terrorism"

First published in Gian Luigi Rondi, *Il Cinema dei Maestri* (Milan: Rusconi, 1980), 341–49. The interview on *Despair* took place on 7 May 1978; the interview on *The Third Generation* on 19 October 1979. Both conversations have been slightly abridged by Michael Töteberg. The text presented here is based on *AP*, 104–7, but has been checked against the Italian original.

124. *Despair:* Nabokov published his own English translation of the novel in 1937.

The Third Generation

First published in *Frankfurter Rundschau*, 2 December 1978; text based on *FbK*, 69–75, except for an omitted section of the final paragraph which has been restored here.

128. Francesco Rosi, Damiano Damiani: See note to page 31, above.

Jonas: A reference to Alain Tanner's film *Jonas, Who Will Be 25 in the Year 2000* (1976).

129. Peter Alexander or Anneliese Rothenberger: West German television entertainers.

130. *The Second Awakening of Christa Klages:* See note to page 34, above.

Germany in Autumn: See note to page 32, above. On Fassbinder's episode for the film, which he refers to in the following passage, see Rentschler 1983.

The Lost Honor of Katharina Blum: See note to page 34, above.

131. Franco Nero: Nero (b. 1942), who later had a leading role in Fassbinder's *Querelle*, starred in Mario Belocchio's film *The Triumphal March* (1976).

Gian-Maria Volonté: Volonté (b. 1930), an Italian leading man of the 1960s, played in Damiani's *La strega in amore* (1966) and *Io ho Paura* (1977).

Rod Steiger: Steiger starred in Francesco Rosi's 1973 film *Re: Lucky Luciano.*

132. Gleiwitz transmitter: Beginning with a reference to the staged attack on a German radio transmitter in Gleiwitz in Upper Silesia (now Gliwice in Poland), which the Nazis used as a pretext to invade Poland in 1939, Fassbinder cites two other famous examples and one not-so-famous instance of such phenomena. The Nazis blamed the burning of the Reichstag in 1933 on the Communist Party, and Fassbinder suggests that reactionary forces in Prague exploited the revolutionary "Spring" of 1968 to justify Russian intervention. Molotov cocktails were not the usual ammunition favored by the Kommune I (KI), a West German anarchistic group of the 1960s that specialized in witty, nonviolent provocations such as pie-throwing.

133. *Conversation Piece:* Luchino Visconti's film has the Italian title

Gruppo di famiglia in un interno (1974). The German title that Fassbinder uses translates as *Violence and Passion.*

"The walls are closing in on us birds of Paradise"

First published in *Theater Heute,* July 1978, 3–4. The text follows the original publication rather than the slightly abridged version in *AP,* 90–93.

135. Schleyer's body: See note on *Germany in Autumn* in note to page 32, above.

136. Horst Söhnlein . . . Andreas Baader . . . Holger Meins: Members of the Red Army Faction, the most publicized West German terrorist organization of the 1970s.

"I'd rather be a streetsweeper in Mexico than a filmmaker in Germany"

First published in *Der Spiegel,* 11 July 1977, 140–42; text based on *AP,* 94–99.

140. Filmverlag der Autoren: See the note to page 33, above.

141. censorship on paper: Fassbinder uses the plural *"Zensuren"* here to play on the double meaning of *"Zensur"* as censorship and evaluation or grade.

French reviews of *Kaspar Hauser:* For a sampling of the French reviews of *Aguirre, the Wrath of God* and *The Mystery of Kaspar Hauser,* see the bibliography in Hans Günther Pflaum et al., eds., *Werner Herzog* (Vienna: Hanser, 1979), 160ff.

142. *Grete Minde:* Film (1976) by Heidi Genée based on the story of the same title by Theodor Fontane.

Heinrich: Film (1976) by Helma Sanders-Brahms based on the life of Heinrich von Kleist.

Group Portrait with Lady: Film (1977) by Alexander Petrovic, a Yugoslavian director, based on Heinrich Böll's novel.

Introductory Remarks on a Projected Feature Film, "Cocaine"

First published in *FbK,* 91–93. The text represents the first part of the exposé for a feature film that was never made.

144. Pitigrilli: Pseudonym for the Italian writer Dino Segre (1893–1975), whose popular novels, including *Cocaina: romanzo* (1922), appeared in German translations in the 1920s. The novel *Cocaine* was banned by the Nazis in 1933 and again temporarily in 1988 when Rowohlt Verlag issued a new edition. The cover of a paperback edition published in Munich in 1982 actually featured the phrase, "The book on which Fassbinder's film is based." Fassbin-

der may have read the novel in the 1979 edition published in Munich by Matthes and Seitz.

144. Tito Arnaudi: The central character in the novel *Cocaine*.

"Images the moviegoer can fill with his own imagination"

First published in *Kino* [West Berlin] 18/19 (1974): 20–30; text based on *AP*, 53–63. The title was formulated by Michael Töteberg.

156. Gustaf Gründgens: The actor and occasional film director (1899–1963) made a film adaptation of *Effi Briest* with the title *Der Schritt vom Wege* (*The Step off the Path*, 1939). Klaus Mann's novel *Mephisto* is a fictional account of Gründgens's life, especially his service as a theater director in Berlin during the Third Reich.

158. Yaak Karsunke . . . Peter Märthesheimer: Karsunke (b. 1934) is an actor, poet, and journalist who played roles in *Love Is Colder than Death* and *Gods of the Plague*. He also supplied the motto for *Katzelmacher,* and in 1974 Fassbinder directed his stage adaptation of Zola's *Germinal*. Peter Märthesheimer, a screenwriter and television producer, collaborated with Fassbinder on several projects, including the screenplay for *The Marriage of Maria Braun*.

159. *Moses the Man:* Fassbinder uses an abbreviated form of the German title, which translates literally as *Moses the Man and the Monotheistic Religion*. The first two parts of *Moses and Monotheism,* as it is called in English, appeared as essays in 1937; they were published together with the third part as a book in 1939. Fassbinder talked about this project as late as 1980 and even named a street after Moses in the cinematic Berlin of *Berlin Alexanderplatz*.

The Cities of Humanity and the Human Soul

First published in *Die Zeit,* 14 March 1980; text based on *FbK,* 81–90. The original context of this essay reflected the cultural authority that Fassbinder exercised at the height of his career. His reflections on Döblin's novel were published as part of the "*Zeit* Library of 100 Books," a collection of essays on "great books" recommended by the distinguished weekly.

162. *Alexanderplatz* film: Piel Jutzi's adaptation, on whose script Döblin collaborated, had its premiere in 1931 and starred Heinrich George as Franz and Bernhard Minetti as Reinhold.

Preliminary Remarks on *Querelle*

First published in *Die Zeit,* 25 May 1982; text based on *FbK,* 116–18. First part of the treatment for the feature film of the same name.

169. to live one's own life: One of many allusions in Fassbinder's work to

the title of Godard's film *Vivre sa vie,* which Fassbinder credited in a 1980 interview with having given him "a lot of strength" and with having "quite a bit to do with my ideas." Cited in Limmer, 72.

"Of despair, and the courage to recognize a utopia and to open yourself up to it"

Section 1 was first published in Horst Laube, ed., *Theaterbuch 1* (Munich: Hanser, 1978), 324–26. Section 2 appeared with the title "Why Despair? Perhaps because it's the essential thing" in the "Television Brochure of the ARD," the First German Television Network (Cologne), April 1981, 137. Section 3 was published for the first time in *AP*; text based on *AP,* 100–103. The title was formulated by Michael Töteberg.

In a Year of Thirteen Moons

First published in *S!A!U!* [Munich] 2 (1978): 52–59; 3 (1978): 45–50; text based on *FbK,* 43–68. The text is the exposé for Fassbinder's film of the same name, for which he wrote the screenplay and did the cinematography, set design, and editing.

185. Their eyes met: The description of Erwin meeting Anton in a bar parallels a scene in Fassbinder's version of *Berlin Alexanderplatz,* in which Franz Biberkopf sees Reinhold for the first time. In both cases, the destructive figure is played by Gottfried John.

193. *World on Wires:* A science fiction novel by Daniel F. Glouye, on which Fassbinder based his 1973 television film in two parts.

Answers to Questions from Schoolchildren

First published in *AP,* 219–23. Written c. 1979–80.

196. The Truth Game: Probably a game played within Fassbinder's circle. There is a "Truth Game" in his film *Chinese Roulette.*

197. Heinrich von Kleist: After making a suicide pact with Henriette Vogel, Heinrich von Kleist shot her and then himself at the Wannsee near Potsdam on 11 November 1811.

Kraftwerk: The German rock band.

Hanna Schygulla

First published in *Hanna Schygulla. Bilder aus Filmen von Rainer Werner Fassbinder* (Munich: Schirmer/Mosel, 1981), 169–87; text based on *FbK,* 97–114.

202. a friend of mine: Christoph Roser, who put up his savings to finance *The City Tramp* (1966) and *A Little Chaos* (1967). Roser also acted in both films.

203. Schwabing: Once the artists' district in Munich, now the center of the city's night life.

Peer Raben: Born Wilhelm Rabenbauer in 1940, Peer Raben would later be best known as a composer. He wrote music for many Fassbinder films and created the sophisticated soundtracks for *Berlin Alexanderplatz, Lili Marleen,* and *Lola.*

Astutuli: Carl Orff (1895–1982) is of course best known for the *Carmina burana* (1937); *Astutuli,* subtitled "A Bavarian Comedy," appeared in 1953.

204. But the show must go on: In English in the original.

206. So what?: In English in the original.

209. *The Criminals:* Ferdinand Bruckner's drama (1928) about the injustices inherent in the judicial system during the period of turbulent social change following the First World War. The play suggests that there are no criminals, only people driven to crime out of economic necessity.

211. *Herr Mockinpott:* A satirical farce (1968) well suited both to the rebellious posturing and the performance technique cultivated by the antitheater.

Hunting Scenes from Lower Bavaria: Based on Martin Sperr's play, which contributed to the revival of the critical *Volksstück.*

Pioneers in Ingolstadt: Fassbinder did a film version of Marieluise Fleisser's play in 1970.

212. *Sickness of Youth:* See the note to page 8, above.

213. emergency decrees: Laws passed by the West German Bundestag on 30 May 1968, which allowed the curtailment of civil liberties.

"Axel Cäsar Haarmann": One of the agit-prop productions of the Action Theater, in which Fassbinder was only marginally involved.

214. so what: In English in the original.

Honni soit . . . : "Shame on him who thinks ill of it," the motto of the British Order of the Garter, which has attained the status of a "familiar quotation." "Honni" is usually spelled "Honi" or "Honny."

The Sad Eyes of Cannes

First published in *FbK,* 119. This text is the first part of an uncompleted essay.

Filmography

The City Tramp. Short film. (1966)
A Little Chaos. Short film. (1967)
Love Is Colder than Death (1969)
Katzelmacher (1969)
Gods of the Plague (1969)
Why Does Herr R. Run Amok? (1969)
Rio das Mortes (1970)
The Coffee House (1970)
Whity (1970)
The Niklashausen Journey (1970)
The American Soldier (1970)
Beware of a Holy Whore (1970)
Pioneers in Ingolstadt (1970)
The Merchant of Four Seasons (1971)
The Bitter Tears of Petra von Kant (1972)
Jail Bait (Wildwechsel) (1972)
Eight Hours Are Not a Day. Television series in five parts. (1972)
Bremen Freedom (1972)
World on Wires. Television film in two parts. (1973)
Nora Helmer (1973)
Martha (1973)
Fear Eats the Soul (1973)
Effi Briest (Fontane Effi Briest) (1974)
Fox and His Friends (Faustrecht der Freiheit) (1974)

Like a Bird on a Wire (1974)
Mother Küsters Goes to Heaven (1975)
Fear of Fear (1975)
I Only Want You to Love Me (1976)
Satan's Brew (1976)
Chinese Roulette (1976)
The Station Master's Wife (Bolwieser). Television film in two parts. (1977) Released as a feature film in 1983.
Women in New York (1977)
Despair—A Journey into Light (Despair—Eine Reise ins Licht) (1977)
Episode for *Germany in Autumn* (1978)
The Marriage of Maria Braun (1978)
In a Year of Thirteen Moons (1978)
The Third Generation (1979)
Berlin Alexanderplatz. Television film in thirteen parts and an epilogue. (1980)
Lili Marleen (1981)
Lola (1981)
Theater in Trance. Documentary. (1981)
Veronika Voss (Die Sehnsucht der Veronika Voss) (1982)
Querelle (1982)

237

Select Bibliography

This bibliography places special emphasis on Fassbinder's interviews. The listing of interviews published in English represents all but a few insignificant items; the German section contains a substantial cross section of the pieces not included in this volume; important interviews in French have been included as well.

The listing of Fassbinder's publications is the most comprehensive published in English to date. Secondary literature on Fassbinder and on the New German Cinema in general has been limited here to a selection of significant publications in English. Previous English translations of the texts published in this volume have not been listed.

Two bibliographies compiled by Michael Töteberg are essential for further research. The bibliography in his article on Fassbinder in the *Kritisches Lexikon zur deutschsprachigen Gegenwartsliteratur* (Fascicle 24, 1986) contains the most extensive bibliography of all secondary literature on Fassbinder, including newspaper articles. Töteberg's "Bibliographie" in the *text + kritik* issue on Fassbinder (103, July 1989) contains the most current listing of Fassbinder's publications as well as the most extensive listing of the interviews (ninety items). The interviews and texts in *FbK* and *AP* not translated in this volume are listed in the bibliography.

Fassbinder's Interviews

In English

Ginsburg, Ina. "On Men, Women, Jews, Germans and Movies . . . Rainer Werner Fassbinder." *Interview* [New York] 10, no. 10 (1980): 46–48.

Haddad-Garcia, George. "A Conversation with Rainer Werner Fassbinder." *Christopher Street* (June 1982): 48–55.

Hughes, John, and Ruth McCormick. "Rainer Werner Fassbinder and the Death of Family Life." *Thousand Eyes* 2 (April 1977): 4–5, 21.

Hughes, John, and Brooks Riley. "A New Realism: Fassbinder Interviewed." *Film Comment* 11, no. 6 (1975): 14–17.

Jagau, Hans-Jürgen. "Interview with Rainer Werner Fassbinder: The Decline of the BRD" (1979). In *The Marriage of Maria Braun,* 190–92.

Lentz, Ellen. "U.S. 'Freedom' to German Director." *New York Times,* 30 July 1977.

Nater, Timothy. "'No Happy Endings.' Interview: Rainer Werner Fassbinder." *Newsweek,* 8 August 1977, 48.

Rayns, Tony. "Forms of Address: Tony Rayns Interviews Three German Film-Makers—Fassbinder, Wenders, Syberberg." *Sight and Sound* 44 (1974/75): 3–7.

Robinson, David. "Fassbinder after *Despair.*" *Sight and Sound* 46 (1977): 216–17.

Sparrow, Norbert. "'I Let the Audience Feel and Think': An Interview with Rainer Werner Fassbinder." *Cineaste* 8, no. 2 (1977): 20–21.

Stoop, Norma McLain. "Rainer Werner Fassbinder and *Fox.*" *After Dark,* February 1976, 43–45.

Thomsen, Christian Braad. "Five Interviews with Fassbinder" (1971–77). Translated by Soren Fischer with Tony Rayns. In Rayns, ed., *Fassbinder,* 82–101. Three of these are also in *AP,* 38–46, 64–81, 86–89.

"Tired of German 'Provincialism': Fassbinder May Move to U.S." *Variety,* 6 July 1977, 6–7.

Tyler, Ralph. "The Savage World of Rainer Werner Fassbinder." *New York Times,* 27 March 1977.

Whitney, Craig. "Fassbinder: A New Director the Movie Buffs Dote On." *New York Times,* 16 February 1977.

Wiegand, Wilfried. "Interview with Rainer Werner Fassbinder" (1974). In Iden et al., *Fassbinder,* 57–82.

In German

Brocher, Corinna. "'Da hab ich das Regieführen gelernt': Rainer Werner Fassbinder erzählt im Gespräch mit C. B. von der Geschichte des antiteaters und ersten Filmplänen" (1973). In *AP,* 15–29.

———. "Rainer Werner Fassbinder." In Barbara Bronner and Corinna Brocher, *Die Filmemacher. Zur neuen deutschen Produktion nach Oberhausen 1962. Mit einem Beitrag von Alexander Kluge,* 171–86. Munich: Bertelsmann, 1973. Includes filmography.

Dullinger, Angie. "Zärtliche Gefühle für den kaputten Star. R. W. Fassbinder über seinen Film *Die Sehnsucht der Veronika Voss.*" *Abendzeitung* [Munich] 12/13 (December 1981).

Fassbinder, Rainer Werner. "Frauen, die Regie führen in einer Männerwelt: R.W.F. interviewt Ula Stöckl" (1974). In *AP,* 202–13.

———. "*Deutschland im Herbst:* R.W.F. interviewt seine Mutter Liselotte Eder" (1977). In *AP,* 214–18.

Fischer, Kurt Joachim. "Fassbinder oder: Der Mut, die Schiffe hinter sich zu verbrennen." *Kirche und Film* 8 (August 1977): 15–18.

Fröhlich, Hans. "Um nicht so schnell verrückt zu werden . . . : Ein Gespräch mit dem Autor und Filmemacher Rainer Werner Fassbinder." *Stuttgarter Nachrichten,* 23 June 1977.

Fründt, Bodo, and Michael Jürgs. "'Egal was ich mache, die Leute regen sich auf': Ein Gespräch mit B. F. und M. J." In *AP,* 167–80.

"Interview mit R. W. Fassbinder." *Der Tagesspiegel* [West Berlin], 29 September 1969.

Jansen, Peter W. "Exil würde ich noch nicht sagen." *Cinema* [Zurich] 2 (May 1978): 10–14.

Karp, Uli. "'. . . der Film wäre ein Molotow-Cocktail geworden . . .' Ein Gespräch mit Rainer Werner Fassbinder." *Stadt-Revue* [Cologne] 3, no. 4 (April 1978): 4–6.

König, Hansheinz. "Ich lege Fussangeln." *Deutsches Allgemeines Sonntagsblatt,* 16 November 1975.

Limmer, Wolfgang. "'Alles Vernünftige interessiert mich nicht': Gespräch mit Rainer Werner Fassbinder" (1980). In *Rainer Werner Fassbinder, Filmemacher,* 49–112. Hamburg: *Spiegel-* Verlag, 1982.

Müller, André. *Entblössungen,* 178–89. Munich: Goldmann, 1979. Three interviews.

"Revolution im Privaten: Gespräch mit Rainer Werner Fassbinder." *Filmkritik* (August 1969): 471–76.

Schidor, Dieter. "Interview." In *Rainer Werner Fassbinder dreht "Querelle,"* 128–39. Munich: Heyne, 1982.

Schütte, Wolfram. "'Wenn ich nicht arbeite—ich weiss gar nicht, wie das so richtig ist': Ein Gespräch mit W. S. über Fassbinders Frankfurter Erfahrungen und den deutschen Film" (1976). In *AP,* 67–81.

Steinborn, Bion, and Rüdiger von Naso. "'Ich bin das Glück dieser Erde/Ach wär' das schön wenn's so wäre': Ein Gespräch mit Rainer Werner Fassbinder." *Filmfaust* 27 (1982): 3–16.

Weber, Ingeborg. "Liebe ist kälter als der Tod." *Abendzeitung* [Munich], 18 June 1969.

In French

Benoussan, Georges, and Florian Hopf. "Entretien avec Rainer Werner Fassbinder." *Cahiers du Cinéma* 322 (April 1981): 15–23.

Grant, Jacques. "Dégager le sens de la réalité: 'Je rejette la tautologie.'" *Cinéma 74* 193 (December 1974): 66–81.

"L'Allemagne en automne: un film, un acte." *Jeune Cinéma* 111 (June 1978): 2–7. Interview with Fassbinder, Schlöndorff, Kluge, E. Reitz, et al.

Sauvaget, Daniel. "Fassbinder." *La Revue du Cinéma* 333 (November 1978): 39–60.

Fassbinder's Publications

In English

The Bitter Tears of Petra von Kant / *Blood on the Neck of the Cat.* Translated by Anthony Vivis. Oxford: Amber Lane Press, 1984.
"In a Year of Thirteen Moons" (Continuity Script). Translated by Joyce Rheuban. In *October* 21 (1982): 5–50.
The Marriage of Maria Braun (Continuity Script). Edited and translated by Joyce Rheuban. New Brunswick, N.J.: Rutgers University Press, 1986.
Querelle. The Film Book. Edited by Dieter Schidor and Michael McLernon. Translated by Arthur S. Wensinger and Richard H. Wood. Munich: Schirmer/Mosel, 1983.
Plays (*The Bitter Tears of Petra von Kant* / *Bremen Freedom* / *Katzelmacher* / *Blood on the Cat's Neck* / *Pre-Paradise Sorry Now* / *Garbage, the City and Death*). Edited and translated by Denis Calandra. New York: PAJ Publications, 1985.
"Talking about Oppression with Margit Carstensen" (1974). In *West German Filmmakers on Film: Visions and Voices,* edited by Eric Rentschler, 168–71. New York: Holmes and Meier, 1988. Also in *AP,* 195–201.

In German

"Acht Stunden sind kein Tag" (1972). In *FbK,* 26ff.
Anarchie in Bayern und andere Stücke (Tropfen auf heisse Steine / *Der amerikanische Soldat* / *Anarchie in Bayern* / *Werwolf).* Frankfurt/M.: Verlag der Autoren, 1985.
Antiteater (Katzelmacher / *Preparadise sorry now* / *Die Betteloper).* Frankfurt/M.: Suhrkamp, 1970.
Antiteater. Fünf Stücke nach Stücken (Iphigenie auf Tauris von Johann Wolfgang von Goethe / *Ajax* / *Die Bettleroper* / *Das Kaffeehaus* / *Das brennende Dorf).* Frankfurt/M.: Verlag der Autoren, 1986.
Antiteater 2 (Das Kaffeehaus / *Bremer Freiheit* / *Blut am Hals der Katze).* Frankfurt/M.: Suhrkamp, 1972.
"Betr. Bundesfilmpreis für *Deutschland im Herbst*" (1978). In *FbK,* 127.
"Betr. Theater und Mitbestimmung" (1973–81). In *FbK,* 124–26.
Bremer Freiheit / *Blut am Hals der Katze.* Frankfurt/M.: Verlag der Autoren, 1983.
"Das bisschen Realität, das ich brauche." Wie Filme entstehen. (With Hans Günther Pflaum). Munich: Hanser, 1976.
Der Film "Berlin Alexanderplatz": Ein Arbeitsjournal. (With Harry Baer). Frankfurt/M.: Zweitausendeins, 1980.
Der Müll, die Stadt und der Tod. Frankfurt/M.: Verlag der Autoren, 1981.
Die Anarchie der Phantasie. Gespräche und Interviews. Edited by Michael Töteberg. Frankfurt/M.: Fischer, 1986.

Die bitteren Tränen der Petra von Kant. Frankfurt/M.: Verlag der Autoren, 1982.

Die bitteren Tränen der Petra von Kant / Der Müll, die Stadt und der Tod. Frankfurt/M.: Verlag der Autoren, 1984; 2nd rev. ed., 1986.

"Die Erde ist unbewohnbar wie der Mond" (Fassbinder's screenplay). In Gerhard Zwerenz, *Die Erde ist unbewohnbar wie der Mond,* 377–573. Herbstein: April, April! Verlag, 1986.

Die Kinofilme I (Der Stadtstreicher / Das kleine Chaos / Liebe ist kälter als der Tod / Katzelmacher / Götter der Pest). Edited by Michael Töteberg. Munich: Schirmer/Mosel, 1987.

"Einer, der eine Liebe im Bauch hat" (1971). In *FbK,* 25.

Fassbinders Filme 2 (Warum läuft Herr R amok?, Rio das Mortes, Whity, Die Niklashauser Fart, Der amerikanische Soldat, Warnung vor einer heiligen Nutte). Edited by Michael Töteberg. Frankfurt/M.: Verlag der Autoren, 1990.

Filme befreien den Kopf. Essays und Arbeitsnotizen. Edited by Michael Töteberg. Frankfurt/M.: Fischer, 1984.

"Im kleinen Leben liegt der grosse Schmerz": Liedertexte von Fassbinder u. a. Edited by Ingrid Caven and Peer Raben. Berlin: Albino, 1983.

Katzelmacher / Preparadise sorry now. Frankfurt/M.: Verlag der Autoren, 1982.

"Notizen zum Spielfilm-Projekt 'Rosa Luxemburg' " (1982). In *FbK,* 131.

"Offener Brief an Franz Xaver Kroetz" (1973). In *FbK,* 123–24.

Querelle. Filmbuch. Edited by Dieter Schidor and Michael McLernon. Munich: Schirmer/Mosel, 1982.

"Schütte. Von der Dialektik des Bürgers im Paradies der lähmenden Ordnung" (undated). In *FbK,* 129–30.

"Sibylle Schmitz. Geschichte für einen Spielfilm" (Treatment for the film *Veronica Voss*). In *text + kritik* 103 (July 1989): 10–19.

Stücke 3 (Die bitteren Tränen der Petra von Kant / Das brennende Dorf / Der Müll, die Stadt und der Tod). Frankfurt/M: Suhrkamp, 1976.

"Wie stelle ich mir meine zukünftige Berufstätigkeit vor?" (1966/67). In *FbK,* 123.

Secondary Literature (in English)

General

Corrigan, Timothy. *New German Film: The Displaced Image.* Austin: University of Texas Press, 1983.

Elsaesser, Thomas. *New German Cinema: A History.* New Brunswick, N.J.: Rutgers University Press, 1989.

Franklin, James. *New German Cinema: From Oberhausen to Hamburg.* Boston: Twayne, 1983.

Helt, Richard C., and Marie E. Helt. *West German Cinema since 1945: A Reference Handbook*. Metuchen, N.J.: Scarecrow Press, 1987.

Kaes, Anton. *From Hitler to Heimat: The Return of History as Film*. Cambridge, Mass.: Harvard University Press, 1989.

Pflaum, Hans Günther, and Hans Helmut Prinzler. *Cinema in the Federal Republic of Germany*. Bonn: Inter Nationes, 1983.

Phillips, Klaus, ed. *New German Filmmakers: From Oberhausen through the 1970s*. New York: Ungar, 1984.

Rentschler, Eric. *West German Film in the Course of Time*. Bedford Hills, N.Y.: Redgrave, 1984.

——, ed. *German Film and Literature: Adaptations and Transformations*. New York: Methuen, 1986.

——, ed. *West German Filmmakers on Film: Visions and Voices*. New York: Holmes and Meier, 1988.

Sandford, John. *The New German Cinema*. London: Oswald Wolff, 1980.

On Fassbinder

Collins, Richard, and Vincent Porter. *WDR and the Arbeiterfilm: Fassbinder, Ziewer and Others*. London: British Film Institute, 1981.

Foss, Paul. *Fassbinder in Review*. Sydney: Australian Film Institute, 1983.

Hayman, Ronald. *Fassbinder, Film Maker*. New York: Simon and Schuster, 1984.

Iden, Peter, et al. *Fassbinder*. Translated by Ruth McCormick. New York: Tanam Press, 1981.

Johnson, Sheila. "A Star Is Born: Fassbinder and the New German Cinema." *New German Critique* 24/25 (1981–82): 57–72.

Kaes, Anton. "History, Fiction, Memory: Fassbinder's *The Marriage of Maria Braun*." *Persistence of Vision* 2 (Fall 1985): 52–60.

——. *From Hitler to Heimat: The Return of History as Film*. Cambridge, Mass.: Harvard University Press, 1989.

Katz, Robert. *Love Is Colder than Death: The Life and Times of Rainer Werner Fassbinder*. New York: Random House, 1987.

Magretta, William R. "Reading the Writerly Film: Fassbinder's *Effi Briest*." In W.R.M. and Andrew Horton, eds., *Modern European Filmmakers and the Art of Adaption*, 248–62. New York: Ungar, 1981.

Markovits, Andrei, et al. "Rainer Werner Fassbinder's *Garbage, the City and Death*: Renewed Antagonisms in the Complex Relationship between Jews and Germans in the Federal Republic of Germany." *New German Critique* 38 (1986): 28–38.

Mayne, Judith. "Fassbinder and Spectatorship." *New German Critique* 12 (1977): 61–74.

"The Other Fassbinder. The Popular / The Historical / The International." *Wide Angle* 12, no. 1 (1990): 5–65. A special issue on the "political Fassbinder."

Raab, Kurt. "My Life with Rainer." *Village Voice,* 3 May 1983, 43–45.
"Rainer Werner Fassbinder: A Special Issue." *October 21* (Summer 1982).
Rayns, Tony, ed. *Fassbinder.* Rev. ed. London: British Film Institute, 1980.
Rentschler, Eric. "Life with Fassbinder: The Politics of Fear and Pain." *Discourse* 6 (1983): 75–90.
———. "Terms of Dismemberment: The Body in/and/of Fassbinder's *Berlin Alexanderplatz." New German Critique* 34 (1985): 194–208.
———, ed. *West German Filmmakers on Film: Visions and Voices.* New York: Holmes and Meier, 1988.
Sontag, Susan. "Novel into Film." *Vanity Fair,* September 1983, 86–90.

Index

Not included are the names and titles in the "Lists" on pages 106–11.

Designed by Bruce Gore

Composed by G&S Typesetters, Inc., in Garamond Book text and Eras display

Printed by The Maple Press Company, Inc., on 50-lb. Glatfelter Eggshell Cream